KANSAS GUIDE 2

Text
Mil Penner and Marci Penner

Photography
Mil Penner

Design
Liz Penner King

Publisher
The Sounds of Kansas
Inman, Kansas

DEDICATION

Kansas Weekend Guide 2 is dedicated to V. Lee, wife and mother, whose constant sustaining love and support made this book possible for both of us.

This book is our gift to all who love Kansas. We have explored many of the towns, highways, backroads, nooks and crannies that make Kansas so rich in adventure and discovery. Many other wonderful places no doubt deserve mention, and we'll continue to hunt for them. Our goal has been to whet your appetite for Kansas journeys so that you will continue your explorations beyond these pages.

Published by The Sounds of Kansas.
Route 1, Box 176
Inman, Kansas 67546
316/585-2389

Designed by Origins Design, Inc.
Edited by Mary Campbell Nielsen
Printed by Mennonite Press, Inc.

Library of Congress Number 93-85570

ISBN: 0-9615597-7-2

CONTENTS

EXPLORE KANSAS

Mini-weekend vacations and day trips in Kansas are becoming increasingly popular as more people discover the byways of Kansas. Roads divide flowering Flint Hills meadows, take roller coaster plunges into oak forests west of Kansas City, float like mirages between fields of golden wheat, fizzle out amid forgotten memories, and enter the choreodrama of the cities.

Exploring Kansas is joyous discovery. The state's beauty, its secrets, and its history are often subtle, wrapped in a veil that yields to patient exploration. Kansas's charm is like a prairie rose at dawn glowing through iridescent dewdrops; you must be there at just the right moment to see its dazzling beauty.

The dictionary defines a tourist as one who travels for pleasure or culture. To get the greatest enjoyment during your Kansas tours, watch for seven elements of rural culture: architecture, art, commerce, cuisine, customs, geography (including flora and fauna), and history. Visit the attractions that display these elements. Focus on them and you'll discover adventure everywhere.

Examine architecture, for example. You can learn a lot by watching for a community's original construction materials: Fort Riley abounds in limestone buildings; the way the stone is trimmed indicates the construction periods. Early Fort Leavenworth was made of clapboard sided buildings. Russell, Lincoln, and Ellis counties feature post rock. Further west, adobe and later brick were prime building materials.

Pete Felten in Hays exemplifies art, Kansas wheat wears the banner of commerce, Hiatt's restaurant in Winfield represents the best in cuisine, tiny Yoder epitomizes customs, the Red Hills flatter geography, and Santa Fe Trail remnants reveal history.

Vacationing in Kansas makes good economic sense too. You save time, gas, and money, while the communities you visit receive income and your money stays in the state.

You'll note in the text that most rural communities have shown a decline in population. Our dying small towns represent an economic and cultural loss to the entire state. Tourism and associated cottage industries do make a difference.

We suggest that you use the phone numbers listed to verify the status of local enterprises, since some business hours can change. For a free Kansas state map call the Kansas Travel and Tourism Division at 1-800/2-KANSAS.

Become an official Kansas Weekend Guide explorer. You'll find it enjoyable and your children will get a priceless Kansas education.

NORTH CENTRAL KANSAS

ABILENE-SALINA SECTION: Abilene, Bavaria, Bennington, Brookville, Chapman, Delphos, Enterprise, Hedville, Minneapolis, Salina. *Page 1 to 7.*

BELLEVILLE SECTION: Agenda, Belleville, Brantford, Courtland, Cuba, Jewell, Kackley, Mankato, Norway, Republic, Scandia. *Page 7 to 9.*

CONCORDIA SECTION: Beloit, Cawker City, Clifton, Clyde, Concordia, Glen Elder, Rice, St. Joseph, Vining. *Page 9 to 13.*

ELLSWORTH-LINCOLN SECTION: Barnard, Carneiro, Denmark, Ellsworth, Geneseo, Kanopolis, Lincoln, Sylvan Grove, Tescott, Wilson. *Page 13 to 18.*

HAYS SECTION: Bison, Bunker Hill, Ellis, Hays, LaCrosse, Liebenthal, Lucas, Luray, Pfeifer, Plainville, Russell, Victoria, Waldo. *Page 18 to 22.*

PHILLIPSBURG SECTION: Athol, Alton, Bogue, Damar, Downs, Harlan, Kensington, Lebanon, Logan, Nicodemus, Osborne, Palco, Phillipsburg, Portis, Smith Center, Speed, Stockton, Woodston. *Page 22 to 26.*

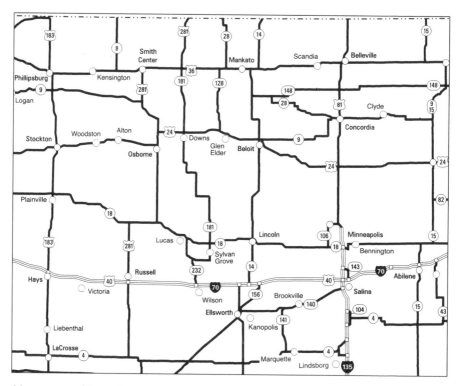

Maps courtesy of Kansas Department of Transportation
Photo opposite side: Geographic Center of the United States, Lebanon

Dr. Brewster Higley and Dan Kelly's folk song, Home on the Range, *was written here near Athol in 1873. Capturing the essence of north central Kansas, the song suggests sweeping verdant landscapes, big blue sky horizons, and pastoral freedom. The wind still sweeps over miles and miles of grassy hills, the skies are still unpolluted blue, and some buffalo still roam.*

The traveler who dares to depart from the twin concrete ribbons called I-70 will discover wonderful places and charming people. The bluest waters in Kansas, stone post fences dividing fields, mysterious hilltop cairns, extraordinarily beautiful stone churches, and much more will vie for your attention.

The people of north central Kansas welcome you. You'll discover through them what it means to be "home on the range."

ABILENE

1990 population 6,242; 1970 6,661. For area accommodations and attractions information call 913/263-2231.

ABILENE VISITORS' CENTER AND HISTORIC TOURS:

201 Northwest Second, Abilene. This beautiful depot is listed on the national register . The lobby is filled with tourist information. Bus tours of historic places start here in the summer, Tuesday through Saturday at 6 p.m. Tour fee. For information call 913/263-2231.

KIRBY HOUSE RESTAURANT:

205 Northeast Third, Abilene. An immaculate lawn, a white picket fence, and a look at the beautifully painted exterior of this Victorian house add to the anticipation of the setting and meal inside. Open daily 11 a.m. to 2 p.m. and 5 to 9:30 p.m.,

Sunday 11 a.m. to 3 p.m. Phone 913/263-7336.

BALFOUR'S HOUSE BED-AND-BREAKFAST:

Three miles south of Abilene on K-15. For a private and cozy country setting with a modern charm, this is the place you're looking for. An indoor pool, spa, and fireplace are available to guests. Phone Gil and Marie at 913/263-4262.

SPRUCE HOUSE BED-AND-BREAKFAST:

604 North Spruce, Abilene. These comfortable guest rooms, named after Hollywood stars, have private baths, but the company of your hosts, Victoria and Earl, is the very best part of this experience. Actors from the East Coast, they have an engaging flair that leaves guests smiling and asking for a return visit. Phone 913/263-3900.

VICTORIAN REFLECTIONS BED-AND-BREAKFAST:

820 Northwest Third, Abilene. The second-floor guest rooms are decorated in the high Victorian style; each room has a private bath. Everything from the beds to the bathroom fixtures is antique in this newly renovated home. Phone 913/263-7774 for reservations.

WINDMILL INN BED-AND-BREAKFAST:

Nine miles south of I-70 exit 286. (Chapman is one mile south of I-70 exit 286.) Watch for the lavender house. Tim and Deb Sanders offer lodging on a working farm near historic Abilene. They also offer evening dining for non-guests as well as guests. Phone a day in advance, and come ready to experience such dishes as Turkey Breast Wellington, Pampered Chicken, Windmill Inn Shrimp Boil, and Flank Steak Stroganoff! Phone 913/263-8755.

SEELYE MANSION:

1105 North Buckeye, Abilene. This 1905 mansion listed on the national register offers one of the premier house tours in the nation. You'll be saying "wow" often, especially when you reach the third floor. It seems there are stairways and bedrooms everywhere in this 25-room Georgian-style private residence. A nearby museum with all the equipment Seelye used to make his patent medicines will soon be open. Tours given at 10 a.m. and 2 p.m. daily, Sunday 2 p.m. only. Admission fee. Phone 913/263-7336.

LEBOLD-VAHSHOLTZ MANSION: 106 North Vine, Abilene. When she was 17, Mrs. Vahsholtz started collecting items hoping that someday they would fill a mansion. Now, as a retirement project, Mr. and Mrs. Vahsholtz have renovated this 1880 Abilene showcase and she has fulfilled her dream. Highlights of this 23-room, six-story house are an 1857 dugout found in the basement and a top floor full of wedding gowns all for use by the Vahsholtz grandkids. Open only by appointment. Admission fee. Phone 913/263-4356.

EISENHOWER COMPLEX: 200 block of Southeast Fourth off South Buckeye, Abilene. The complex includes the Eisenhower family home; an 11-foot statue of President Eisenhower; the burial site of Dwight, wife Mamie, and first-born son, Doud Dwight; and the museum. Open daily 9 a.m. to 4:45 p.m. Phone 913/263-4751.

EISENHOWER MUSEUM: Part of Eisenhower Complex, Abilene. From a photo of Ike on the Abilene High School baseball team to photos and displays of his family life, military endeavors, and presidential days, these exhibits have a powerful effect. Open daily 9 a.m. to 4:45 p.m. Admission fee. Phone 913/263-4751.

DICKINSON COUNTY HISTORICAL SOCIETY MUSUEM: 412 South Campbell, Abilene. Displays are done superbly according to a timeline that begins B.C. and continues through the days of the Indians, cattle drives, and agriculture. Open daily April through October 10 a.m. to 8 p.m., Sunday 1 to 5 p.m.; November through March, Monday through Friday 9 a.m. to 4 p.m. Admission fee. Phone 913/263-2681.

MUSEUM OF INDEPENDENT TELEPHONY: 412 South Campbell, Abilene. This is fascinating! You'll see telephones from every era. You can even call a friend across the room on some of the older phones. Learn about the history of telephones and operators. Same hours and phone as Dickinson County Museum.

MUSEUM OUTBUILDINGS: Behind the museums. You'll feel like you're on someone's 1915 farm rather than at a museum complex. In the brooder house see hens sitting on their eggs. In the barn wipe away cobwebs, look for the cat, dodge the barn swallows, and get a good whiff of an old barn smell. Relax on the porch of the log cabin and watch the carousel across the way. This is the site of the summer Pioneer Camp for Children. For information about the camp call 913/263-2681.

C.W. PARKER CAROUSEL: Behind the museums. Pick your favorite hand-carved rocking pony and take a ride on this national historic landmark that was built in 1901. Carnival music will accompany your ride, and a lasting memory is almost promised. Fee for rides. Open during museum hours.

GENNY'S CUPBOARD: 300 North Broadway, Abilene. Head behind the shelves and displays of gift items and antiques for sandwiches, salads, soups, and delicious pies! Fun place to eat or shop with pressed tin ceiling overhead. Open Monday through Saturday 8 a.m. to 5:30 p.m. Phone 913/263-4714.

GREYHOUND HALL OF FAME: 407 South Buckeye, Abilene. Read these tributes to great racing dogs and their owners. Open daily April through October 9 a.m. to 8 p.m., November through March 9 a.m. to 5 p.m. Free. Phone 913/263-3000.

PLAZA THEATER: 408 Northwest Second, Abilene. Open for nightly movies at 7:30 p.m. It may be hard to see the art deco ceiling and tapestry walls, but give it a try. Sit on the main floor or in the balcony on slightly uncomfortable but very nostalgic original wooden seats. This is where Dwight D. Eisenhower announced his intent to run for the presidency. Phone 913/263-1612.

BOW STUDIO AND GALLERY: 921 South Buckeye, Abilene. Bob and Inga Bow make all their ceramics, sculptures, and fountains out of Kansas clays. Their studio and retail gallery are found tucked under the trees of their country home. Open daily 10 a.m. to 7 p.m. Phone 913/263-7166.

FARMERS AND DROVERS GALLERY: 309 North Buckeye, Abilene. Excellent Kansas art to browse through or buy. Open daily 10 a.m. to 5:30 p.m., Sunday noon to 5 p.m. Phone 913/263-7250.

ANTIQUES: Abilene. Half a dozen shops are available in the area. Start on Buckeye Street.

CHICKEN CROSSING ANTIQUES: South of Abilene. Head south on Buckeye, cross the Smoky Hill River, and take the first turn east.

This barn houses all sorts of antiques. Saddles and toys can be found upstairs. Open most of the time. Phone 913/263-3517.

OLD ABILENE TOWN: 100 Southeast Fifth, Abilene. Find gift shops, recreated buildings from cattle drive days, and a restaurant. Open Memorial Day through Labor Day. Phone 913/263-4194.

HISTORICAL MARKER: Third and Buckeye, Abilene. This granite memorial, dedicated to the pioneers of Dickinson County, marks the end point of the Chisholm Trail.

RV PARKS: Covered Wagon RV Park, 803 South Buckeye, Abilene. New owners. Open year-round. Phone 913/864-4053. Four Seasons RV Acres, six miles east of Abilene on I-70 at exit 281. Phone 1-800/658-4667.

ENTERPRISE ECOLOGICAL GARDENS: Downtown Enterprise. A great idea — converting a three-acre undeveloped tract into an OWLS (Outdoor Wildlife Learning Sites) project. Watch this one grow. Trails and footbridges are in place. Stop in the library and ask to see photos of Carrie Nation coming to Enterprise. Talk to either Dale Anders or Reed Hoffman at the bank about the park. Phone 913/263-8400.

SALINA

1990 population 42,303; 1970 37,714. For additional accommodations or attractions information call 913/827-9301.

LAKEWOOD PARK: One mile east of Santa Fe on East Iron, Salina. Enter this urban wildlife sanctuary by crossing a one-lane bridge, then take the second right to the beginning of the wood-chip walking trails. On a breezy day cottonwood leaves mute the distant sounds of city traffic. Phone 913/826-7335.

OAKDALE PARK: Turn north on Oakdale from East Iron, Salina. This is a beautiful park filled with trees and flower gardens to drive through or relax in. Take some time to walk over one of the three suspension bridges that cross the Smoky Hill River. A Statue of Liberty replica is found here as well as playground equipment.

DOWNTOWN ARCHITECTURAL TOUR: Salina has a wealth of architectural gems and historic buildings throughout the business and residential districts. Extensive use of terra cotta in the business district gives it an artistic flavor. Pick up an architectural tour brochure at Downtown, Inc., 106 West Walnut, or call 913/825-0535.

SALINA ART CENTER: 242 South Santa Fe, Salina. Adults will appreciate the exhibits by regional and national artists. Kids will like the hands-on art experience laboratory! Open Tuesday through Saturday noon to 5 p.m., until 7 p.m. on Thursday, and Sunday 1 to 5 p.m. Phone 913/827-1431.

BLUESTEM GALLERY: 636 East Iron, Salina. Located in a 120-year-old building listed on the state and national registers, this cooperative gallery features 12 central Kansas artists. Artistic media range from photography to pastels. New works are displayed bimonthly. Free. Open Thursday through Sunday 1 to 5 p.m. Phone 913/826-9816.

SMOKY HILL MUSEUM: 211 West Iron, Salina. Get acquainted with the history of the county here. Open Tuesday through Friday noon to 5 p.m., Saturday 10 a.m. to 5 p.m., and Sunday 1 to 5 p.m. Phone 913/826-7460.

CENTRAL KANSAS FLYWHEELS MUSEUM: 1100 West Diamond Drive, Salina. Just northwest of the I-70 and U.S. 81 (Ninth Street) junction. The main floor and balcony of this huge metal building are full of everything from machinery manuals to a threshing machine and just about anything in between that you'd find on a farm or in a farmhouse. Open April through September daily 1 to 5 p.m. Admission fee. Phone 913/825-8473.

AULD LANG SYNE: Corner of Santa Fe and Iron, Salina. This former bank now holds a wealth of antiques, art, and Kansas food products. Even the vaults are full of treasures. Food is catered in at noon some days. Open Tuesday through Saturday 10 a.m. to 6 p.m. and Sunday 1 to 5 p.m. Phone 913/825-0020.

THE KOCHS' HOUSE: 155 North Broadway, Salina. You'll be offered coffee or tea when you enter this house full of wonderful gift items like soaps, candles, coffees, teas, truffles, and much more. Open Monday through Saturday 9:30 a.m. to 5:30 p.m. Phone 913/825-2780.

HUNTER'S LEIGH BED-AND-BREAKFAST: 4109 East North, Salina. As you drive up take a good look at the house, because when you go in you'll meet the designer and builder, Wynona Mason. After you step in, you'll crane your neck to see what all the color is in the gazebo-styled room. Its from all the ribbons Wynona and her horse have won. Wynona was one of the top pros during her riding days and now teaches classical riding. The upstairs rooms are cozy, the kitchen table conducive to long chats, and you can see the Smoky Hill River from the back window. Ask for Wynona's special granola strawberry and yogurt breakfast! Phone 913/823-6750.

GIORGIO'S ITALIAN RESTAURANT:
1200 East Crawford, Salina. All the Giorgio Restaurants in the state were designed by Wynona Mason, owner of the Salina Hunter's Leigh Bed-and-Breakfast. Her choices of colors and design go superbly with the delicious Italian food. Open Monday through Sunday 11 a.m. to 9 p.m. Phone 913/825-0200.

SCHEME RESTAURANT:
123 North Seventh, Salina. The many plants in here look great against the barn wood walls. You'll love the deep-dish homemade pizza! Open for Thursday and Friday lunch, supper Thursday through Saturday. Phone 913/823-5124

SCENIC DRIVE: Go west from Salina on I-70 and get off at the Hedville exit (exit 244) to see the real Kansas. There's not much to see in Hedville, but keep going south and keep your eyes open for the Rolling Hills Ranch. You'll see buffalo,

camels, and Belgian horses on this picturesque ranch. As much as you'll want to, don't stop in unless you're with a group that has an appointment (913/827-9488). Continue on to Bavaria and take a drive through what is left of the town. Go west on K-140 through Brookville. (See Brookville entries.) Continue on K-140 to Carneiro. You'll miss this ghost town if you're not observant. Turn south into Carneiro and look for buildings behind the foliage. Mushroom Park is south of Carneiro. Continue on to K-111, turn north and then go northeast on K-156 to return to I-70. The countryside along this route will vary from no trees to thick groves of trees and rock outcroppings. It's winding and rolling and especially inspiring in the spring.

BROOKVILLE

1990 population 226; 1970 238.

BROOKVILLE HOTEL: Downtown Brookville. If you've never been to

Brookville Hotel restaurant, Brookville

Brookville you're in for a real treat, and if you have been here we know you'll return. You'll be eating the famous family-style chicken dinner on fabric tablecloths in this old hotel and bank in a comfortable but classy setting. Relax on benches out front after the meal. Street lamps border the hotel sidewalk. Open Tuesday through Friday 5 to 8:30 p.m., Saturday 4 to 8:30 p.m., Sunday 11 a.m. to 7:30 p.m. Reservations required. Phone 913/225-6666.

ROSIE'S: Next to the post office, Brookville. Curtains accent storefront windows and give this attractively painted antique store some quaint charm. Usually open on weekends. Phone 913/225-6877.

BROOKVILLE MERCANTILE: Next to Rosie's, Brookville. Just another abandoned building in Brookville that has been turned into a classy gift store using the old wall shelves. Open Tuesday through Saturday 5 to 9 p.m. and Sunday 11 a.m. to 8 p.m. Phone 913/225-6668.

BENNINGTON

1990 population 568; 1970 561.

LARRY'S PHARMACY: Downtown Bennington. Get your sundries or ice cream sundaes here at the old-fashioned soda fountain and drug store. Try to avoid the after-school crowd! Open daily 9 a.m. to 5 p.m., Sunday 1 to 5 p.m. Phone 913/488-3942.

BENNINGTON ANTIQUE PLAZA: 107 North Nelson, Bennington. The hardware business moved out and the antique people moved in. Duane Walls, who plans the annual Bennington Rodeo, has old saddles, harnesses, and other cowboy things for sale here. Good place to

find Van Brigle and Roseville, too. Hours are Monday through Saturday 11 a.m. to 5 p.m. (closed Wednesday) and Sunday 1 to 5 p.m. Phone 913/488-2230.

MEMORY LANE ANTIQUES: North Nelson and Washington, Bennington. Behind the two-room house full of antiques is an old lumber yard with everything from old doors and chairs to potbellied stoves. Open Monday through Friday 9 a.m. to 5 p.m. and Saturday and Sunday 1 to 5 p.m. Phone 913/488-2206.

PRAIRIE LAKE CAFE: Five miles north and one mile east of Bennington. The cafe snuggles alongside the Ottawa County State Lake. The homemade food is as good as the view. Open Thursday 4 to 9 p.m., Friday and Saturday 11 a.m. to 9 p.m., Sunday 8 a.m. to 9 p.m. Phone 913/488-3967.

MINNEAPOLIS

1990 population 1,983; 1970 1,971.

ROCK CITY: Three miles southwest of Minneapolis. This patch of 200 sandstone concretions is a surprise to find in the midst of crop and prairie grasses. These sturdy rocks can be touched and climbed on. See if you can figure out which ones are named Widow's Tunnel, Twin Sisters, Kissing Rocks, and Doughnut Rock! Fee per car. Phone 913/392-3068.

OTTAWA COUNTY RED POST TOURS: Four self-guided auto tour brochures of the county are available at the Chamber of Commerce office, 213 West Second, Minneapolis, or by phoning 913/392-3068. These town and countryside tours feature one-room schoolhouses, churches, cemeteries, memorials, two ghost towns, and more! Just follow the red posts!

OTTAWA COUNTY MUSEUM:
110 South Concord, Minneapolis. Come here to appreciate and learn about county history. Open Tuesday through Friday 9 a.m. to 5 p.m., Saturday morning. Closed Monday. Donations appreciated. Phone 913/392-3321.

GEORGE WASHINGTON CARVER MARKER: A half block north of Second on Sheridan, Minneapolis. Located next to the public library, this marker is at the site where Carver attended school in Minneapolis.

MINNEAPOLIS COUNTRY CLUB: 728 East Laurel or K-106, Minneapolis. Nonmembers are welcome to play this nine-hole course. Golf carts available. Green fee. Public restaurant for lunch and supper. Closed Sunday evening and Monday. Phone 913/392-3300.

DELPHOS

1990 population 494; 1970 599.

LETTER TO LINCOLN: Northwest corner of downtown square, Delphos. As a young girl, Grace Bedell Billings wrote Abe Lincoln a letter and said that if he grew a beard some of her brothers would vote for him. A monument shows the letter Grace wrote to Lincoln and Lincoln's reply. Grace lived her married life in Delphos.

J.J.'S BEST YET GROCERY: Downtown Delphos. This grocery has been around as long as the wooden floors. Open Monday through Friday.

PIKE'S ROUTE MONUMENT: 5-1/2 miles northwest of Delphos on an unpaved road. The view of the rolling hills is excellent on your drive to this hilltop memorial. Grain elevators mark surrounding towns. This is a good place to imagine Zebulon

Pike's trek across these hills. Please sign the guest book!

BELLEVILLE

1990 population 2,517; 1970 3,063. For additional Belleville accommodations information call the Chamber of Commerce, 913/527-5519.

THE GOOSE CROSSING: 1820 M, Belleville. This gift shop with the pressed tin ceiling has a marble countertop soda fountain and swivel stools. Order fountain treats or sandwiches! Phone 913/527-5998.

CROSSROADS MUSEUM:
2726 U.S. 36, Belleville. The photo display of Republic County barns is especially interesting. Local dance bands, seed sacks, railroad exhibits, and quilts are other highlights. Open daily 1 to 4 p.m., Sunday 1:30 to 4:30 p.m. Free. Phone 913/527-5971.

BELLEVILLE MURALS: See a Birger Sandzen mural at the Belleville post office, 1119 18th, during daily lobby hours, and the Mary Ann Walker murals of county scenes in the library, 19th and N. Library open afternoons Monday through Saturday.

HANZLIK RUSTIC FURNITURE: Ninth and N, Belleville. Hedgewood fenceposts are turned into intriguing barstools, chairs, stools, and tables. No two pieces are ever alike and each piece is full of character. No nails used, just dowel and peg. Call Bud or Pat at 913/527-2427.

COUNTY FAIRGROUNDS: The Belleville High Banks, site of the Midget National Auto Race Championships, was a WPA project. A lake can be found behind the fairgrounds on Twelfth.

OLD BARN ANTIQUES: Seven miles north of Belleville on U.S. 81.

This barn houses wagons, buggies, horse-drawn farm machinery, and the usual antiques. Usually open 9 a.m. to 5:30 p.m. during the week. Phone 913/729-3329.

PAWNEE INDIAN VILLAGE: Located at the end of K-266 in Republic County. Pawnee lodges once housed 1,000 Indians at this state historic site. The village was abandoned in 1830, but one lodge has been excavated and a building erected over it. The earthen floor is exposed for public viewing. A sound and light program tell about the floor. Outside, a sidewalk guides you to other lodge depressions. A monument to Zeb Pike marks the place where he lowered the Spanish flag and raised the U.S. flag. Open Tuesday through Saturday 10 a.m. to 5 p.m., Sunday 1 to 5 p.m. Donations appreciated. Phone 913/361-2255.

SCANDIA

1990 population 421; 1970 567.

SCANDIA MUSEUM: Fourth and Grant, Scandia. Enter through library. Museum has some unique displays, including a hand-carved exhibit of a wagon train attack and another of Dodge City. Open Memorial Day to Labor Day Monday through Saturday 2 to 4 p.m. Phone 913/335-2271.

CERAMIC TILE MURAL: Fourth Street, Scandia. This border mural spans three businesses across from the library. Note the Swedish symbols around town. The red brick home at 313 Washington is worth a slow drive by.

SVENSK BUTIK: Downtown Scandia. Open Monday through Saturday 9 a.m. to 4 p.m., closed for lunch. Buy some crafts or come on Saturday for the food sale.

HISTORICAL MARKER: U.S. 36, Scandia. A historical marker tells about the country of the Pawnee. A stone monument commemorates the first Scandinavian colony house built nearby in 1868.

NORWAY: About seven miles south of Scandia on a county road to K-148. A big white sign lets you know you're in Norway. Underneath the sign a monument rock honors veterans. A 1917 church is at the end of the main street. On the north side of K-148 is the O. Blosser home built in 1906. Private residence.

KACKLEY: Several miles west of Norway on K-148. Once a Swedish settlement. Abandoned houses are now seen behind overgrown trees. A marker on the east side of town has an etching of what the school looked like. The school was closed in 1966.

JEWELL

1990 population 529; 1970 569.

CITY PARK: Downtown Jewell. This park, in the middle of the downtown square, has playground equipment. A memorial commemorates Fort Jewell, built in 1870 to protect settlers.

HIGHWAY 14 ANTIQUES: K-14 in Jewell city limits. Great antique shopping here. Usually open during the week. Phone 913/428-3611.

HAVEL'S ANTIQUES: 300 Delaware, Jewell. Do some antique shopping in this red brick corner building. Usually open during the week. Phone 913/729-3329 or 913/428-3564.

M AND M ANTIQUES: A few stores east of Havel Antiques, Jewell. Usually open during the week. Phone 913/428-3672.

SCENIC DRIVE: K-14 to K-128 via Jewell State Fishing Lake. These unpaved roads will take you by some great backroads scenery. It's rolling hill after rolling hill, then a valley where you'll find the secluded, peaceful state lake. In season the hills may be filled with grazing cattle or wildflowers.

BUFFALO ROAM STEAK-HOUSE: U.S. 36, Mankato. 1990 population 1,037; 1970 1,287. Great place for hearty eating. Open Monday through Friday 11 a.m. to 1:30 p.m. and daily 5 to 9 p.m. Closed Sunday. Phone 913/378-3971.

COURTLAND

1990 population 343; 1970 403. This is another town of Swedish heritage. The newspaper editor says that irrigation has helped keep the rural culture alive here. Some days 30 semi-trucks of grain come in. Two railroads cross here.

DEPOT-MARKET AND CIDER MILL: From U.S. 36 turn south to Courtland. The old Courtland Santa Fe depot now is full of fresh produce. Apples are the feature. Some of the 45 varieties include Arkansas Black, Winter Banana, and Golden Russett. Watch cider being made in September and October. Pumpkins and sweet corn sold during the season. Apple butter, jellies, syrups, and Kansas products sold here. In November and December local crafts are available. Open early July until Christmas daily 9 a.m. to 5:30 p.m. Closed Sunday. Phone 913/374-4255.

CUBA: Nine miles east of Belleville on U.S. 36, then south on K-139. 1990 population 242; 1970 290. Home of the annual March week-long rock-a-thon, Cuba calls itself an antique town, not a ghost town. To take part in the round-the-clock rocking or for more information call 913/729-3623.

AGENDA: Turn south off K-148 to find Main Street. 1990 population 81; 1970 107. You'll get curious glances from the locals at the Agenda Cafe in the old bank building.

BRANTFORD: Community members are keeping Brantford rural culture alive by renovating the old one-room school into a community center. Keep the outdoor basketball goal!

STRAWBERRY TOWNSITE MARKER: Two miles east of Brantford on K-148 in Washington County. The lifespan of this town, named after the wild strawberries that grew here, was 1868 to 1951. No evidence of the town can be seen.

CONCORDIA

1990 population 6,167; 1970 7,221. For more information about area accommodations and attractions call 913/243-4290.

BROWN GRAND THEATRE: 310 West Sixth, Concordia. This

Brown Grand Theatre, Concordia

painstakingly restored early 1900s opera house is a rare treat. Sit in one of the padded wooden theater seats on the main floor or in the balcony and enjoy the richness of the gold lattice on the cream-colored ceiling, the gold decorative molding and lights around the proscenium arch, the brass rails in front of the box seats, and the forest green curtain behind them. Just stop in and look Monday through Friday 9 a.m. to noon and 1 to 4 p.m.; Saturday 10 a.m. to noon and 1 to 4 p.m.; Sunday 1 to 3 p.m.; or call 913/243-2553 for tour or coming attractions.

BROWNSTONE MANSION: End of West Sixth, Concordia. This grand old limestone house was built in 1906 by the original owner of the Brown Grand Theatre, Napoleon Bonaparte Brown. Private residence.

CLOUD COUNTY STAINED GLASS DRIVING TOUR: This is a wonderful way to experience Cloud County. A self-guided auto tour of the county will direct you to almost 20 sites of stained-glass beauty including churches, a convent, and a museum. The brochure also lists restaurants and lodging in the seven towns featured and can be picked up at the Brown Grand Theatre, 310 West Sixth, Concordia, or call 913/243-2553.

LESTER'S SWEET SHOP: 210 West Sixth, Concordia. Lester's has been newly renovated but still houses one of the grandest old-fashioned working soda fountains in Kansas. The long marble-top counter was featured at the 1901 Chicago World's Fair, and the wooden back bar with big mirrors adds to the delight of sipping a malt. The mauve and white swirling colors of the fountain stand out against the stools and brass footrail. Eat deli sandwiches and ice cream treats in a booth or at the counter and let your kids enjoy a 10-cent ride on the electric horse. Open daily 9 a.m. to 5 p.m., closed Sunday. Phone 913/243-4440.

CLOUD COUNTY HISTORICAL MUSEUM: 635 Broadway, Concordia. Large museum depicts every aspect of life since the 1870s. Wicks Direct electric pipe organ, 1928 Lincoln-Page airplane, 20-by-40-foot frame of 1870s barn using wooden pegs. Large display of machinery and farm tools includes McCormick-Deering tractors, 1898 Holsman, bright red 1950 IHC pickup, 1937 truck, and stationary balers. Open Tuesday through Saturday 1 to 5 p.m. Donations appreciated. Phone 913/243-2866.

FRANK CARLSON MEMORIAL LIBRARY: Seventh and Broadway, Concordia. Library includes memorial room to Concordia native Frank Carlson, who served in the U.S. House of Representatives and as Kansas governor. Open daily 9 a.m. to 5 p.m., closed Sunday. Phone 913/243-2250.

WET PAINT GALLERY: Corner of Sixth and Washington (top floor), Concordia. Go up the stairs, and down the hallway, and you'll find your way to this highly creative and personable Kansas artist's domain. She does a variety of work but is probably best known for her north central Kansas watercolors. Hours are by chance or appointment. Don't hesitate to call 913/243-4612 or 913/243-3770.

NANCY'S FANCY: 101 East Sixth, Concordia. This former corner bank with the wraparound iron steps is listed on the national register and is now home to a shop full of Victorian antiques. Open most days, closed Sundays. Phone 913/243-2502.

KANSAS BACKROADS: On West Eleventh, 1-1/4 miles west of U.S. 81, Concordia. Antiques, collectibles, furniture, gifts and crafts, furniture refinishing, framing and matting, photo restoration. Open Monday through Saturday 9 a.m. to 5 p.m. or call 913/243-7783.

BOBBIE AND DOT'S: 101 West Sixth, Concordia. The cinnamon rolls and pie are some of the best around. Also, full meals, sandwiches, and salad bar. Open Tuesday through Saturday 10 a.m. to 9 p.m., Sunday 11 a.m. to 2 p.m. Phone 913/243-3040.

CRYSTLE'S BED-AND-BREAK-FAST: 508 West Seventh, Concordia. Crystle McDowell lived in this house for 60 years. After her death, her granddaughter turned it into a bed-and-breakfast. All the furniture is original. You'll find surprises throughout the house, like the steamer oven built into the radiator! The five guest rooms are delightfully unlike home. Relax on the porch, play the Steinway piano, or ask innkeeper Jone what there is to do in the Concordia area. Phone 913/243-2192.

PRISONER-OF-WAR CAMP: Two miles north and one mile east of Concordia. Guard tower and other scant remains of a World War II German prisoner-of-war camp can be seen from the road.

SCENIC STONE BRIDGE: From U.S. 81 and K-9 junction go 5-3/5 miles east to the unincorporated town of Rice. Turn north into Rice, take the first turn west, and follow the dirt road to the river. A huge cottonwood tree stands by this limestone arch over the Republican River. Take the stone staircase down to the river and treat this old relic with care.

CLYDE

1990 population 793; 1970 946.

CLYDE HOTEL: 420 Washington, Clyde. Once inside this old-fash-

ioned lobby you'll be eager to see where the curved staircase takes you. Each upstairs room has its own new design with original woodwork and private bath. The hotel first did business in 1870. Phone 913/446-2231 for reservations.

VAN DEMARK HOUSE: 504 Washington, Clyde. It seems the large windows, big doorways, wooden floors, plants, and ceiling fans in this 1884 historic home make the meals a bit more tasty. Everything from breads to soups is homemade. Open Tuesday through Saturday 7:30 a.m. to 1:30 p.m. and 5:30 to 8 p.m., Sunday 8:30 a.m. to 1 p.m. Phone 913/446-3770.

CLYDE COMMUNITY MU-SEUM: North Green, Clyde. This two-room museum is just right. See a gun from the War of 1812, miniature farm buildings, and an Edison disc player. People with Clyde connections will want to spend some time looking at old photos. Open Sunday 2 to 4 p.m. or call Steve at 913/446-2812 or Leola at 913/446-3361.

MARCOTTE SCHOOL: Next to museum, Clyde. A one-room school scene is recreated superbly here with three rows of old-fashioned desks, kerosene lamps mounted on the walls, a pot-bellied stove, and two wooden baseball bats resting against the blackboard. Open during museum hours or call Steve or Leola.

1872 JAIL: North Green, Clyde. Look in the windows any time and see how the interior has been refurbished.

SAINT JOSEPH'S CHURCH: Five miles south of Clyde. The twin towers on this red brick building with white stone arches and stained glass windows can be seen from miles away. The parish has recently disbanded and local citizens are making efforts to save the church.

CLIFTON-VINING COUNTRY MUSIC FESTIVAL: Held the third weekend in August. Clifton and Vining host over 25 musicians who come here to compete for prize money. Phone 913/455-3345. Clifton 1990 population 561; 1970 718. Vining 1990 population 55; 1970 84.

LCL BUFFALO RANCH: Two miles northwest of Clifton on K-9 or six miles east of Clyde on K-9. Most often you can see a small buffalo herd from the road, but make sure you pull into the yard and look for Lester. Unless he's out tending to his five pastures of over 160 buffalo, he'll be found here, and he loves visitors. Don't be shy! You can buy buffalo steaks or buffalo sticks for the road in his meat shop. Phone 913/455-3707 to make sure he'll be home.

CLIFTON MUSEUM: Clifton and Railroad, Clifton. Located in the old Missouri Pacific depot. Open June through September 2 to 4 p.m. For an appointment call 913/455-3763 or 446-2284.

BELOIT

1990 population 4,066; 1970 4,121.

BELOIT INFORMATION: Chamber of Commerce, 123 North Mill, Beloit. Stop in or call 913/738-2717 for additional Beloit area accommodations and attractions information. Pick up a walking tour brochure of historical downtown buildings and take a walk down the red brick streets.

CARL'S: Corner of Mill and Main, Beloit. This gift shop has a wonderful 1909 soda fountain with a marble counter. Sit on ice cream parlor chairs or at booths to enjoy your soda foun-

tain treats. Open Monday through Saturday 9 a.m. to 5 p.m. Phone 913/738-5644.

SAINT JOHN CATHOLIC CHURCH: 701 East Court, Beloit. Step inside to see this Romanesque and Gothic style church, listed on the national register. It was the first church in the nation to have flying buttresses and a stone ceiling. Note the painted ceilings.

MITCHELL COUNTY COURTHOUSE: East end of central business district, Beloit. This courthouse, built in 1902 in the Romanesque Revival style, is one of the more striking in the state.

LITTLE RED SCHOOLHOUSE: Located in rest area one mile east of the junction of K-14 and K-9/U.S. 24. This schoolhouse was built to preserve the tradition of all the one-room schoolhouses in the county. Open Friday through Monday 1 to 4 p.m. Phone 913/738-5301.

MITCHELL COUNTY MUSEUM: 402 West Eighth, Beloit. Four floors of displays tell the story of the county. A spiral staircase leads to the fourth floor. It's like exploring grandma's attic. Open daily 1 to 5 p.m. Closed Saturdays. Phone 913/738-5355.

CHAUTAUQUA PARK: K-14 and Roosevelt Avenue lead to Chautauqua Drive, Beloit. The Solomon River provides a nice backdrop for the playground, recreational facilities, camping area, and RV hookups. Phone the Chamber of Commerce at 913/738-2717.

BUTTERFIELD'S MEAT SHOP AND BUFFALO HERD: From U.S. 24 and K-14 junction north of Beloit, go one mile west and 1/4 mile south to the store. Get buffalo meat in all forms. To get to the nearby buffalo herd go three miles west and two miles north of the junction. Phone 913/738-2336.

GLEN ELDER STATE PARK:
Between Cawker City and Glen Elder on U.S. 24. This popular camping park also provides great fishing, nature trails, paved roads for bicycling, and a prairie dog town. Efforts are being made to create a replica of Waconda Springs and a Heritage Village area including a school and a church that will be used by camp visitors. Camping and vehicle permits required. Phone 913/545-3345.

COUNTRYSIDE MARKET:
Downtown Glen Elder. 1990 population 448; 1970 422. Staying at the lake and needing some groceries? This grocery with the wooden floors and pressed tin ceiling is open daily 8 a.m. to 6 p.m. Closed Sunday. Phone 913/545-3565.

NORTHSIDE CAFE DINING HALL:
Downtown Cawker City. 1990 population 588; 1970 726. Pick a booth or a spot at the counter. Basic fare. Open daily 6:30 a.m. to 10 p.m. Phone 913/781-4741. Look for the big ball of twine in this town.

LAKESIDE GOLF COURSE:
First exit east of Cawker City on U.S. 24, south side of road. Public course, green fee.

HISTORICAL MARKER:
North side of Lake Waconda on U.S. 24/K-9. This marker tells about Waconda, the Indian maiden who followed her mortally wounded lover into a spring.

LINCOLN

1990 population 1,381; 1970 1,582. For additional accommodations and attractions information call the Chamber of Commerce, 913/524-4934 .

VILLAGE LINES:
139 West Lincoln, Lincoln. Not only does Marilyn carry interesting Kansas and north central Kansas products, she's an excellent source of area tourist information. Ask her about local art galleries and wheat harvest tours! Open Monday through Saturday 9 a.m. to 5:30 p.m. Phone 913/524-5133.

PENNY'S WOODEN WONDERLAND:
Fifth and Court, Lincoln. The front of the store sells Penny's handcrafted wood products and antiques as well. Look carefully to find the penny that Penny packages in each furniture piece. The Lincoln penny is his personal trademark. It's dated the year he made the piece and signifies that the wood came from Lincoln county! Penny cuts the wood in his own sawmill. Ask for tours of his workshop. The shop is open in the summer Monday through Friday and catch-as-catch-can in the winter. Phone 913/524-4294.

J.J. COUNTRY CRAFTS:
137 East Lincoln, Lincoln. These creators and makers of Deelehopper dolls are doing a booming business. Hand carved whimsical wooden animal-faced dolls are flexible. Dressed in doll clothes, they're quickly becoming collectors' items. Public welcome to see work in progress. Phone 913/524-4626.

LINCOLN ART CENTER:
East Lincoln, Lincoln. Local artwork featured here on a rotating basis. Open Tuesday through Friday 12:30 to 4:30 p.m., Saturday 10 a.m. to 2:30 p.m., Sunday 1 to 3 p.m. Donations appreciated. Phone 913/524-3241.

LINCOLN COUNTY COURTHOUSE:
East Lincoln and Second, Lincoln. Completed in 1900, this Romanesque Revival-styled limestone building is listed on the national register. During business hours feel free

to tour the interior. A monument on the courthouse lawn honors Union soldiers and sailors.

KYNE HOUSE MUSEUM: Lincoln and Fifth, Lincoln. This interesting county museum and house are open April through September on Sunday 1 to 4:30 p.m. or by appointment. Donations appreciated. Phone 913/524-5133.

THE YOHE HOUSE: 316 South Second, Lincoln. Group tours are offered of this private Queen Anne home by appointment. Fee. Phone 913/524-4648.

LINCOLN CEMETERY: Located on K-18, Lincoln. Two interesting gravestones in this cemetery include the Suitcase gravestone and a memorial to a Civil War flag carrier. Look for a four-walled limestone structure on the west side of the cemetery. In front of it is a tombstone with an inscription and an etching of a boy carrying a flag. The suitcase is located on the cemetery's east side.

WOODY HOUSE BED-AND-BREAKFAST: K-18 and North Avenue, Lincoln. This Queen Anne home on the edge of town offers a warm and friendly respite in Victorian comfort. Reading a book on the porch is a marvelous way to spend a few hours! Hosts Michael and Ivona have the inside track on area tours. Phone 913/524-4744 for reservations.

DANISH WEEKEND: WANTED: Six couples per weekend interested in a unique Danish experience. Three couples stay at the Spillman Creek Lodge in Denmark, the other three at the Woody House in Lincoln. The package includes a Danish meal served by women in costume, a tour of a Danish home, church, and community hall, and the option of a character portrayal by Bev Nelson.

Offered April through October. Phone 913/524-4744 or 913/277-3424.

SPILLMAN CREEK LODGE: Edge of Denmark. This farm, that has been in the Nielsen family since 1870, has two homes on it. Guests stay in one and eat breakfast in the limestone family home. The Nielsens are an enthusiastic source of information about the resurgence of the unincorporated town of Denmark. Phone 913/277-3424.

TESCOTT MUSEUM: Minnesota off K-18, Tescott. 1990 population 317; 1970 393. This old schoolhouse displays local exhibits including a personal collection of World War II concentration camp photos that were smuggled out of Germany. Open by appointment only. Stop at the bank during the day and inquire or call 913/283-4389, 283-4302, or 283-4722.

BETTY'S RESTAURANT: Downtown Barnard, beside the post office. 1990 population 129; 1970 190. This little town boasts one of the great local cafes in the state. Famous for its homemade pies, this cafe was once featured in the *Los Angeles Times*. Open daily 6 a.m. to 2 p.m., closed Sundays. Phone 913/792-6323.

SYLVAN GROVE

1990 population 321; 1970 403.

S.M. LAWSON HARDWARE STORE: Downtown Sylvan Grove. People say it's easier to find older hardware here than in most places. The wooden floors and pressed tin ceiling haven't changed either. Open weekdays 9 a.m. till noon. Phone 913/526-7197 or 526-7190.

CATTLE AUCTION: Turn east at the bank in Sylvan Grove. Cattle auction held every Friday afternoon. Watch the auction from a window seat in the restaurant. Closed during harvest. Phone 913/526-7123.

SYLVAN CAFE: Downtown Sylvan Grove. Open Monday through Friday 7 a.m. to 7 p.m. Phone 913/526-7254.

YESTERDAY MUSEUM: Downtown Sylvan Grove. The museum is housed in one of the many limestone buildings in Sylvan Grove. Post rock tools and a barbed wire collection are featured at the museum. Open May through October weekends 9 a.m. to 5 p.m. or phone 913/526-7270. Donations appreciated.

THE COUNTRY SHOPPE: Second and Main, Sylvan Grove. Local crafts are featured here. Open Monday through Saturday 10 a.m. to 5 p.m. Phone 913/526-7288.

VONADA STONE COMPANY: 6-1/2 miles north of Sylvan Grove on K-181 and 1/2 mile west. The father-son team of Duane and Damon Vonada founded the Vonada Stone Company in 1986. People are welcome to stop by and see exhibits of post rock, antique stone drills, and post rock artwork. The Vonadas made the city signs for Lincoln, Lucas, Sylvan Grove, Tescott, Tipton, and Wilson, to name a few. For demonstrations of extracting post rock call in advance. Fee for demonstration. Phone 913/526-7391.

VONADA STONE QUARRY: Six miles north of Sylvan Grove on K-181. Watch for the stone sign. Open the gate and drive up to the quarry (beware if muddy). You'll be able to see the post rock layer of the Greenhorn formation. The view overlooks Spillman Creek and the Blue Hills and is a wonderful place to observe a Kansas sunrise or sunset.

The Vonadas quarrying post rock, Sylvan Grove

POST ROCK COUNTRY TOURS: An all-day tour of post rock country can be arranged. Tours feature ghost towns, working farms and ranches, the stone arch bridge, limestone quarries, timber claims, dugout ruins, the town of Denmark, the Vonada Stone Company, the Garden of Eden, and much more. Expert step-on guides (available for a fee) elaborate on the history of the Smoky Hills and post rock country. Phone 913/526-7391 for this adventure and ask about various tour plans.

STONE ARCH BRIDGE: About eight miles north of Sylvan Grove on K-181. A rest-area park is being developed to feature the stone twin arch bridge, which will be restored to its original 1908 condition.

WILSON

1990 population 834; 1970 870.

KANSAS ORIGINALS MARKET: Just north of I-70 on K-232, Wilson. More than 330 Kansas artists display their folk art, crafts, fine art, and food products here. Often Kansas foods are offered for sampling. The shop was opened to help improve the north central Kansas rural economy, so your purchases are for a good cause. A hospitality room allows space to spread out maps, pore over area history, or peruse any of the 100 statewide brochures supplied here. Open daily 8 a.m. to 8 p.m., Sunday noon to 6 p.m. Phone 913/658-2602.

SCENIC DRIVE: From Kansas Originals head north on K-232. At the Wilson Reservoir dam go east on K-181 to Sylvan Grove, then to Lucas on K-18, returning to Kansas Originals on K-232. This is the heart of farm and post rock country. The mist in the early morning gives the hills their smoky blue tint and the evenings bring a gorgeous sunset. Ask Marge Lawson of Kansas Originals about this drive.

WILSON LAKE: Eight miles north of I-70 exit 206 on K-232. Noted for its clear water, Wilson Lake has all the usual federal and state recreational, hunting, and fishing facilities found at large reservoirs. A three-mile hiking loop offers access to diverse prairie grasses, plants, and unique geological formations in the Rocktown Natural Area. Entrance fee charged in state park. Phone 913/658-2551.

BUR OAK NATURE TRAIL: Below the Wilson Dam and adjacent to Sylvan Park. Self-guided 3/4-mile trail with 23 stops described in a brochure. Trail explains area's ecology.

WILSON OPERA HOUSE AND MUSEUM: Downtown Wilson. Built in 1901, this opera house has been renovated over the years and is still the scene of local dances. In the basement, the House of Memories Museum is in an area once used as the Sokol gymnasium. The post rock walls are full of fossils, and displays relate Wilson's Czechoslovokian heritage. Open by appointment. Phone the Chamber of Commerce at 913/658-2211 or Jeanie or Peppy Joe at 913/658-3343.

LIONS PARK: City band concerts with music that includes polkas and marches are held here every Saturday night in the summer if the weather cooperates. Phone 913/658-2211.

SHAW'S GROCERY: 417 25th, Wilson. *Vitame vas* (welcome) to the home of Shaw's Homemade Sausage. In 1930 Roy Shaw learned the art of sausage making from Tony Sula, a Czech sausage maker from Moravia. Generations later sausages like Moravian Klobasi, Jaternice, Holsteiner summer sausage, Bavarian beef, and bratwurst are still some of Shaw's specialties. Open daily 8 a.m. to 8 p.m., Sunday noon to 4 p.m. Phone 913/658-2120.

STONE JAIL: Look for a sign on Main that will take you a half block down an alley. This unique stone jail was built in the late 1880s.

MORGAN'S THIS N' THAT SHOP: Old Highway 40, Wilson. This well-organized antique and collectibles store is open Monday through Saturday 9 a.m. to 5 p.m. Phone 913/658-3455.

WILSON RECREATION CENTER CAFE: Around the corner from the opera house, Wilson. Good food for dining in or a chicken picnic packed to go. Open daily 8:30 a.m. to 8 p.m. Phone 913/658-9311. In the cafe basement is an old six-lane bowling alley. Inquire at cafe desk. Fee.

ELLSWORTH

1990 population 2,294; 1970 2,080. For additional Ellsworth accommodations, and attractions information call Georgina at 913/472-4071.

ELLSWORTH COUNTY HISTOR-ICAL MUSEUM: 104 South Main, Ellsworth. This museum complex includes the Hodgen House, livery stable, one-room schoolhouse, caboose, church, and agricultural exhibits. Open May through October Tuesday through Saturday 9 a.m. to noon and 1 to 5 p.m., Sunday 1 to 5 p.m. Rest of year open Tuesday through Friday 1 to 5 p.m. Free. Phone 913/472-3059.

ART GALLERY: 204 Douglas, Ellsworth. Monthly displays feature local artists as well as special exhibitions. Open Tuesday through Friday noon to 4 p.m., Saturday 10 a.m. to 3 p.m., Sunday 1 to 3 p.m. Buy or browse.

ELLSWORTH MUNICIPAL GOLF COURSE: Located off K-156 at the bridge overpass. Golf carts are available at this nine-hole course. Green fee. Phone 913/472-4236.

K A N O P O L I S

1990 population 605; 1970 626.

WHITE'S STATION: Downtown Kanopolis. Owner Annette White is known as the Cave Lady because of her dedication to reopening the nearby Faris Caves. She is an avid student of local Pawnee Indian history. The front room of her store has local crafts; go to the back room to see Annette's beadwork crafted in the traditional style, dream makers, and photos and articles about the nearby Faris Caves. Hours are irregular. Phone 913/472-5422

FORT HARKER GUARDHOUSE MUSEUM: West side of Kanopolis. One of four Fort Harker buildings left, this Dakota sandstone structure has exhibits that tell the story of the fort. Note the stretched bar on the upstairs west window. Legend has it

that Satanta was being held in the guardhouse and escaped through those bars. Open daily 9 a.m. to noon and 1 to 5 p.m., Sunday 1 to 5 p.m. Closed Monday. Donations appreciated. Phone 913/472-5733.

OROZCO'S PORTALES CAFE: Downtown Kanopolis. This family-owned and -operated restaurant brings Old Mexico-style food to the area. Open most days for breakfast, lunch, and supper. Phone 913/472-4226.

KANOPOLIS DRIVE-IN: North end of Main, Kanopolis. Tony Blazina, Kanopolis resident, built this outdoor theater over 40 years ago. It's become a legend, and people continue to flock to the 170 parking spaces. There are benches for kids up in front. Open April into the fall depending on the weather. Phone 913/472-4786 for recorded show schedule.

KANOPOLIS RESERVOIR: Southeast corner of Ellsworth County. Excellent fishing and skiing here. Also camping, hiking, swimming, and boat rental. Phone 913/546-2294.

KANOPOLIS LAKE LEGACY TRAIL: This self-guided auto tour, a round trip of about 70 miles, takes you to 27 historical sites. The tour includes Faris Caves, Mushroom Rock State Park, Horsethief Canyon, Carneiro, Fremont's Knob, Scates Cemetery, Buckeye Cemetery, petroglyphs, and more. Phone 913/546-2294 to obtain a brochure or pick one up at the Kanopolis Lake Information Center or the marina.

FARIS CAVES: Follow the signs going east from Kanopolis, get directions at White's Station, or follow the Legacy Trail brochure. The caves were originally dug by Charles Griffee in the 1880s for shelter. Later the Faris family used the caves as a spring house, generator room, and schoolhouse.

BUFFALO TRACK CANYON NATURE TRAIL: East shore area of Kanopolis Lake. Walk up a sandhill to begin this adventurous 1-1/2-mile trail through a box canyon, past caves, and among the yucca. Located just before Horsethief Canyon area in the state park.

MUSHROOM ROCK STATE PARK: South of Carneiro off K-140 or follow the Legacy Trail brochure. This little park has a trail around and among very unusual limestone rocks that dominate this area. Cross the footbridge and find the rock to the east (left) with an inscription of the U.S. flag.

GENESEO MUSEUM: 907 Silver, Geneseo. 1990 population 382; 1970 453. This yellow house is full of local spaceship lore and area history displays. It's a tribute to the townspeople's desire to keep their rural culture alive. Free. Call Silvey at 316/824-6250 or knock on her door at 708 Tenth.

HAYS

1990 population 17,767; 1970 15,396. Hays is a city of poignant contrasts. On the west side of town the old military Fort Hays and venerable Fort Hays State University stand strong and massive, built from native limestone. Along Vine Street on the east side of town, neon lights, gaudy facades, and fast-food drive-ins represent the faster pace of modern life. Legendary citizens of the Old West, once Hays residents, now lend their names to street markers. Beyond the city, the rolling prairie lands dominate the scene as they always have. Write Hays Convention and Visitors' Bureau for information at 1301 Pine Street, Suite B, Hays, Kansas 67601. Phone 1-800/569-4505.

TWILIGHT TOURS: Free guided bus tours of Hays region featuring points of interest depart from all Vine Street motels. A great idea sponsored by the Hays Convention and Visitors' Bureau. Tour destinations vary— Cathedral of the Plains, band concerts, Philip Ranch, Walter Chrysler home, and more. For a schedule call 1-800/569-4505.

DOWNTOWN WALKING TOUR: This brochure guides you to 25 bronze plaques that mark historic places throughout downtown Hays. Pick up brochure at the Visitors' Bureau, 1301 Pine, or call 1-800/569-4505.

ROOFTOPS RESTUARANT: Fifth floor of the Emprise bank building at 1200 Main, Hays. Take the elevator up to a delightful experience of fine food, atmosphere, and service. Open weekdays 11 a.m. to 2 p.m., Monday through Saturday 5:30 to 9:30 p.m. Phone 913/628-8631.

STERNBERG MUSEUM: 600 Park, Fort Hays State campus, Hays. A place every Kansan should visit to recall the dawn of time. Displayed here are fossils of large fish and reptiles from the sea that once covered Kansas, and bones of camels, elephants, and giant bison that inhabited the land after the sea subsided. Most famous fossil is a fish-within-a-fish. Free. Open Monday through Friday 9 a.m. to 5 p.m., Saturday and Sunday 1 to 5 p.m. Large groups please call ahead, 913/628-4286.

WHEELS AND SPOKES: At intersection of I-70 and U.S. 183, Hays. A classic auto display featuring Mopar performance cars. Admission fee. Open weekdays 8 a.m. to 6 p.m., Saturday 10 a.m. to 5 p.m. Closed Sundays and holidays. Phone 913/628-6477.

STONE GALLERY: Shinbone Alley between Sixth and Seventh, Hays. Studio and exhibit gallery of Pete Felten, acclaimed sculptor. Note Felten limestone sculptures throughout Hays. Visitors welcome during business hours and by appointment. Phone 913/625-7619.

FORT HAYS STATE UNIVERSITY CAMPUS: Southwest corner of Hays. Picturesque campus of post rock limestone buildings.

FORT HAYS NATIONAL HISTORIC SITE: 1472 Bypass U.S. 183, Hays. Fort Hays was constructed in 1867 to provide protection for settlers and railroads pushing westward into Indian country. Excellent visitors' center. Note the Pete Felten buffalo sculpture at the entrance and the live buffalo pasture across U.S. 183. Open Tuesday through Saturday 9 a.m. to 5 p.m., Sunday and Monday 1 to 5 p.m. Closed major holidays. Phone 913/625-6812.

FRONTIER PARK: South end of Main at Bypass U.S. 183, Hays. Good place to stretch out. Enjoy a walk over the suspension bridge!

ELLIS COUNTY HISTORICAL MUSEUM: 100 West Seventh, Hays. More than 10,000 artifacts display Ellis County pioneer life. Free. Open Tuesday through Friday 10 a.m. to 4 p.m.; open summer afternoons on Saturday and Sunday. Phone 913/628-2624.

ELLIS

1990 population 1,814; 1970 2,137.

ELLIS RAILROAD MUSEUM: 915 Washington, Ellis. Ellis at one time was a Union Pacific Division Center with a roundhouse and railroad shops. This rich, rich history is represented by real rolling stock, a photo section, a continuous projection room, model trains, and a Union Pacific memorabilia store. Open daily 9 a.m. to 7 p.m., Sunday 1 to 7 p.m. For information call 913/726-4493.

WALTER CHRYSLER HOME: Tenth and Washington, Ellis. White picket fences identify the early home of Walter Chrysler, founder of the Chrysler Corporation. Chrysler learned his mechanical skills in the Ellis railroad shops. Free. Open daily May through September 9 a.m. to 5 p.m., Sunday 1 to 5 p.m.

LANDMARK CRAFT CO-OP: 822 Washington, Ellis. Eight local crafters and artists display and sell their products here — gold-leaf pictures, quilts, ceramics, hand-painted eggs, and more. Open Tuesday through Saturday 9 a.m. to 5 p.m. Phone 913/726-3465.

WAGON WHEEL ANTIQUES: North Washington, Ellis. Burgess Bieler "scrap metal art," monkey wrenches, pitcher pumps, lanterns.... Open Monday through Saturday 9 a.m. to 5 p.m. Phone 913/726-4666.

MAIN STREET COTTAGE: 807 North Washington, Ellis. This cottage is full of everything from antiques and collectibles to Kansas food products, cookbooks, and innumerable gift items. Open Monday through Saturday 9 a.m. to 5 p.m. Phone 913/726-3760.

WILDLIFE: Wildlife is abundant in the Hays region but may be difficult to see. Heavier concentrations of wildlife in the Wilson Lake and Cedar Bluff areas make watching a pleasure. White-tailed and mule deer, turkeys, pheasants, cottontails, jackrabbits, and Canada geese are species you can expect to see as you drive or hike. Foxes and bobcats are there too but a little harder to find. Some eagles may be seen in winter. Watch for magpies; note their graceful lilting-gliding style of flight.

SCENIC ROUTE: South on U.S. 183 from Plainville to Hays. The bluffs and rolling hills are picturesque along this 23-mile route.

CATHEDRAL OF THE PLAINS: Victoria. 1990 population 1,157; 1970 1,246. The most dramatic of all post rock structures is the Cathedral of the Plains, also known as Saint Fidelis Church. The twin towers, visible from I-70, rise 141 feet.

PFEIFER: This unincorporated town is about ten miles south of Victoria on a county road. One of the most beautiful of the Ellis County churches is Pfeifer's Holy Cross Shrine.

LIEBENTHAL

1990 population 112; 1970 169.

DECHANT & SONS ANTIQUES AND COLLECTIBLES: South Main, beside St. Joseph Church, Liebenthal.

Decant and Sons Antiques and Collectibles, Liebenthal

Enter the screen door into the "biggest little store in Kansas," an antique lover's delight. Dave tries to be open Monday through Saturday 10 a.m. to 6 p.m. Phone 913/222-3267.

PAT'S BEEF JERKY: 401 Main, Liebenthal. Stop in at this red brick corner store and watch Pat cut up beef, or buy some of the excellent peppered beef jerky, hot beef sticks, or beef bologna made on the premises. Open Monday through Saturday 9 a.m. to 5 p.m. Phone 913/222-3341.

LIEBENTHAL POST OFFICE: If you're looking for a picture-perfect old-time post office, take your photo in front of this quaint building.

LACROSSE

1990 population 1,427; 1970 1,583.

POST ROCK FENCEPOST: Just about anywhere in Rush County you'll find seemingly endless rows of post rock fencepost. Think of all the work it took to extract the rock, dig the holes, and set in the posts.

MUSEUM COMPLEX: Three small but unique museums are located on the south side of LaCrosse and are open Monday through Saturday 10 a.m. to 4:30 p.m. and Sunday 1 to 4:30 p.m. Phone 913/222-2719. Free camping at adjoining park.

POST ROCK MUSEUM: A model quarry and tools explain how post rock was extracted and used.

BARBED WIRE MUSEUM: LaCrosse is the Barbed Wire Capital of the World, and this museum displays over 500 varieties of barbed wire, fencing tools, and related items.

RUSH COUNTY HISTORICAL MUSEUM: The story of the county is told in the old Timken Depot.

BISON: 1990 population 252; 1970 285. In the spring, trees almost hide the museum located downtown and the bench in front of the grocery looks particularly inviting. During business hours go inside the bank and see the prints of Bison's historic buildings.

RUSSELL

1990 population 4,781; 1970 5,371. For accommodations information call the Chamber of Commerce, 913/483-6960.

DEINES CULTURAL CENTER:

820 Main, Russell. Permanent display of wood engravings of nationally known artist E. Hubert Deines. This elegant center also features the traveling exhibits of other distinguished artists. Truly an inspiring visual experience. Free. Open Tuesday through Sunday 1 to 5 p.m. Phone 913/483-3742.

OIL PATCH MUSEUM: Visible

from the intersection of I-70 and U.S. 281, Russell. Authentic displays of rigs and artifacts telling the "black gold" story in Russell County. Free. Open Memorial Day through Labor Day Tuesday through Saturday 9 a.m. to 6 p.m., Sunday 1 to 5 p.m. Phone 913/483-6640.

FOSSIL STATION MUSEUM:

331 Kansas, Russell. Formerly the county jail, this fine example of post rock construction tells the story of Russell County. Free. Open Memorial Day to Labor Day Tuesday through Sunday 1 to 4 p.m. Phone 913/483-3637.

SCENIC SALINE RIVER VALLEY

DRIVES: The argument rages on—which is the most beautiful drive through the Saline River Breaks in Russell County? You decide.
#1. Drive U.S. 281 north to the Saline River. You will be impressed.
#2. Continue on through Waldo and

Fossil Station Museum, Russell

Luray, then go south on a county blacktop to Bunker Hill. Now wasn't that pretty? #3. Canyon Road (unsurfaced) west out of Russell on 15th Street meandering in northwest direction, ending up in Paradise. Note how these Smoky Hills are more abrupt than the Flint Hills.

WALDO: 1990 population 57; 1970 123. Located in northern Russell County on U.S. 281. Crumbling town, all too representative of waning Kansas communities.

LURAY: 1990 population 261; 1970 303. This town is on the comeback trail. Beautiful restored buildings.

BUNKER HILL CAFE: Go north from I-70 exit 193 to downtown Bunker Hill. 1990 population 111; 1970 181. In this old native stone building, coal-oil lamps, antique tables with oil-cloth spreads, and a wood fire provide a romantic atmosphere, with Tom and Janet Taggart providing the delicious home-cooked meals. Twice-baked potatoes and homemade raisin bread are trademarks. Open Wednesday through Saturday 5 to 10 p.m. For reservations call 913/483-6544.

LUCAS

1990 population 452; 1970 524.

GARDEN OF EDEN: Second and Kansas, Lucas. Without a doubt the most bizarre sight in Kansas. See Cain and Abel, Adam and Eve, the Goddess of Liberty, and more full-sized images sitting in concrete trees. A *Ripley's Believe It or Not* feature. Admission fee. Open daily April through November 10 a.m. to 5 p.m. Phone 913/525-6395.

BRANT'S MEAT MARKET: Main Street, Lucas. Secret old-world recipes, oak and fruitwood smoke tang, and the old-fashioned wood-and-glass meat counter haven't changed since the thirties. Enjoy the flavor of Czech, Bavarian, and Italian sausages. Phone 913/525-6464.

Brant's Meat Market, Lucas

GRASSROOTS ART GALLERY: Downtown Lucas. A grassroots art gallery built around the Inez Marshall limestone art collection is coming soon. Call the Chamber of Commerce for details, 913/525-6288.

LUCAS COUNTRY INN: 229 South Main, Lucas. Reasonable, clean, with separate bathrooms for men and women. Phone and TV in lobby. Fishing guide service available. Phone 913/525-6358.

PHILLIPSBURG

1990 population 2,828; 1970 3,241. Located in north central Kansas at the intersection of U.S. 36 and 183. There are good motels along U.S. 36 in Smith Center and Phillipsburg. For information call the Phillipsburg Chamber of Commerce, 913/543-2321.

SCOTT-MCCOPPIN BOOK STORE: 767 East Third, Phillipsburg. For some home-town travel advice stop here and ask for Stephanie or Ron.

GRANNY'S OVEN: Across from the courthouse square, Phillipsburg. This is a good place to plan your travel strategy as you munch one of 11 flavors of English muffins, sample pastries, eat lunch, or just sip coffee. Open Monday through Friday 6 a.m. to 5 p.m. and Saturday 6 a.m. to 1 p.m. Phone 913/543-6331.

FORT BISSELL: West side of Phillipsburg on U.S. 36. The name of this excellent attraction derives from a protective stockade built by settlers in the 1870s. Original log cabins, a sod house, an 1885 store building, a one-room school, and a blacksmith shop all display furniture and tools of the period. The extensive Kingery gun collection is housed in a log cabin. Open April through October Tuesday through Friday 9 a.m. to 4 p.m., Saturday and Sunday 1 to 4 p.m. Closed for the noon hour. For guided group tours call 913/543-6212 or Beth Freeman at 913/543-5373.

KANSAS'S BIGGEST RODEO: About 1-1/2 miles north of Phillipsburg. First week in August. Call Steve

Bruning for information, daytime 913/543-5246, evening 913/543-6301, or Rod Innes, 913/543-6160. Kansas's Biggest Bull Ride takes place the second Saturday each June.

CARMEN HOUSE: Visible at mile 143 on U.S. 36 west of Phillipsburg. This abandoned farmhouse was built with rock quarried locally from the Niobrara chalk formation. An example of pioneers making do with resources at hand. This is private property; view and photograph from the side road.

KIRWIN NATIONAL WILDLIFE REFUGE: About 16 miles southeast of Phillipsburg. Over 10,000 acres of water, grasslands, and crops for sightseeing, nature observation, hiking, camping, boating, fishing, and hunting on this North Fork Solomon River refuge. Phone 913/543-6673.

THE BRANDING IRON: Located in downtown Speed, 11 miles southwest of Phillipsburg on K-9. 1990 population 64; 1970 58. Don't expect paved roads or much of a town here, but you will get one huge hamburger. Open daily 11 a.m. to 2 p.m., Sunday noon to 2 p.m. Phone 913/543-6176.

STOCKTON

1990 population 1,507; 1970 1,818. Call 913/425-6162 for accommodations and attractions information.

ROOKS COUNTY HISTORICAL MUSEUM: South U.S. 183, Stockton. The exhibits in this new museum will tell the county story in an interesting fashion. Phone 913/425-6162 or 425-7217 for hours.

THE OLD LOG HOTEL: Main and Cypress, Stockton. This once served as a hotel in the early days of Stockton.

The roomy, shaded city park is located behind.

CINDY LOU'S: 409 Main, Stockton. Reuben sandwiches, charbroiled burgers, and baked potatoes with a number of toppings are the specialties here. Open Monday through Saturday 11 a.m. to 8 p.m., closed Wednesday at 5:30 p.m. Phone 913/425-7135.

WEBSTER RESERVOIR AND HIKING TRAILS: Eight miles west of Stockton on U.S. 24. This reservoir has camping, boating, and fishing. The Webster and South Solomon River Hiking Trail is a rugged ten-mile route that follows the north bank of Webster Reservoir and the South Solomon River. The trailhead is located at Marina Cove. Phone 913/425-6775.

NICODEMUS: Thirteen miles east of Hill City on U.S. 24. Nicodemus is unincorporated and has no businesses, but it is the only black Kansas settlement to have survived in Kansas. Named after a legendary slave who was the first to buy his freedom, Nicodemus celebrates the Emancipation Get-Together the last weekend of every July. Recognized as a national historic landmark, it still has a church, a community hall, and a few residents. Led by the efforts of Angela Bates, Nicodemus is intent on making a comeback. Phone 913/674-3311.

BOGUE: Junction of U.S. 24 and K-18. 1990 population 150; 1970 257. Note the stone used to build the Township Hall and High Tower Park.

DAMAR: K-18 six miles southeast of Bogue. 1990 population 112; 1970 245. Interesting town with individual buildings as in the early days. Twin tower limestone Catholic church is a landmark. A memorial to veterans is in front of the post office.

COUNTRY CREATIONS FLOWER'S AND GIFTS: Five

miles south of Damar, downtown Palco. 1990 population 295; 1970 398. The wood floor and pressed tin ceiling are in keeping with delightful flowers, plants, and gifts. Open weekdays 9 a.m. to 5 p.m., Saturday 9 a.m. to noon. Phone 913/737-2331.

WOODSTON: Ten miles east of Stockton on U.S. 24. 1990 population 121; 1970 211. Drive down Woodston's Main Street before you head for the Big Barn. Note the abandoned high school at the east end of Main.

THE BIG BARN: About three miles east of Woodston on U.S. 24 (look for sign), then north two miles on unpaved road. This 100-foot-long, 64-foot-wide and 64-foot high barn with an unobstructed haymow is under continuous renovation. Take the stairway up to see the vastness of the haymow. The plan is to have a museum of horse-drawn farm equipment inside. Sign register, donations appreciated. Phone 913/994-6246 or 994-6253.

ALTON

1990 population 115; 1970 214. Eight miles east of Woodston on U.S. 24.

THE BLUFFS: Follow Alton Main Street south of town, across the bridge, and to the bluffs. You'll come to a T. Take the west fork and then the first turn south up into the bluffs. Drive slowly and look for the vantage point where Alton and the vast surrounding area can be seen. The east fork provides a different vantage point.

ALTON MIDWAY CO-OP: North Mill, Alton. Stop here for gas, and a few groceries, or to ask these friendly people about the bluffs. They might also have information about Russell

Stover, the candy magnate, who grew up southwest of Alton. Open weekdays 8 a.m. to 5 p.m., Saturday until noon. Phone 913/984-2214.

HISTORICAL MARKER: In front of the post office, Alton. This marker tells about General Bull, one of the founders of Alton. Alton was once named Bull City.

HISTORICAL MARKER: On U.S. 24 between Bloomington (unincorporated) and Osborne. Keep your eyes open for this stone marker that tells about the last Indian fight in Osborne County. The 1870 victory for the white man must have felt like doomsday to the Indians.

OSBORNE

1990 population 1,778; 1970 1,980.

THE LOFT BED-AND-BREAKFAST: 520 North First, Osborne. As Irene says, the house is furnished in early homemaker. Russ and Irene are as comfortable to be around as their two rooms are to sleep in. They have great rocking chairs upstairs, a big flower and vegetable garden out back, and a swimming pool within a block. Phone 913/346-5984 for reservations.

OSBORNE LIVESTOCK COMMISSION: West Adams, Osborne. Cattle auction every Wednesday afternoon. Lunch served. No sale during harvest. Phone 913/346-2351.

OSBORNE COUNTY COURTHOUSE: Two blocks west of business district. This courthouse, with historical displays inside, has had a working outdoor clock since 1907. If you look closely you'll see a portrait on the south side of the tower. It's the face of the sidewalk superintendent who was such a nuisance when the courthouse was built that they decided to sculpt his image in the courthouse walls.

FLOWER GARDEN: Main and Second, Osborne. Wouldn't it be nice if every town had a little spot like this? Benches, fountain, flowers. Rest room available here.

OSBORNE COUNTY GOLF COURSE: Follow West Main outside of town, pass the scout cabin, and follow river to parking lot at dam. Walk across the river dam bridge and follow the shade tree tunnel to the first tee. This nine-hole grass-green course has a self-pay station at the first hole. A nature trail is being planned along the fairways, but you're welcome to find your own way now. A sand-green golf course is available north of town on U.S. 281.

HISTORICAL MARKER: Located in park at junction of U.S. 24 and U.S. 281. This marker tells about the geodetic center of North America located eighteen miles to the southeast.

OSBORNE COUNTY MUSEUM: Second and U.S. 24, Osborne. The old Osborne depot holds county displays featuring the doctor who made all his house calls in black top hat and tux. Open by appointment or Sunday 2 to 5 p.m. in the summers. Donations appreciated. Call Gladys 913/346-2626 or Lillian 913/346-2418.

TOWN AND COUNTRY GROCERY: Downtown Osborne. The prices in this small-town grocery are often better than those in the big towns. A deli in the back of the grocery can fix you up with soup and sandwiches to eat there or carry out. Open daily for lunch and supper. Closed Sunday. Phone 913/346-2600.

STUFF AND SUCH: 801 Morgan, Downs. 1990 population 1,119; 1970 1,268. The renovated Lipton Hotel,

built in 1880, is a gift oasis in north central Kansas. You'll find everything from fabrics and cookbooks to brass, crystal, baskets, and handmade crafts. Open daily 9 a.m. to 5:30 p.m. Closed Sunday. Phone 913/454-3416.

PORKY PIG MARKER: South edge of Portis. 1990 population 129; 1970 178. This marker is in memory of Tubby Miller, animator for the Looney Tunes Porky Pig cartoons. Miller grew up in Portis.

THE FRONTIER INN: Downtown Portis. Evening menu offers a variety from steaks to frog legs. Open Wednesday and Sunday 11 a.m. to 2 p.m. and Friday and Saturday night 5:30 to 9 p.m. Make sure you look at the sign on the north outside wall of the cafe. Phone 913/346-5407.

HISTORICAL MARKER: South of Portis on U.S. 281. This marker tells about the only completed stockade in Osborne County. Enjoy this scenic drive in the High Plains Blue Hills region between Osborne and Portis.

NICHOLS HARDWARE: On U.S. 281, Harlan (unincorporated). Just turn into town and look for the store overflowing with inventory. It 's true that the inventory seems to have been there a while, but then owner Kelly Nichols started business in 1928. The most dedicated of antique hunters will enjoy a trip through the crowded aisles. Kelly's open just about every day. Phone 913/697-2922.

SMITH CENTER

Junction of U.S. 36 and U.S. 281. 1990 population 2,016; 1970 2,389.

INGLEBORO RESTAURANT: 319 North Main, Smith Center. Let David Haug and staff provide you with a fine dining experience in this

1883 Victorian mansion. Serving hours Monday through Friday and Sunday 11 a.m. to 2 p.m. and evenings 5 to 9 p.m. Open Saturday 5 to 10 p.m. Phone 913/282-3798.

DUTCH MILL AND WAGNER PARK: One block east on Third, Smith Center. The Dutch windmill was originally built near Reamsville in the 1870s. It supplied power to grind corn and wheat unil 1914, when a kerosene engine was installed. The millworks have been removed and the mill's interior now serves as a meeting hall. Lots of shade for picnics in the park, playground for children. Free.

GEOGRAPHIC CENTER OF THE UNITED STATES: One mile north of Lebanon and one mile west on K-191. An attractive marker here indicates the geographic center of the 48 contiguous states. A picnic shelter and a small chapel are here also. Lebanon 1990 population 364; 1970 517.

HOME ON THE RANGE CABIN: One mile west of Athol (west of Smith Center on U.S. 36), eight miles north, and 3/4 mile west on a gravel road. In 1873, Dr. Brewster Higley wrote the words to "My Western Home," now known as "Home on the Range," in a little log cabin on the banks of Beaver Creek. His restored cabin is located on the farm of Mrs. Ellen Rust, who graciously says the public is welcome any time.

WAITES SUNDRIES AND FOUNTAIN SERVICE: 123 South Main, Kensington. 1990 population 553; 1970 653. This marble soda fountain is magnificent among limestone walls, pressed tin ceiling, and wooden floors. Open Monday through Saturday 8 a.m. to 6 p.m. Phone 913/476-2651.

NORTHEAST KANSAS

ATCHISON SECTION: Atchison, Doniphan, Hiawatha, Highland, Iowa Point, Lancaster, Troy, Wathena, White Cloud, Whiting. *Page 27 to 30.*

COUNCIL GROVE SECTION: Admire, Burlingame, Bushong, Council Grove, Herington, Lincolnville, Lyndon, Miller, Osage City, Overbrook, Vassar. *Page 30 to 34.*

KANSAS CITY SECTION: Bonner Springs, Fairway, Kansas City, Lenexa, Olathe, Overland Park, Shawnee, Stilwell. *Page 35 to 38.*

LAWRENCE SECTION: Baldwin City, Lawrence, Lecompton, Tonganoxie. *Page 38 to 43.*

LEAVENWORTH SECTION: Leavenworth, McLouth, Meriden, Nortonville, Oskaloosa, Ozawkie, Valley Falls. *Page 43 to 47.*

MANHATTAN SECTION: Alma, Alta Vista, Clay Center, Junction City, Longford, Manhattan, Milford, Olsburg, Onaga, Paxico, Riley, St. Marys, Wabaunsee, Wakefield, Wamego, Westmoreland. *Page 47 to 52.*

MARYSVILLE SECTION: Blue Rapids, Bremen, Hanover, Marysville, Morrowville, Oketo, St. Benedict, Seneca, Washington, Waterville, Vermillion. *Page 52 to 56.*

OTTAWA SECTION: Gardner, Hillsdale, Louisburg, Paola, Osawatomie, Ottawa, Spring Hill. *Page 56 to 59.*

TOPEKA SECTION: Big Springs, Holton, Topeka. *Page 59 to 62.*

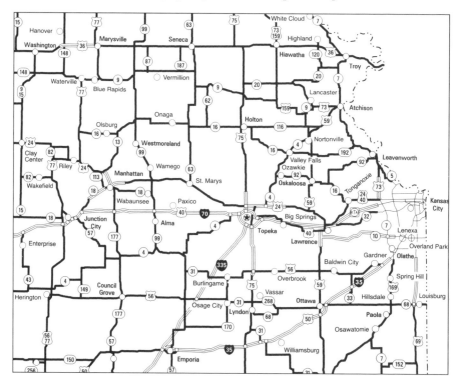

Photo opposite side: Osage County Quilt Factory, Overbrook

Steamboats on the big rivers, freight and pioneer wagons lumbering westward, and the turbulent politics of territorial Kansas may be history, but their influence lingers here. Amid the high-rises of Johnson County are rich farmland and bustling commerce. Grand old mansions, temporary capitols, trail ruts, and museums full of memorabilia still recall early Kansas.

Evidence of other eras and cultures also remains: Red quartzite rocks scattered in fields and pastures are reminders of the ice age. Forts, old missions, and the pay station at St. Marys bring to mind our republic's questionable dealings with native Americans . Old barns in the countryside and forgotten filling stations in small towns speak of a transition some call progress.

Northeast Kansas offers metropolitan comfort and drama alongside bucolic farms and villages. Each season brings fresh beauty as colors change from emerald green to autumn gold to winter white. Meander on the byways and backways, remember what was and rejoice in the beauty that is now.

ATCHISON

1990 population 10,656; 1970 12,565. Located on the Missouri River near the northeast corner of Kansas at the junction of U.S. 73, U.S. 59, and K-7. Organized in 1854 as a town company, Atchison became a staging area for travelers headed westward. The ageless Missouri River and the bluffs overlooking it, the old limestone Santa Fe depot, and stately homes built in the mid-1800s are alongside contemporary foundries, agribusiness, and yarn mills. It's easy to recall the excitement of a time when wagons were outfitted here for journeys west. Call 1-800/234-1854 for area information.

SANTA FE DEPOT VISITORS' CENTER: Located 1/2 block north of the intersection of U.S. 59 and 73 (200 South Tenth), Atchison. A wonderful place to start your Atchison region journey. The depot building itself, constructed in 1880 of native limestone, is worth a stop . Detailed information about Atchison city attractions is supplied here. Ask for step-on guides for bus tours. Open weekdays 8 a.m. to 5 p.m., Saturday 10 a.m. to 4 p.m., Sunday noon to 4 p.m. Closed on holidays. Phone 1-800/234-1854.

ATCHISON COUNTY HISTORICAL MUSEUM: Old freight room in the depot visitors' center. Museum features personal effects of Amelia Earhart, railroad and antique farm memorabilia, Indian artifacts, and guns. Vintage railroad rolling stock is displayed outside. Admission fee. Hours same as visitors' center.

ATCHISON WALKING/DRIVING TOUR: Start from the visitors' center. A free brochure guides you to 18 structures on the National Register of Historic Places that reflect affluence, luxury, and craftsmanship in early Atchison.

EVAH C. CRAY HISTORICAL HOME MUSEUM: 805 North Fifth, Atchison. A rare treat — an ornate 25-room Victorian mansion furnished in luxurious period decor. Open to the public. Admission fee. Open daily May through October 10 a.m. to 4 p.m., Sunday 1 to 4 p.m. Phone 913/367-3046.

AMELIA EARHART BIRTHPLACE: Overlooking the Missouri River at 223 North Terrace, Atchison. Earhart is famous for her 1932 transAtlantic solo flight and many other aviation firsts. Her plane disappeared near Howland Island in 1937 on her attempt to fly around the world.

Open daily 9 a.m. to 4 p.m., Sunday 1 to 4 p.m. Admission fee. Phone 913/367-4217.

INTERNATIONAL FOREST OF FRIENDSHIP: Near Warnock Lake in the southwest part of Atchison. What a lovely idea. Embedded in the walkway entrance Joyce Kilmer's immortal poem, *Trees,* sets the mood for a contemplative walk that integrates the states of our union and many nations of the world through the medium of trees indigenous to each region. Walk the paths quietly, enjoy the call of the birds, and let your eyes feast on the rich colors of the season. Near Warnock Lake is a playground for children. Open always. Free.

DRURY-PENNELL HOUSE: 519 North Fifth, Atchison. Elegant stained-glass windows and intricately carved woodwork highlight 1870s affluence in this fine restaurant. Lunch and dinner Wednesday through Saturday only. Call 913/367-4996 for reservations.

PAOLUCCI'S RESTAURANT: 115 South Third, Atchison. Enjoy Italian food in this cozy family restaurant. Open Monday through Saturday 7 a.m. to 9 p.m., Sunday 8 a.m. to 1 p.m. Phone 913/367-6105.

ALLEN HOUSE BED-AND-BREAKFAST: 623 North Fifth, Atchison. An example of the magnificent homes built in early Atchison, only a few blocks from the Missouri River and the birthplace of aviator Amelia Earhart. Call 913/367-6380 or 913/367-1884.

THE WILLIAMS HOUSE BED-AND-BREAKFAST: 526 North Fifth, Atchison. Located in the heart of Atchison. Phone 913/367-1557.

ATCHISON MALL: A charming hometown shopping mall located in the heart of Atchison. After two devastating floods in 1958 and the construction of flood-prevention dams, downtown Atchison was rebuilt in a unique manner, becoming a prototype for malls across the nation.

DONIPHAN: Take the Scenic River Road north out of Atchison, always bearing east when you reach a fork in the road until you reach the Doniphan County line. This is not an all-weather road, and there are no road markers here, so you'll need to explore or ask for help. The only readily visible remnant of Doniphan is the mercantile building's red-orange brick front facade. Doniphan was a busy steamboat port on the Missouri River until the town was left high and dry when a series of floods after the Civil War moved the river two miles east.

WÅTHENA

1990 population 1,160; 1970 1,150.

A TASTE OF COUNTRY: 401 Saint Joseph, Wathena. Beefburgers and the Sunday buffet are the house specialties but it's the house itself that's really the most special. The atmosphere created by the brick walls, wooden floor, and screen door in this century-old bank building make this an intriguing dining experience. Open daily 6 a.m. to 2 p.m. Phone 913/989-2182.

TROY

1990 population 1,073; 1970 1,047.

TALL OAK, INDIAN MONUMENT: South lawn Doniphan County courthouse, Troy. Impressive 27-foot monument sculpted from a large bur oak by Peter Toth. This is the 29th in Toth's "Trail of Whispering Giants" series placing one sculpture in each of the 50 states. The court-house, built in 1906, is on the national historic register.

NELSON HOME TOWN PHAR-MACY: 219 South Main, Troy. It's a dying breed, but you'll find a soda fountain here. Sit on the red stools, sip on a malt, and ask questions about Troy. Open Monday through Satur-day 9 a.m. to 6 p.m. Phone 913/985-2314.

SIMPSON HARDWARE: 101 South Main, Troy. Walk through these narrow white double doors, look at the 1929 receipt book and the wooden drawers and counter, then find something to buy. Owner Gary knows a lot about Troy history. Open Monday through Saturday 8 a.m. to 6 p.m. Phone 913/985-3641.

IOWA POINT: South of White Cloud on K-7. Not on most maps. Some residences remain in what was once the second largest steamboat town on the Missouri River. During the Civil War opposing factions burned each other's businesses and homes. Later the fickle Missouri moved a mile and a half east, leaving the town stranded.

WHITE CLOUD: Extreme northeast corner of Kansas on K-7. Four states may be viewed from a high bluff north of town.

HIGHLAND

1990 population 942; 1970 899.

IOWA, SAC, AND FOX MIS-SION: Two miles east of Highland. A State Historical Society restoration. Andy Clements, curator, is a great source of information. The story of the mission and its era is essential to understanding the flesh-and-blood history of Doniphan and Brown coun-ties. Open Tuesday through Saturday 10 a.m. to 5 p.m., Sunday 1 to 5 p.m. Phone 913/442-3304.

DONIPHAN COUNTY BARN TOUR: Barns are disappearing across Kansas, but Doniphan County has a number of barns on or eligible for the national historic register. Barn tour information may be obtained from Andy Clements at the Iowa, Sac, and Fox Mission. The barns are on private property but may be seen and pho-tographed from the road.

HIAWATHA

1990 population 3,603; 1970 3,365.

DAVIS MEMORIAL: Mount Hope Cemetery, Hiawatha. Eleven life-size marble and granite characters and a poignant vacant chair represent the lives of John and Sarah Davis. Ask townspeople why John may have had mixed motives in spending a half-million dollars on Sarah's tomb.

Davis Memorial, Hiawatha

BROWN COUNTY HISTORICAL MUSEUM: 611 Utah, Hiawatha. Spacious museum depicting Brown County history. Open Monday through Saturday 1 t o 4 p.m. Phone 913/742-3330.

KILLOREN EXOTIC BIRD AND ANIMAL FARM: On FAS 60 between Powhattan and U.S. 73. Take a trip around the animal world right here. Sicilian donkeys, llamas, ostriches, Dall sheep, pygmy goats, and more. Best to call first, 913/474-3539.

KENNEKUK: One mile south of Horton on U.S. 159, then two miles east on county road. Unincorporated. Main attraction in this old Pony Express village is the whimsically decorated Francis During house. Thousands of reflectors on a white frame house contrast incongruously with a nearby abandoned pioneer store.

WHITING

1990 population 213; 1970 256.

PORCELAIN TREASURES: Whiting. Quite a surprise here in a small, tumbling-down town. Sally Bottorff moved here from Chicago to make and teach others to make fine porcelain dolls from imported China clay. Call Sally for information at 913/873-3566.

WHITING CAFE: Downtown Whiting. Rosa and her Mom, Gwyn, cook up some mighty good food at this small cafe with the U-shaped counter. Open daily 6:30 a.m. to 4 p.m. Closed Sunday. Phone 913/873-3125.

LANCASTER

1990 population 299; 1970 279.

HADERWAY HOUSE TEA-ROOM: East side of Lancaster, nine miles west of Atchison on U.S. 73. Pamper yourself with a cup of tea in a luxurious Victorian home. Full tea consists of a salad; an antique crystal platter filled with English scones, breads, and sweets; your choice of entree; a

dessert; and English tea or coffee. Top off the experience with a round of croquet on the lawn if you like. Serving February, March, July, and August Thursday through Saturday 11 a.m. to 3 p.m.; the rest of the year open Tuesday through Saturday 11 a.m. to 3 p.m. Closed in January. For reservations call 913/874-5771.

COUNCIL GROVE

1990 population 2,228; 1970 2,403. For more information phone 1-800/732-9211. The city of Council Grove has been designated a National Historic Landmark. Santa Fe Trail history saturates this town like a morning mist. Indeed, phantom bullwhackers of the mid-1800s would still recognize landmarks such as the Kaw Mission, the Last Chance store, and possibly the Old Calaboose, where some of them may have spent a sobering night. In 1860, 3,000 wagons, 7,000 people, and 60,000 mules passed through the city.

Cradled in the Neosho River Valley, Council Grove is located in the heart of summer grazing country among the Kansas Flint Hills at the intersection of K-177 and U.S. 56, which stair-steps along the old Santa Fe Trail. Almost modestly, the town features its history and discreetly calls attention to its attractions.

COTTAGE HOUSE HOTEL: 25 North Neosho, Council Grove. Advertised as having "modernistic comforts in nostalgic surroundings." All rooms are decorated and furnished in keeping with the time when they were built: 1870, 1898, and 1913. Private baths for each room. We highly recommend this fine old hotel for your lodging pleasure. Call 1-800/727-7903 for reservations.

FLINT HILLS BED-AND-BREAK-FAST: 613 West Main, Council Grove. This 1913 American Four-Square, the boyhood home of former congressman John Rhodes, is full of antiques and is located on the old Santa Fe Trail. Phone 316/767-6655.

HAYS HOUSE: 112 West Main, Council Grove. Built by Seth Hays in 1857 as a tavern and hostelry, this is the oldest restaurant in continuous use west of the Mississippi River. Rick and Alisa Paul, the present owners, continue the famous fine dining tradition of the Hays House. Open Monday through Friday 7 a.m. to 9 p.m., weekends 6 a.m. to 9 p.m. Call 316/767-5911 for a great dining experience.

THE CANOPY: Across from the Hays House, Council Grove. Be good to yourself. Enjoy old-fashioned ice-cream treats, munchy cookies, and soft drinks (yogurt too) at the Canopy window service from 3 to 10 p.m. during the summer. In the spring, fall, and winter enter at the Aldrich Apothecary for soda fountain service inside (open daily 9 a.m. to 5 p.m., Sunday 12:30 to 4:30 p.m.). You'll like the gift shop and Kansas souvenirs too. Phone 316/767-6210.

KAW METHODIST MISSION: 500 North Mission, Council Grove. A good place to start your Council Grove explorations. The mission dates back to 1849 when white missionaries sought to proselytize young Native Americans. Ron Parks, site curator, tells the story of European intrusion into what became the Kansas Territory and the opening of the Santa Fe Trail. The building itself and pioneer exhibits complete the story. Open Tuesday through Saturday 10 a.m. to 5 p.m., Sunday 1 to 5 p.m. Phone 316/767-5410.

D.A.R. MARKERS: In the early 1900s the Daughters of the American Revolution placed red or gray granite markers at key points along U.S. 56 and other roads to mark the Santa Fe Trail. Aficionados of the Santa Fe Trail may want to use Simmons's book, *Following the Santa Fe Trail,* for supplemental information.

OLD CALABOOSE: Main and Railroad Avenue, Council Grove. Starting point of self-guided walking tour. Old jail, 1870, built of oak timbers.

COUNCIL OAK: Near Third and Main, Council Grove. The old oak stump under a canopy marks the site of the 1825 treaty with the Osage people permitting safe passage on the Santa Fe Trail. Council Grove is named after the grove of large bur oaks in which this important treaty council was held. Several of these venerable trees are still growing along Main Street.

POST OFFICE OAK: Almost two blocks west of the Council Oak, Council Grove. Purportedly the site of a letter drop for trail travelers.

MADONNA OF THE TRAIL: Neosho River and Main, Council Grove. A moving tribute to the courage of pioneer women. Note the determined expression and the resolute step forward. A series of 12 similar statues were placed along the old National Road of which the Santa Fe Trail was a segment.

LAST CHANCE STORE: Main and Chautauqua, Council Grove. Once the last trading post where supplies for the journey to Santa Fe could be bought. Council Grove was also the last place where hardwood trees for spare wagon axles and tongues were found on the trail. Similar trees are still growing along the river.

FARMERS AND DROVERS BANK:
Main and Neosho, Council Grove. An eye-catching example of Eclectic architecture featuring Romanesque arches and Byzantine minarets and domes. Constructed in 1902 (note the high floor level to escape flooding). It makes you stop to think about what motivated the early prairie settlers to go to great effort and expense for beautiful structures that are longer-lived than our new buildings.

COUNCIL GROVE LAKE:
On the Neosho River just northwest of Council Grove. The usual services and facilities associated with large reservoirs are found here, including camping, fishing, hunting, sightseeing, and boating. For information call 316/767-5195.

HERINGTON

1990 population 2,685; 1970 3,165.

TRI-COUNTY HISTORICAL MUSEUM AND TRAIN ANNEX:
800 South Broadway, Herington. The Rock Island Railroad and Dickinson, Marion, and Morris counties are represented in museum displays. Open Monday through Friday 10 a.m. to 4 p.m. Free. Phone 913/258-2842.

BOELLING'S PHARMACY:
2 West Main, Herington. You can get sandwiches as well as ice cream treats at this soda fountain. Open daily 9 a.m. to 6 p.m., closed Sunday. Phone 913/258-3703.

TIEMEIER'S STORE:
Downtown Lincolnville. 1990 population 197; 1970 218. The wide screen doors on this red brick building are your first clue that you're about to have a nostalgic experience. This grocery and mercantile has modernized somewhat over the years, but the wooden floors, pressed tin ceilings, roomy aisles, and old meat counter and checkout counters will still take you back decades. Open daily 8 a.m. to 5:30 p.m., closed Sunday. Phone 316/924-5523.

BUSHONG:
Seventeen miles east of Council Grove on U.S. 56. 1990 population 57; 1970 39. Almost a ghost town. The business section of town is abandoned. Question: Should you stop at stop signs in a ghost town?

ADMIRE:
South of U.S. 56 and K-57 intersection. 1990 population 147; 1970 144. This is a thriving town compared to Bushong, with a cafe, post office, and tire shop open. Heartland America is dying, is anybody watching?

MILLER:
South on spur K-78 from U.S. 56. Unincorporated. Main Street business is dead, but there is a poignant beauty and charm manifest as you travel the tree-canopied, unpaved back streets. Kids ride bikes on shaded streets.

OSAGE CITY

1990 population 2,689; 1970 2,600.

OSAGE RAILROAD AND MINING MUSEUM:
508 Market, Osage City. Osage County and Santa Fe Railroad exhibits in a little museum featuring the coal-mining era. The museum is housed in a unique Spanish Mission-style depot. Open Tuesday, Thursday, and Sunday 1 to 4 p.m. Call Belle Youngers at 913/528-3835 or 528-4530 for special tours.

MIDWEST SPORTS RACING, INC.:
512 Main, Osage City. Race cars and more race cars! Want to rent a Shelby Can-Am? Here's your chance. Steven Fenske invites you to stop by and actually see fine racing cars being assembled, painted, and set

up for racing. Just call 913/528-4125 for your personal tour.

BURLINGAME

1990 population 1,074; 1970 999.

BURLINGAME: "Where Trail meets Rail." The Santa Fe Railroad crosses over U.S. 56 at the east edge of town near the point where the trail and rail first intersected in 1869. Travel on the Santa Fe Trail ebbed as quickly as the railroads moved west. Camera buffs will find a great picture where K-31 enters Burlingame from the west as you look down from the crest of the hill. Note the center street parking downtown.

COAL MINE REMNANTS: Coal mining was an important industry in Osage County till the early 1900s. The mine shafts are all closed now, but as you drive through the countryside you may see gray and sometimes red piles of tailings as evidence of shaft locations. If you stop to visit with some old-timers, they'll tell you about miners working all day in "drifts" only 30 inches high.

SANTA FE TRAIL RUTS: Go west of Burlingame on K-31 about three miles to Dragoon Creek, named after a contingent of dragoons (mounted infantry) who crossed here in the 1850s. Go another mile and a half to a D.A.R. trail marker on the north side of the road. On the opposite side of the road faint trail ruts are visible going southwest. In the spring be sure to note the beautiful wildflowers here.

HAVANNA STAGE STATION: Go almost 1/4 mile east of the D.A.R. trail marker. On the south side of the road a weathered loading chute marks the point where you may see the limestone walls of the Havanna Stage Station. A nearby red barn will

verify the location. Private property, view from the road.

SCENIC DRIVE: Continue to the intersection west of the D.A.R. marker. (You're now five miles west of Burlingame). Go 1/2 mile south on a rock road. You'll find a wonderful canopy of giant hardwood trees overhanging the road. In season enjoy the wildflowers including spiderwort, butterfly milkweed, and daisy fleabane. Stop a while, listen to the birds in the trees. Caution: the roadside is covered with poison ivy.

STATION AT 110 MILE CREEK: Also known as the McGee Tavern. This old Santa Fe ruin is a bit hard to find but it's worth it. From the intersection of U.S. 56 and U.S. 75 go approximately 1/2 mile south to a D.A.R. marker on the west side. At this point you'll see a faint trail leading west-southwest. Follow it on foot for 3/10 of a mile. When foliage is heavy you won't see the building till you're right on it. Then it will pop out at you like a specter. Another hundred yards down the trail you will find more ruins. View and take photos from the trail only.

OVERBROOK

1990 population 920; 1970 748, a healthy 23 percent increase. Overbrook is a paradox. The initial appearance is one of decline, but as you explore you find a spark that has flickered into a flame. There is rebuilding from within going on.

TOPPING'S FINE FOODS: 309 Maple, Overbrook. Undoubtedly the best chocolate chess pie in Kansas. The delicious luncheon menu includes light sandwiches, so your calorie bank can afford the homemade desserts featured here. Topping's is an example of the positive Overbrook spirit. A car crashed through the front window, so Rosemary operates the business in the back room while she slowly rebuilds the front room. Open Monday through Saturday from 11:30 a.m. to 1:30 p.m. Phone 913/665-7331.

OSAGE COUNTY QUILT FACTORY: 400 Walnut, Overbrook. As you walk into this converted church be ready to be transported to quilt heaven. For creative quilters, this shop supplies everything you'll ever need or ever wanted to know about quilts. Open Tuesday through Saturday 10 a.m. to 5 p.m. Phone 913/665-7500.

FIELDSTONE, A BED-AND-BREAKFAST: Rural Overbrook. Another gem in the Overbrook collection. This time it's a converted barn that deserves the accolades. A charming place with stone walls, exposed timbers, and nearby vineyards and apple orchards. The luxurious suite on the third floor is a must for that special occasion. Call 913/665-7643 for reservations and location.

Fieldstone, A Bed-and-Breakfast, Overbrook

LYNDON

1990 population 964; 1970 958.

KNIGHT'S PHARMACY SODA FOUNTAIN: Downtown Lyndon.

It's a formica counter instead of marble, but the stools work just fine and the hand-packed ice cream tastes mighty good. Stop in for coffee. Open Monday through Friday 8:30 a.m. to 6 p.m., Saturday 9 a.m. to 2 p.m .

HEADMASTER'S BARBER SHOP AND ANTIQUES: Downtown Lyndon. Look for the swirling red, white, and blue barber pole. You don't have to get a haircut to be allowed inside. In fact, it's hard to find the barber chair amidst all the used books and antiques. Open Tuesday through Saturday 8 a.m. to 4 p.m. Phone 913/828-4507.

MELVERN RESERVOIR AND EISENHOWER STATE PARK: Located in southwest Osage County. Take the Lebo exit on I-35 and go north or take exits on U.S. 75. Hiking and equestrian trails, camping, swimming beach, boating, fishing. Entrance fee. Phone 913/528-4102 for a brochure or information.

THE GERMAN HAUS: Downtown Vassar north of K-268. Unincorporated. This place is reason enough to stop in Vassar. You'll find all sorts of things here from furniture, Persian rugs, flowers, and some German gifts to a little grocery including German meats and sausages! Open Monday through Saturday 9 a.m. to 6 p.m. and Sunday 11 a.m. to 5 p.m. Phone 913/828-3451.

POMONA RESERVOIR: East side of Osage County. Fishing, boating, camping, swimming beach, Deer Creek Nature Trail, equestrian trails, and the Pine Ridge Interpretive Center. Entrance fees. Phone 913/453-2201 for brochure or information.

KANSAS CITY

1990 population 149,767; 1970 168,213. For lodging and cultural events information call the the Kansas City Convention and Visitors' Bureau at 913/321-5800.

As you drive in the Kansas City region horizons come and go. One minute you may see the shimmering towers of Kansas City, Missouri, across the Missouri River. The next minute the road plunges into an ancient wooded valley, and then you might crest a hill and see only rows and rows of houses under construction. Street markers bear names of a civilization vanquished long ago — Quivira, Shawnee — and other markers pay tribute to the evolution of Kansas City — Santa Fe, Shawnee Mission, Metcalf....

You will discover the Kansas City region to be one of the most beautiful in Kansas. Side by side are robust high-tech development, quiet shaded streets, and natural places that scarcely reflect human influence. For your enjoyment we encourage you to explore the byways and backways of the western side of Kansas City.

STRAWBERRY HILL MUSEUM AND CULTURAL CENTER:

720 North Fourth, Kansas City. This museum represents a unique Croatian enclave bounded by the Kansas River on the east and Minnesota Avenue on the north. At the turn of the century many European immigrants to Kansas City settled in distinct cultural communities. The Strawberry Hill community, made up originally of Croatians working in large packing houses across the river, is still identifiable today. Houses are small but neat and characterized by displays of flowers. You may drive through the area any time. The museum is open Saturday and Sunday noon to 5 p.m. Phone 913/371-3264.

JENNIE'S RESTAURANT:

402 North Fifth, Kansas City. A chance to experience authentic Croatian food and conversation in a small neighborhood cafe. Open Monday through Friday 10:30 a.m. to 3 p.m. and 5 to 7:30 p.m. Phone 913/621-4222.

BOAT RIDES: One River City Drive, Kansas City (coming from the west take I-70 Exit 423B). Enjoy the romance of cruising the Missouri River on the 600-passenger *Missouri Queen* or the elegant *America*. Call 1-800/373-0027 or 913/281-5300 for schedules, rates, and reservations.

A Missouri River cruise boat, Kansas City

HURON BURIAL GROUND:

One-half block west of Sixth and Minnesota, Kansas City (just west of the library). This old Indian cemetery is a poignant example of the juxtaposition of two cultures.

GRINTER PLACE: 1420 South 78th, Kansas City. Moses Grinter operated a ferry here across the Kaw (Kansas) River serving Indian, Military Road, and Oregon Trail travelers from 1831 to 1870. Grinter and his wife Anna built the present two-story red brick house in 1857. Curator Rodney Staab is an excellent interpreter of history. Free. Open Tuesday through Saturday 10 a.m. to 5 p.m., Sunday 1 to 5 p.m. Phone 913/299-0373.

THE WOODLANDS: 99th and Leavenworth Road, Kansas City. Greyhound racing September to May, horse racing May to September. Phone 913/299-9797.

F A I R W A Y

1990 population 4,173; 1970 5,227.

SHAWNEE METHODIST MIS-SION: 3403 West 53rd, Fairway (one block north of Shawnee Mission Parkway at Mission Road). This mission school was established in 1839 as a manual labor school for Indian children. In 1855 after adjourning in the first territorial capitol at Fort Riley, the legislature met here to pass the "Bogus Laws" in an effort to make Kansas a slave state. Tour guide Alice Stein and curator Lee Wright make history exciting. Free. Open Tuesday through Saturday 10 a.m. to 5 p.m., Sunday 1 to 5 p.m. Phone 913/262-0867.

S H A W N E E

1990 population 37,993; 1970 20,946.

JOHNSON COUNTY HISTORI-CAL MUSEUM: 6305 Lackman Road, Shawnee. The museum features permanent and changing exhibits, hands-on activities for children, and workshops. Free. Open Tuesday through Saturday 10 a.m. to 4:30 p.m., Sunday 1 to 4:30 p.m. Phone 913/631-6709.

OLD SHAWNEE TOWN: Three blocks west of Nieman Road on 57th, Shawnee. A recreated pioneer town and craft shop. Free. Open Tuesday through Friday 10 a.m. to 5 p.m., Saturday and Sunday noon to 5 p.m. Phone 913/268-8772.

GOVERNOR'S MANSION RESTAURANT: 60th and Nieman, Shawnee. This was the first territorial governor's home. Popular place for chicken, steak, and grilled catfish. Open Tuesday through Saturday 11 a.m. to 2 p.m. and 5 to 9:30 p.m., Sunday 11 a.m. to 3 p.m. Phone 913/962-9999.

O V E R L A N D   P A R K

1990 population 111,790; 1970 77,934. For accommodations and attractions information call 1-800/262-PARK.

NCAA VISITORS' CENTER: 6201 College Boulevard, Overland Park. The National Collegiate Athletic Association Visitors' Center is a tribute to college athletics and a celebration of the drama intercollegiate competition fosters. The 21 NCAA sports are featured in two galleries displaying over 850 photographs. Gift-shop merchandise features national championship items. Admission fee. Open daily 10 a.m. to 6 p.m., Sunday noon to 5 p.m. Phone 913/339-0000.

DEANNA ROSE CHILDREN'S FARMSTEAD: 135th and Switzer streets (on K- 150), Overland Park. A heartwarming country treasure hidden in the city. Wander down cozy garden paths to visit ducks, geese, sheep, goats, horses, and pigs, many with babies at their sides. Free. Horse and wagon rides for a nominal charge. Open every day April through October 9 a.m. to 5 p.m. Phone 913/897-2360.

JOE'S BARN: 14885 Metcalf, Overland Park. Elegant this is not, but if you are a serious eater this buffet is for you. Open Monday through Friday 11 a.m. to 8:30 p.m. and Saturday and Sunday 8 a.m. to 8:30 p.m. Ideal for large groups if you call ahead to 913/681-2556.

HERITAGE CENTER ANTIQUES AND GIFTS: 6995 West 151st Street (downtown old Stanley), Overland Park. An old church and parsonage full of old-style new furniture, home decor, year-round Christmas shop, and antiques. Open Tuesday through Saturday 10 a.m. to 5 p.m. This church paradoxically is closed Sunday mornings. Phone 913/897-4241 or 913/897-4330.

OLD STILWELL COUNTRY STORE: Main and Broadway, Stilwell. Country antiques, primitives, and collectibles. Free gourmet coffee and penny candies for the kids. Open daily 10 a.m. to 5 p.m., Sunday noon to 5 p.m. Closed Monday and Tuesday. Phone 913/897-3004.

ROUND BARN: 1-7/10 miles east of U.S. 69 on 199th Street, north side, Stilwell. A decaying round barn and a tile silo lend rustic charm to a new housing development.

O L A T H E

1990 population 63,352; 1970 17,917. For accommodations and attractions information call Olathe Convention and Visitors' Bureau at 913/764-1050.

MAHAFFIE FARMSTEAD AND STAGECOACH STOP: 1100 Old Kansas City Road, Olathe. A stone farmhouse used as a stagecoach stop from 1865 to 1869, a wood-peg barn, and a stone ice house have been carefully restored by the City of Olathe. A barnyard dotted with farm implements and an orchard reflect a working 19th-century farm. Admission fee. June, July, and August tours are available Wednesday through Sunday at

10:30 a.m. and 1:30, 2:30, and 3:30 p.m. September through May open afternoons Monday through Friday. Closed in January. For group tours call 913/782-6872.

ERNIE MILLER NATURE PARK: K-7 and 131st Street, Olathe. Two miles of hiking trails, a 1/4-mile self-guided nature trail, and a nature center. Trails open dawn to dusk, center open Tuesday through Saturday 9 a.m. to 5 p.m., Sunday 1 to 5 p.m.

PRAIRIE CENTER STATE PARK: Four miles west of courthouse on 135th Street, Olathe. A place to experience the prairie as it was. Follow six miles of trails on 293 acres of prairie grasses and forbs. Open dawn to dusk. For information and conversation about the prairie ecosystem call Steve Case, 913/884-8832.

L E N E X A

1990 population 34,034; 1970 5,549. For information about accommodations and attractions call 1-800/950-STOP.

LEGLER BARN MUSEUM: 14907 West 87th, Lenexa. A restored stone barn built in 1864 houses pioneer artifacts and a gift shop. Nearby an old depot, a caboose, a prairie schooner, and a park with playground equipment make this a nice family stop. Free. Open Tuesday through Saturday 10 a.m. to 4 p.m., Sunday 1 to 5 p.m. Phone 913/492-0038.

B O N N E R S P R I N G S

1990 population 6,413; 1970 3,884

AGRICULTURE HALL OF FAME: 630 North 126th (north 1/4 mile from the junction of I-70 and K-7), Bonner Springs. A great attraction for anyone whose roots go back to agriculture (that includes all of us). Exhibits depict almost every facet of rural life and trace the development of farm machinery. The Agriculture Hall of Fame honors 32 agriculturists and lists their accomplishments. Admission fee . Open seven days a week April through December 9 a.m. to 5 p.m., Sunday 1 to 5 p.m. Phone 913/721-1075.

WYANDOTTE COUNTY MUSEUM:

631 North 126th Street, Bonner Springs (across the road from the Agriculture Hall of Fame). Exhibits here trace the county's history through 350-million-year-old fossils, native Kanza Indian culture, emigrant Indian cultures, the 1850s turbulent river port era, pioneer days, and modern Kansas City. Free. Open Tuesday through Saturday 10 a.m. to 5 p.m., Sunday 1 to 5 p.m. Phone 913/721-1078.

PORTER HOUSE RESTAURANT:

13020 Kansas Avenue (intersection of K-7 and Kansas Avenue), Bonner Springs. A comfortable family restaurant just out of the big city yet close enough to be convenient. Open Tuesday through Thursday 7 a.m. to 8 p.m., Friday and Saturday 7 a.m. to 10 p.m., Sunday 7 a.m. to 3 p.m. Phone 913/441-3942.

RENAISSANCE FESTIVAL:

Agriculture Hall of Fame grounds. Go back in time to 16th-century Merry Olde England. Enjoy games, performances, and food. Admission fee. Continues for seven weekends beginning Labor Day weekend 10 a.m. to 6:30 p.m. Phone 816/561-8005.

SANDSTONE AMPHITHEATER:

633 North 130th Street, Bonner Springs. An outdoor amphitheater presenting top recording artists May through October. For specifics call 913/721-3300.

BEDKNOBS AND BISCUITS BED-AND-BREAKFAST: 15202

Parallel, Basehor. 1990 population 1,591; 1970 724. A nice modern small-town home close to all the attractions north of Bonner Springs. Call 913/724-1540 for reservations.

LAWRENCE

1990 population 65,608; 1970 45,698. The Lawrence Convention and Visitors' Bureau (734 Vermont, Lawrence) is an excellent place to pick up brochures about local attractions, food, and lodging. If you have questions ask for Judy or Joan. Phone 913/865-4411. Lawrence also provides a 24-hour information hotline, 913/864-3506.

Lawrence is first in culture per capita in American cities under 100,000 and has the most vibrant downtown shopping district in the state. Rated as America's least stressful city to live in under 100,000, Lawrence was founded in 1854 by the New England Emigrant Aid Society determined to keep the territory free from slavery.

THE HALCYON HOUSE BED-AND-BREAKFAST: Tenth and

Ohio, Lawrence. The halcyon is a mythical bird that can charm the sea winds and waves into calmness. The eight guest rooms reflect that charm and calmness with their airy, modern, and individual style. Enjoy your own private area, until you meet for breakfast in the kitchen with its south wall of windows. You're within walking distance of downtown or campus, and you can count on thoroughly enjoying your stay. Phone 913/841-0314.

THE ELDRIDGE HOTEL: Seventh

and Massachusetts, Lawrence. This is a very, very nice place to stay. Some rooms have fireplaces and jacuzzis, others have balconies. Each has a sitting room and kitchenette. Phone 1-800/527-0909.

TELLER'S: 746 Massachusetts, Lawrence. This was once a bank, thus the name. The three levels of eating area offer a nice mix of formal, casual, and artsy. The high ceilings are painted a soft purple, and ceiling lamps of all sizes hang down at various lengths. An abstract Stan Herd mural adorns one wall, and the works of other local artists are placed tastefully throughout the building. The bathrooms are in the vault! Oh, by the way, the food is excellent and the menu features brick-oven pizza, salads, and pastas. Open daily 11:30 a.m. to 10 p.m. Phone 913/843-4111.

AMERICAN BISTRO: Seventh and Massachusetts, Lawrence. A first-class menu and wine list complement the formal yet comfortable atmosphere. Open daily 7 a.m. to 2 p.m. and 5 p.m. to 9 p.m. Phone 913/841-8349.

PARADISE CAFE: 728 Massachusetts, Lawrence. This easy-going place is a Lawrence favorite. Everything is made from scratch. Open daily 6:30 a.m. to 2:30 p.m. and 5 to 10 p.m., Sunday 8 a.m. to 2:30 p.m. Phone 913/842-5199.

BLUE BIRD DINER: 814 Massachusetts, Lawrence. Get espresso and cappuccino here along with just about anything healthy — and that means nothing fried! The chrome, the checkered floors, and the fluorescent pink and blue lights make this a fun experience. Open daily 7 a.m. to 10 p.m. and Sunday 8 a.m. to 2 p.m. Phone 913/843-2473.

FREE STATE BREWERY: 636 Massachusetts, Lawrence. The good food is almost overlooked because of the unique experience of eating inside a brewery! Local musicians often play here in the evening. Open daily 11 a.m. to 10 p.m., Sunday noon to 10 p.m. Phone 913/843-4555.

FULL MOON CAFE: 803 Massachusetts, in the back of the Sunflower International Casbah store, Lawrence. Step out of the mainstream and come here to enjoy Mediterranean food, home-brewed tea, local musicians, art, and discussion of social issues. Open Tuesday through Saturday 11:30 a.m. to 10 p.m. Phone 913/832-0444.

HERBIVORE'S: 9-1/2 East Eighth, Lawrence. Exclusively vegetarian! A one-of-a-kind menu in a small but friendly restaurant. Open daily 9 a.m. to 8 p.m., Sunday 11 a.m. to 7 p.m. Phone 913/749-2477.

JOE'S BAKERY: 616 West Ninth, Lawrence. Be like the college students and go on a "Joe's run" for hot glazed doughnuts that will make you drool. Watch for the neon light in the window (usually late at night) that announces when the doughnuts are hot! Fresh egg salad, tuna, turkey sandwiches and more at noon for carry-out. Open during the school year. Phone 913/843-4720.

PYWACKET'S: 10 East Ninth, Lawrence. This smoke-free environment features the work of local artists and a menu with chicken, turkey, and seafood. Open Monday through Saturday for breakfast and lunch, Sunday brunch 9 a.m. to 2:30 p.m. Phone 913/749-3883.

MAD GREEK: 907 Massachusetts, Lawrence. Authentic Greek food cooked by Greek natives Peggy and George. Pleasant setting. Open daily 11 a.m. to 9 p.m. Phone 913/843-2441.

CORNUCOPIA: 1801 Massachusetts, Lawrence. If you have an appetite for a salad bar, fettuccine,

N O R T H E A S T   K A N S A S

crepes, or an ice cream treat, you'll find all that and much more here. Children's menu. Open daily 11:30 a.m. to 9 p.m. Phone 913/842-9637.

WILD OATS GROCERY STORE AND DELI: 1040 Vermont, Lawrence. This is a grocery store with a purpose — an environmental one. If you're looking for organic produce, bulk items, or "natural" meats you can fill up your cart here. There's a deli featuring fruit smoothies and salads. Open daily 7 a.m. to 10 p.m. Phone 913/865-3737.

SOUTH PARK CONCERTS: South Massachusetts, Lawrence. Band concerts are held every Wednesday night in June and July. Bring lawn chairs or blankets. Free. Phone 913/841-4411.

BROWN-BAG CONCERTS: Ninth and Massachusetts, Lawrence. Thursday noons June through August bring your sack lunch to this First National Bank area and enjoy some great music. Sit curbside or on benches. Phone 913/841-4411.

HARMONY HALL: 10 East Ninth, Lawrence. A variety of music is offered in this smoke- and alcohol-free setting on weekends. Phone 913/749-0202.

LIBERTY HALL: 642 Massachusetts, Lawrence. See classic, foreign, and art house movies here nightly. Alternating monthly, the public is invited to be the studio audience for "Imagination Workshop," a live radio comedy and drama show, or "Goodtime Radio Revue," an old-fashioned radio variety show featuring local performers. Phone 913/749-1972 or 749-1912.

JAZZHAUS: 926-1/2 Massachusetts, Lawrence. Live and recorded jazz, reggae, or local rock featured here most evenings. Phone 913/749-3320.

THE LIED CENTER: West Campus, Lawrence. This newly opened cultural center is state-of-the-art making any event a pleasure to attend. Call the box office (913/864-ARTS) for a schedule.

SPENCER MUSEUM OF ART: Behind the student union on the north edge of the KU campus, Lawrence. Impressive from its black-and-white photos of pioneers to the Flag Story Quilt. Enjoy ever-changing galleries that show over 4,000 years of world art history. Open Tuesday through Saturday 8:30 a.m. to 5 p.m. and Sunday noon to 5 p.m. Free. Phone 913/864-4710.

MUSEUM OF NATURAL HISTORY: Dyche Hall, University of Kansas campus near the student union, Lawrence. One of the nation's top five university natural history museums. The fossil collection is astonishing. Exhibits of reptiles, birds, mammals, and amphibians are on four floors. An exhibit on the Indians at Little Big Horn is especially moving. Donations appreciated. Open daily 8 a.m. to 5 p.m., Sunday 1 to 5 p.m. Phone 913/864-4540 or 864-4450.

UNIVERSITY OF KANSAS MUSEUM OF ANTHRO-POLOGY: Located across from the Museum of Natural History on the KU campus, Lawrence. Plains Indian artifacts to African thrones are on display here. Open Monday through Saturday 9 a.m. to 5 p.m. and Sunday 1 to 5 p.m. Free. Phone 913/864-4245.

WATKINS COMMUNITY MUSEUM: 1047 Massachusetts, Lawrence. Acquaint yourself with the story of Lawrence here. Ask Steve or Judy where to find the markers that tell where the Quantrell's raiders massacres occurred, as well as the memorial to those killed at Oak Hill cemetery. Open Tuesday through Saturday 10 a.m. to 4 p.m., Sunday 1:30 to 4 p.m. Donations appreciated. Phone 913/841-4109.

THE UNIVERSITY OF KANSAS CAMPUS: Lawrence. The many historic buildings and Campanile Hill above Potter's Lake are highlights of one of the most beautiful campuses in the nation. Call 913/864-3506 for upcoming campus and community events.

HASKELL INDIAN JUNIOR COLLEGE: 23rd and Barker, Lawrence. Over 100 tribes are represented in the student body. A self-guided walking tour of the campus features the Haskell Totem Medicine Pole and the Medicine Wheel field art. Obtain a tour map at the Lawrence Convention and Visitors' Bureau. Phone 913/749-8404.

ERNST AND SON HARDWARE: 826 Massachusetts, Lawrence. This old hardware store doesn't seem to fit in modern downtown Lawrence. Maybe that's what makes it so unique. Open Monday through Saturday 8 a.m. to 5:30 p.m., Thursday till 8 p.m. Phone 913/843-2373.

SUNFLOWER OUTDOOR AND BIKE SHOP: 804 Massachusetts, Lawrence. You'll feel more ready for any outdoor adventure just by walking in the door. This is the place to get gear for camping, hiking, canoeing, bicycling and more. Open Monday through Saturday 8 a.m. to 5 p.m., Thursday until 8 p.m. Phone 913/843-5000.

GALLERIES AND STUDIOS: Lawrence. Pick up a gallery and studio guide at the Convention and Visitors' Bureau at 734 Vermont or call 913/865-4411. The Lawrence Arts Center is located at 200 West Ninth.

FARMERS MARKET: 1000 block of Vermont, Lawrence. Find fresh fruits, vegetables, baked goods, herbs, and homemade condiments here. Open May through November Saturday 6:30 to 10:30 a.m. and Tuesday and Thursday 4 to 6:30 p.m.

HIKING AND BIKING TRAIL INFORMATION: For a listing of trails in the Lawrence area call the Lawrence Parks and Recreation at 913/832-3450 or write to the department at City Hall, Sixth and Massachusetts, Lawrence, Kansas 66044.

KANSAS RIVER LEVEE: Located north of the Kansas River bridge in north Lawrence. This ten-mile stretch of biking or jogging trail is in excellent condition atop the levee.

KAW RIVER TRAIL: Entrance is just west of the U.S. 24, 40 and 59 junction, Lawrence. This narrow walking trail along the river is four miles long.

BURCHAM PARK: Second and Indiana, Lawrence. Enjoy the pleasant picnic area among huge cottonwood trees or take the half-mile walk to Constant Park at Sixth and Tennessee along the river.

WELLS OVERLOOK: Several miles south of Lawrence on U.S. 59 look for the brown sign leading you to Wells Overlook. Climb the tower to enjoy the view.

LONE STAR LAKE: Twelve miles southwest of Lawrence. The marina rents a variety of boats between April and October. Phone 913/748-0866 or 748-0829.

CLINTON LAKE: Three miles southwest of Lawrence on West 23rd. Camping, fishing, boating, a swimming beach, and picnic areas can be found here. Explore 30 miles of bridle and rustic hiking trails in the

Rockhaven area. The North Shore Trail is for mountain bikes. Phone 913/843-7665 for information.

CLINTON LAKE MUSEUM: Located in the Bloomington area of Clinton Lake. If you've never been to a museum in a milkshed, you must experience this. Open May through October Friday and Sunday 1 to 5 p.m. and Saturday 10 a.m. to 6 p.m. Phone 913/748-0800.

B A L D W I N   C I T Y

1990 population 2,961; 1970 2,520.

PEACHEY'S GROCERIES AND MORE: Downtown Baldwin City. Antiques and groceries are mixed together here. You'll wish your town had a little store like this. Open Monday through Saturday 10 a.m. to 6 p.m. Phone 913/594-3277.

VICHEE'S: 713 High, Baldwin City. The Italian food tastes really good in this low-key, relaxing setting. Open Monday through Saturday for lunch and supper. Phone 913/594-6900.

BLACK JACK PARK: Three miles east of Baldwin City on U.S. 56. The first armed confrontation involving federal troops leading up to the Civil War occurred here when John Brown captured pro-slavery forces under the direction of Captain Henry Pate. This historic park also includes Santa Fe Trail ruts, a log cabin, black jack oaks, and an outstanding grove of maples once used to make maple syrup. Always open.

MIDLAND RAILROAD EXCURSION RIDES: The depot at High Street next to the grain elevator, Baldwin City. How about a trip to "Nowhere" in a passenger car or a caboose — seven miles of clickety-clack on a line first used in 1867. Train runs May through October on Saturdays, Sundays, and holidays. Departure times are 11:30 a.m., 1:30, 2:30, and 3:30 p.m. Phone 913/594-6982. For dinner train schedules call 1-800/637-1693.

QUAYLE RARE BIBLE COLLECTION: Located in Collins Library, Eighth and Elm, Baldwin City. Included among the 700 volumes and manuscripts are ornately decorated Bibles, a synagogue roll, and Bibles signed by every U.S. President since World War II. Open Monday through Friday 9 a.m. to 4 p.m. Phone 913/594-6451, extension 414.

PARMENTER HALL: North side of Baker University, Baldwin City. The cornerstone was laid here for Kansas's oldest four-year college. Abe Lincoln contributed money for this limestone building.

OLD CASTLE MUSEUM: 515 Fifth, Baldwin City. This museum features community and university exhibits. The Palmyra Post Office and Blood's Grocery Store open between 1857 and 1862 are nearby as is the 1857 Kibbee Cabin. Museum hours are Tuesday through Friday 10 a.m. to 4:30 p.m. Open weekends in the summer. Phone 913/594-6809.

BALDWIN CITY HISTORIC SITES: An excellent booklet details 60 historic landmarks in the area and may be picked up at Old Castle or the Midland Railway depot or from local merchants.

T O N G A N O X I E

1990 population 2,347; 1970 1,717.

ALMEDA'S INN: 220 South Main, Tonganoxie. This old bus stop and hotel now serve as a bed-and-breakfast. There's nothing particularly modern about this place, and its best feature is the old-fashioned hospitality. It's especially enjoyable to relax on the narrow front porch. Phone 913/845-2295.

EVERLASTING SPECIALTIES:
421 South Main, Tonganoxie. This old Union Pacific Tonganoxie depot has been converted into a dried-flower wholesale and retail warehouse. This is the place to get your eucalyptus, boxwood, silver queen, sweet annie and more! Open Monday through Friday 9 a.m. to 2:30 p.m. Phone 913/845-2099.

LECOMPTON

1990 population 619; 1970 434.

LECOMPTON: Northwest of Lawrence on U.S. 24 to Perry, then south to Lecompton on county road. This sleepy little town once had high hopes of being the capital city of Kansas. A wagon train was dispatched from here in the town's glory days to explore the possibility of platting a town in Colorado. The decision was made here to name the town Denver.

CONSTITUTION HALL: North Elmore Street, Lecompton. Another site, circa 1855, built to accommodate the Kansas Territorial Legislature . The famous Lecompton Constitution was written here. Drive by. Phone 913/887-6285.

LANE UNIVERSITY MUSEUM: East side Lecompton. This limestone building was originally planned to be the Kansas state capitol, but construction was temporarily halted when it became clear the capitol would be in Topeka. Open Sunday afternoons March through October. Phone 913/887-6285.

LEAVENWORTH

1990 population 38,495; 1970 25,147. Write or call the Leavenworth/Lansing Convention and Visitors' Bureau, 518 Shawnee, Box 44, Leavenworth, Kansas 66048, for area accommodations and self-guided tour booklet. Phone 1-800/844-4114 or 913/682-4113. The tour will give you an enjoyable overview of Leavenworth. Ironically, the tour begins with a state prison to the south and ends with the federal penitentiary on the north end of town. Guided tours for groups of 15 or more may be arranged by calling Connie Boyd at the number above.

LEAVENWORTH: Founded in 1854, Leavenworth is the oldest city in Kansas. The city's early history, in a time when adventurers and pioneers crossed the Missouri here to go west, is reflected in well-preserved brick and clapboard buildings, elaborate mansions, street names and layouts. The character of the city is also shaped by the Missouri River, the hills and bluffs, and nearby Fort Leavenworth and the federal penitentiary.

LEAVENWORTH COUNTY MUSEUM: 1128 Fifth, Leavenworth. (Due to street renumbering, old literature shows a different address.) Also known as Leavenworth's Victorian Carroll Mansion. The lavish carved woodwork in this 16-room mansion will amaze you, especially when you consider that the house was built in 1867. Admission fee. Open Tuesday through Sunday 1 to 4:30 p.m. Phone 913/682-7759.

LEAVENWORTH LANDING: The 100 and 200 blocks of Delaware near the Missouri River, Leavenworth. This area was the hub of activity during the days of the steamboats from 1854 to 1870. Thousands of

Oregon Trail pioneers arrived by boat and bought their wagons, oxen, and supplies here. The Landing now consists of original warehouses restored as a delightful shopping mall. Most shops in this area are open Monday through Saturday 10 a.m. to 5:30 p.m., Thursday evening until 8 p.m.

FULLER GALLERY OF FINE ART:
205 Delaware in the Leavenworth Landing block, Leavenworth. The gallery displays the original work of award-winning Kansas artist Lu Fuller. Redbirds in each painting are her trademark. Phone 913/651-7940.

COUNTRY CUPBOARD:
203 Delaware, Leavenworth. One of the neat shops you'll find in the Leavenworth Landing Mall. Handcrafted furniture, gifts, and collectibles. Open Monday through Saturday 10 a.m. to 5:30 p.m., Thursday until 8 p.m. Phone 913/682-4522.

EL SAMBRE RESTAURANT:
781 Shawnee, Leavenworth. Listed in your self-tour guide as the Old Santa Fe Depot. Great Spanish-style architecture, even greater Mexican food. Open daily 11 a.m. to 10 p.m. Phone 913/682-3200.

NORTH ESPLANADE STREET:
Houses numbered 203-515 North Esplanade Street are listed on the national historic register. This street also is a lovely river drive.

OLD UNION STATION:
123 South Esplanade Street, Leavenworth. Now known as the Leavenworth Riverfront Community Center. The lobby inside takes you back to the days of steam locomotives. Windows on the east side provide an unusually good view of the Missouri River. Open Monday through Friday 6 a.m. to 9 p.m., Saturday 9 a.m. to 7 p.m., Sunday 1 to 6 p.m.

HARVEY GIRL LUNCHEONS:
Leavenworth Riverfront Community Center, 123 South Esplanade Street, Leavenworth. A reminder of the good old days when Harvey Girls waited on Santa Fe railroad passengers. Groups of 15 or more will be served. Reservations are requested two weeks in advance. Phone 913/651-2132.

THE SKYVIEW RESTAURANT:
504 Grand Avenue, Leavenworth. Fine American cuisine in an authentic 1892 Victorian antique-filled house. Full bar available. Lunch Tuesday, Wednesday, and Thursday 11 a.m. to 1:30 p.m; dinner Tuesday through Saturday 5:30 to 8:30 p.m. For reservations call 913/682-2653.

SALT CREEK BED-AND-BREAKFAST:
16425 Fort Riley Road north of Leavenworth. Spend the night here in this rustic old stagecoach house built in 1854. Phone 913/651-2277.

FORT LEAVENWORTH:
On U.S. 73 just north of Leavenworth. Established in 1827, it is the first continuously occupied non-native American settlement in Kansas. Its original purpose was to protect Santa Fe Trail traffic. By the 1840s travelers destined for Oregon and California were passing through the post. In 1846 the fort was an important staging point in the Mexican War. Fort Leavenworth is an active military installation.

SELF-GUIDED TOUR OF FORT LEAVENWORTH:
For information and maps call the Leavenworth/ Lansing Convention and Visitors' Bureau at 1-800/844-4114. For guided group tours call the fort public affairs office at 913/684-5604.

BUFFALO SOLDIER MONUMENT:
Grant Avenue, Fort Leavenworth. This impressive bronze statue of a mounted buffalo soldier is dedicated to the all-black 9th and 10th

Cavalry Regiments. There are two schools of thought about why the soldiers were given this nickname during the Indian war era. One claims it was because of their valor; others believe it was because their hair resembled a buffalo's coat . Monument always open to the public.

FRONTIER ARMY MUSEUM: Reynolds Avenue, Fort Leavenworth. Have you wondered what a surrey, a landau, a tally-ho break, an opera omnibus, or a phaeton was? Well, they're all here for you to enjoy. Featured are army and civilian horse-drawn vehicles: a 10-team prairie schooner, a stagecoach, and a covered wagon, all meticulously authentic. Free. Open weekdays 9 a.m. to 4 p.m., Saturday 10 a.m. to 4 p.m., Sunday noon to 4 p.m. Closed major holidays. Phone 913/684-3191.

THE ROOKERY: 12 to14 Sumner, Fort Leavenworth. The oldest house still occupied in Kansas, circa 1832. Douglas MacArthur lived here in the early 1900s. Drive by only.

U.S. DISCIPLINARY BAR-RACKS: McPherson Avenue, Fort Leavenworth. This is a military prison housing up to 1,800 prisoners. Drive by only.

NORTONVILLE

1990 population 643; 1970 727.

MIKE'S PLACE: Downtown Nortonville. A charming restaurant with high wooden ceilings and a wood floor. Open daily 8 a.m. to 9 p.m., Sunday 11 a.m. to 2 p.m. Phone 913/886-3003.

LIBERTY'S ROSE: Downtown Nortonville. This old bank building has become a quaint craft shop. The vault is filled with work by Kansas

artists. Open Monday through Saturday 10 a.m. to 5 p.m. Phone 913/886-3565.

THE NORTONVILLE CRAFT MALL: Downtown Nortonville. Open daily 9 a.m. to 5 p.m. and Sunday noon to 3 p.m. Phone 913/886-8411.

THIS OLD HOUSE: Three miles north of Nortonville on U.S. 159, then 1/2 mile east on K-116. Everything in This Old House is handmade or antique. The only commodities are roomfuls of fabric, quilts, and antiques. You might find June at work on her machine quilts. Open Monday through Saturday 9 a.m. to 5 p.m. Phone 913/886-6685.

JEFFERSON COUNTY SODA FOUNTAINS: Nortonville, Valley Falls, Oskaloosa, and McLouth. This is the soda fountain county of Kansas. There isn't anything particularly ornate about these drug store fountains. They have formica counters, but the stools all swivel and the ice cream is hand-packed and still goes down real good, so get out there before the school kids do.

HISTORICAL MARKER: On U.S. 59 between Nortonville and Oskaloosa. This marker describes the pro-slavery and free-stater Battle of Hickory Point. The marker also tells about John Steuart Curry's boyhood home once nearby. Note the combination silos and tin grain elevators on this road.

VALLEY FALLS

1990 population 1,253; 1970 1,169.

THE BARN BED-AND-BREAK-FAST: Rural Valley Falls. This 100-year-old barn is full of modern comforts. Each of the 18 rooms has a private bath and king-size bed, there's an indoor heated pool, an exercise room, air conditioning, a conference room, a fireplace, large living rooms, and a dining room full of windows. Take a walk on the grounds or the country roads. This is an ideal accommodation for a family reunion or large group. Phone 913/945-3225.

FRANK'S PHARMACY: 324 Broadway, Valley Falls. Great place for a soda fountain treat. Frank can answer questions about the area. Open Monday through Saturday 8 a.m. to 6 p.m., Saturday until 2:30 p.m. Phone 913/945-3711.

STEWART O'STORE HARD-WARE AND GIFTS: 412 Broadway, Valley Falls. Once inside the screen doors, you'll realize this place has whatever you're looking for — including nostalgia! Open Monday through Saturday 8 a.m. to 5 p.m., Wednesday until 7 p.m. Phone 913/945-333 2.

G W CRAFTS: 510 Broadway, Valley Falls. Stop in and see Wayne or Georgiann at work on their various wood crafts. They're friendly people and can answer questions about Valley Falls. Pick up a community tree tour brochure here. Open daily 8:30 a.m. to 5 p.m., closed Sunday. Phone 913/945-6659. Check out the Valley Falls Craft Mall and the electric needle quilting shop also in downtown Valley Falls.

OZAWKIE

1990 population 403; 1970 137.

APPLE VALLEY FARM: Ozawkie. East side of Lake Perry; from Perry take FAS 1280 north, then follow signs to Apple Valley Farm. What a great country setting for a fun evening! The Farmhouse Restaurant serves Mexican food Thursday evening 5 to 8 p.m., ribs and chicken Friday and Saturday 5 to 9 p.m., and plate dinners Sunday 11:30 a.m. to 3 p.m. But there's more! The milk barn is full of crafts and antiques, the rustic Granary Saloon serves steaks and hamburgers, and the highlight is the Ric Averill Players Theater in the barn. Thursday at 8 p.m. is a squeaky-clean family performance; Friday and Saturday enjoy comical melodrama at 8:30 p.m. Call 913/876-2114 for restaurant and melodrama reservations.

LAKE PERRY: Located in Jefferson County between Topeka and Lawrence. Excellent lake for sailing. Also hiking and equestrian trails, boat rental, golfing, and camping. Entrance fee. Phone 913/246-3449 or 876-2274 for information.

VILLAGE INN: Rural Meriden. 1990 population 622; 1970 472. Six guest rooms overlook the Village Greens Golf Course. Each room has a private bath, jacuzzi tub, king-size bed, and TV. Phone Ed or Donna at 913/876-2835 for a reservation.

OSKALOOSA

1990 population 1,074; 1970 955.

YOUR FAVORITE THINGS: 313 Jefferson, Oskaloosa, in the Tin Roof Plaza building. Nothing historic about this building's interior, and the gifts are the kind you'd expect to find in a metropolitan area. But Carol's shop deserves mention because of her belief that a business like this can work in rural Kansas. Other shops in the Tin Roof Plaza include an antique and collectible store. Open daily 8 a.m. to 5:30 p.m., Sunday 11:30 a.m. to 5 p.m. Phone 913/863-3222.

SNICKERDOODLES TEA ROOM: 313 Jefferson, Oskaloosa, in

the Tin Roof Plaza. Aren't snicker doodles the best cookies to dip in coffees and teas? They're ever-present here, ready for dipping. Lunch menu consists of soups, salads, muffins, and sandwiches. Open daily 8 a.m. to 5 p.m., lunch served 11 a.m. to 2:30 p.m.

OLD BANK CAFE: Downtown Oskaloosa. This limestone corner bank building with the high ceilings and wainscoting serves breakfast and lunch.

OLD JEFFERSON TOWN: U.S. 59, Oskaloosa. A collection of vintage Jefferson County buildings and artifacts — John Steuart Curry home, McLouth blacksmith shop, Winchester jail (a jail without a lock), Reynolds General store, 1891 chapel, windwagon sculpture, 1875 bowstring bridge, and much more. Open weekend afternoons May through September. Phone 913/863-2182 or 913/863-2070.

ROUND BARN: East of Oskaloosa two miles from the Conoco Station on a gravel road. Private property, view from the road.

MANHATTAN

1990 population 37,712; 1970 27,575. Home of Kansas State University, the first land-grant college in the United States. Current enrollment is about 19,000. Manhattan is situated in the Flint Hills along the Kansas River and near Tuttle Creek Lake. For lodging information call the Manhattan Convention and Visitors' Bureau, 1-800/528-4748 or 913/776-8829.

SUNSET ZOO: 2333 Oak, Manhattan. Let's take a little side trip to the Outback of Australia or the African Veldt, or how about Tibet to see wallabies, cheetahs, snow leopards, and red pandas. Admission fee. Open

every day except winter holidays. Phone 913/587-APES.

RILEY COUNTY HISTORICAL MUSEUM: Adjoining Goodnow House at 2309 Claflin, Manhattan. Features Riley County history. Donations appreciated. Open Tuesday through Friday 9 a.m. to 5 p.m., Saturday and Sunday 2 to 5 p.m. Phone 913/537-2210.

GOODNOW HOUSE: 2301 Claflin Road, Manhattan. A furnished limestone house, barn, and carriage house once owned by Isaac Goodnow, who helped organize Kansas State University in 1863. Free. Open Tuesday through Saturday 10 a.m. to 5 p.m., Sunday 1 to 5 p.m. Phone 913/539-3731.

WOLF-BUTTERFIELD HOUSE: 630 Fremont, Manhattan. Presumed to have been built in 1865 and operated as an inn and tavern serving the Butterfield Overland Dispatch stagecoach line. Check with Riley County Museum for details.

COUNTRY GIFT SHOP: 2206 Fort Riley Road (K-18), Manhattan. This inviting city-country store offers Kansas gifts, dolls, wheat weaving, brass.... Open daily 10 a.m. to 5:30 p.m. Open Sunday afternoons in December.

KIMBLE CLIFF BED-AND-BREAKFAST: 6782 Anderson Avenue (five miles west of Manhattan). A lovely drive overlooking Wildcat Creek brings you to this cozy limestone home, circa 1894. Phone 913/539-3816.

TUTTLE CREEK LAKE: Five miles north of Manhattan on K-13. Offers all the recreational, fishing, and hunting opportunities provided by federal and state lakes. Fees required in certain areas. Phone 913/539-7941 or 913/539-8511.

SCENIC DRIVE: Highway K-13 across Tuttle Creek Dam and on north several miles. Recent road cuts through hills reveal layered appearance of sedimentary rock formations.

RILEY

1990 population 804; 1970 668.

CALICO INN: Main Street, Riley. Quaint — shingle front, tin roof, bright pastoral scene on door framed by barn wood. Stop for a bite and information about antique shops in town. Open daily 11 a.m. to 8 p.m. Closed Monday. Phone 913/485-2622.

TRIX'S RILEY ROOMER: 104 North Hartner, Riley. Colorful, homespun bed-and-breakfast, plus a nice family cottage with kitchen. Phone 913/485-2654.

CLAY CENTER

1990 population 4,613; 1970 4,963.

C AND C AUCTION: 416 Court, Clay Center. Two to three hundred people, including people from out of state, find their way to Clay Center the first Sunday of every month at 10 a.m. for this auction. Dennis Hamilton's sales are known for their fine items. Sale items vary from month to month but include rare and unusual pieces as well as estate sale items. Phone 913/632-6021.

CLAY CENTER MUSEUM: 2121 Seventh, Clay Center (in the old hospital). Over 40 rooms of Clay County memorabilia including a Regina 1896 music box, a doll collection, and a turn-of-the-century Swedish loom. Open Tuesday through Saturday 2 to 4 p.m. and Sunday

afternoons in the summer. Phone 913/632-3786.

CLAY CENTER ZOO: Fourth and Clay, Clay Center. This is a small zoo with some monkeys, one bear, small animals, and birds. Open 8 a.m. to 9 p.m. Free. Phone 913/632-2137.

THE COACHLIGHT: 311 Weda, downtown Longford. 1990 population 68; 1970 99. They say it's like going home to stop in here for the specialty of the house, fried chicken. Open Tuesday through Saturday 8 a.m. to 8 p.m., Sunday 11 a.m. to 2 p.m., and Monday 8 a.m. to 2 p.m. Phone 913/388-2437.

WAKEFIELD

1990 population 900; 1970 583.

KANSAS LANDSCAPE ARBORETUM: Just south of Wakefield on Dogwood Street. This natural prairie woodland with wildflowers, butterflies, bluebirds, and adventurous nature trails, also has a section of memorial trees. You're welcome to stop at the Arboretum House. Phone 913/461-5259.

LAKEVIEW RESTAURANT: West side of Wakefield on K-82 overlooking Milford Lake. Good home cooking. Open 8 a.m. to 7:30 p.m. Closed Monday. Phone 913/461-5469.

WAKEFIELD'S COUNTRY BED-AND-BREAKFAST: Rural Wakefield. Three generations have owned and operated this grain and livestock farm. Enjoy a stay in the country. Phone 913/461-5533.

MILFORD

1990 population 384; 1970 296. This town had to start over again. The original town is at the bottom of Milford Lake.

MILFORD LAKE: Four miles north-west of Junction City on K-57. Largest lake in Kansas. Recreational and camping facilities. Hunting and fishing. Phone 913/238-5714.

MILFORD NATURE CENTER: Near spillway of dam on Milford Lake. One of the best exhibits of Kansas flora and fauna — terrestrial and underwater dioramas, live animals, nature trails. State-of-the-art fish hatchery. Free. Open, weekdays 10 a.m. to 4 p.m., weekends spring and summer afternoons only. Closed winter holidays. Call 913/238-LEAF for hatchery tours.

FORT RILEY: Take I-70 exit 301 or enter on K-18 from either Junction City or Ogden. K-18, marked as Huebner Street on the fort, gives you a good overview of the complex. You hardly notice the modern cars and paved streets as you drive along the wooded avenues of stately limestone structures built in the 1880s. An information booth on Huebner Street will provide you with guide maps to points of interest. Fort Riley, home of the Big Red One, is an active military base.

U.S. CAVALRY MUSEUM: Henry Avenue and Custer Avenue, Fort Riley. Main body of structure built in 1850s (note how flat limestone walls mark the older section). Military displays feature horse soldiers from Santa Fe Trail era to present. Original works by artist Frederic Remington are displayed. Open Monday through Saturday 9 a.m. to 4:30 p.m., Sunday noon to 4:30 p.m. Phone 913/239-2737.

FIRST TERRITORIAL CAPITOL: Fort Riley, on K-18 (East Huebner Road). First, very temporary, capitol in Kansas. Donations appreciated. Open 10 a.m. to 5 p.m., Sunday 1 to 5 p.m., closed Monday. Phone 913/784-5535.

JUNCTION CITY

1990 population 20,604; 1970 19,018. For information in Junction City call the Geary County Convention and Visitors' Bureau, 1-800/JCT-CITY.

FREEDOM PARK: I-70 exit 301, then short distance east, Junction City. Have you ever wondered about the big cannon on top of the hill east of Marshall Field? You'll find steps leading to the hilltop in Freedom Park. The view on top is great.

INDIAN STATUE: I-70 exit 299 east to J-Hill Road, 3-8/10 miles southwest to Skiddy Road, then 1/8 mile east. View from road. Not a great work of art but a poignant reminder of the Native American's plight. Stop at Glen Dotson's house, 4015 J-Hill Road, for the sad story of a memorial forgotten and defamed. For an appointment call 913/238-7072.

ONAGA

1990 population 761; 1970 761.

ONAGA SALE BARN: Onaga. This is an unusual eight-cornered sale barn. Livestock sale every Wednesday. Phone 913/889-4700.

DOUGHBOY STATUE: Fourth and Leonard, Onaga. A statue commemorating the "doughboys" of World War I.

WESTMORELAND

1990 population 541; 1970 485. This is the county seat of Pottawatomie County. During the Oregon Trail years hundreds of wagons rendezvoused here near Scott's Spring, which is still flowing. Nice museum open May through October.

HAND-DUG WELL: Located in a small park on K-99 beside the swimming pool, Westmoreland. Completed in 1914, the well was 38 feet deep and the inside diameter was 25 feet. The stone pump house was later moved to Second and Main and presently serves as the City Hall.

OREGON TRAIL MONUMENT: One mile south of Westmoreland on K-99. Prairie art at its finest. New in 1993. A full-sized steel replica of a covered wagon pulled by a yoke of bronzed oxen. Crafted and painted so skillfully that the wagon looks like the real Oregon Trail prairie schooner. Scott's Spring is nearby.

O L S B U R G

1990 population 192; 1970 151.

THE KAFFE HAUS: Downtown Olsburg. The Kaffe Haus is famous for its cinnamon rolls but all the cooking is homestyle. Try the noon buffet and ask here about the scenic drive on Carnahan Road south of Olsburg. This drive is especially beautiful when the colors start to change. Open Tuesday through Saturday 7 a.m. to 2 p.m., Sunday 11 a.m. to 2 p.m. Phone 913/468-3665.

S A I N T   M A R Y S :

1990 population 1,791; 1970 1,434.

INDIAN PAY STATION: First and Mission, Saint Marys. A small stone structure where Potawatomi Indians were paid their meager allotments in exchange for land. In operation 1857 to 1870. Now a part of the Saint Marys Historical Society complex. Adjoining barn museum offers a look into the pioneer era. Summer hours are 1 to 4 p.m. Other seasons stop at City Hall for guide or call Julia Bork, 913/437-2391.

BAYER STONE COMPANY: 120 North Sixth, Saint Marys. Ever wonder whether there are any modern-day stone cutters? Well, this is the place where they do it in a massive way. Giant lazer-guided saws cut stone quarried in Kansas. For tours call 913/437-2781 in advance.

JEFFREY ENERGY CENTER: Six miles north of Saint Marys on K-63. Giant power plant visible for miles. Groups of 15 to 45 people may tour this Kansas Power and Light plant. For more information call Lisa Jenkins two weeks in advance. Phone 913/575-6468.

W A M E G O

1990 population 3,706; 1970 2,507.

DUTCH MILL: Wamego City Park, 1/4 mile east of K-99 and Fourth Street intersection, Wamego. Bring your camera — especially in late April when tulips color the terraces below this old mill. Originally in service in the 1870s, this authentic Dutch mill still grinds wheat and corn. Drive by any time. Operating hours are afternoons late April to Labor Day. Call 913/456-7849.

COLUMBIAN THEATRE: 521 Main Street (K-99), Wamego. Imagine an ornate theatre, built in 1895 and abandoned in 1950, hovering like a phantom over Main Street for 40 years, then coming back to life and yielding a three-quarter million dollar lost treasure. Explore Wamego and discover what the 1893 Chicago World's Fair, allegorical works of art, and Wamego have in common. The restored Columbian Theatre is scheduled to open in 1994. Meanwhile stop by and ask Colonel Ray Morris to tell you the story. Call 913/456-2029.

THE DITTO/LEACH HOUSE:
Fifth and Poplar, Wamego. Styled after a Sicilian Villa, this 1890s home has 14 gables! View this private residence from your car. For a group tour call 913/456-7688.

FRIENDSHIP HOUSE: 507 Ash (west of park), Wamego. Stop in this lovely old house for sandwiches featuring Dutch Mill stone-ground flour. Open Tuesday through Saturday 9 a.m. to 5 p.m. Phone 913/456-9616.

CAROLYN'S: 515 Lincoln, Wamego. A charming gift shop with lots of Kansas souvenirs and books. Open Monday through Saturday 9 a.m. to 5:30 p.m. Phone 913/456-7600.

LOUIS VIEUX ELM: Wamego. From intersection of K-99 and U.S. 24 drive four miles east, then north three miles on the Onaga Road, then 1/2 mile west. This elm, the largest in the world, stands near where the Oregon Trail crossed the Vermillion River. Two historic cemeteries, the Louis Vieux and the Oregon Trail Cholera Cemetery, are nearby. The stones tell the story.

BEECHER BIBLE AND RIFLE CHURCH: One-fourth mile south of K-18 at Wabaunsee (unincorporated). Pre-Civil War colony here was named the Beecher Bible and Rifle colony because famed abolitionist and preacher Henry Ward Beecher contributed Sharps rifles and Bibles to the colony. This church still holds services. Seems to be a derelict John Deere tractor on every corner in this decaying town.

ALTA VISTA

1990 population 477; 1970 402.

DUGAN'S GALLERY: 519 Main, Alta Vista. Enter town from K-177 north to gain the true bucolic ambience of this Flint Hills town. Stop at the gallery for hand-crafted furniture — cradles, gun racks, shelves; antiques; and Kansas-made jellies, candles, popcorn.... Open Thursday through Saturday 9 a.m. to 3 p.m. Phone 913/499-6605.

ALTA VISTA SUNDRIES: Alta Vista. Strange situation. This old store has all the elements of an old-fashioned soda fountain, tin ceiling, wood floor, fountain-ice cream, syrups, soda water but Clelen says, "Nobody has ever asked me to make an ice cream soda." Open Monday to Saturday 8 a.m. to 5:30 p.m. Phone 913/499-6610.

SKYLINE MILL CREEK DRIVE: Start northeast corner Alta Vista. About 20 miles of scenic rocky road to Alma. Good panoramic vistas of Flint Hills pasture country and limestone farm buildings. Drive continues on south from Alma on a circuitous route to Paxico. Great scenery finally becomes redundant on another 20 miles of rock road.

ALMA

1990 population 871; 1970 905.

WABAUNSEE COUNTY HISTORICAL MUSEUM: Alma. Features pioneer main street shops — shoe cobbler, blacksmith, general store. Open afternoons to 4 p.m. Tuesday through Sunday. Enjoy driving the streets of this "limestone" town and look for the bakery and cheese factory.

PAXICO

1990 population 174; 1970 216.

MILL CREEK ANTIQUES: 109 Newbury, Paxico. Continue east

one mile on county road from Fields of Fair or enter from east on exit 335. Antiques, collectibles, soda bar, deli, and candy counter. This shop and six more in a whole town of antiques and collectibles will delight antique buffs. Open Monday through Saturday 10 a.m. to 5 p.m., Sunday 1 to 5 p.m. Phone 913/636-5520.

FIELDS OF FAIR WINERY:
Paxico exit on I-70 (exit 333). First licensed winery in Kansas. Tours and tasting available, call 1-800/732-1984.

DOROTHY'S LAND OF AHS:
Paxico exit, inside Fields of Fair building. Kansas art — stone, brass, walnut, glass, and clay — plus cheeses, jellies, honey, flour, and much more can be found in this gift shop. Open daily 8 a.m. to 6 p.m. Phone 913/636-5360.

MARYSVILLE

1990 population 3,359; 1970 3,588. For accommodations information call 913/562-3101.

PONY EXPRESS BARN AND MUSEUM: 106 South Eighth, Marysville. Said to be the only Pony Express barn still existing. Except for the boardwalk through the stone barn, the floor is dirt as it was then, the manger is full of hay, and bridles, harnesses, horse collars, and saddles hang everywhere, as do kerosene lamps. The museum contains Pony Express items, a Pony Express video, and displays of Marysville's history. The loft houses county pioneer exhibits. Open daily 9 a.m. to 5 p.m. May through September or by appointment. Phone 913/562-3825.

PONY EXPRESS PRIVATE MUSEUM: 1002 Jenkins, Marysville. Ken and Arleta Martin invite you to see their private collection of Pony

Express memorabilia. They have collected 27 maps of the Pony Express route, photos or etchings of eight of the ten Kansas stations, three of Henry Jackson's prints depicting Pony Express riders, and much more. Ken, a former president of the National Pony Express Association, will be able to answer most of your questions about this exciting period in the American West. Open weekends or evenings by appointment. Free. Phone 913/562-3615.

BRONZE PONY EXPRESS HORSE AND RIDER: West of Marysville on U.S. 36. Touch this bronze statue and remember the 120 Pony Express riders who completed all but one schedule during the 18 months of this colorful era in American history.

Pony Express rider, Marysville

KOESTER HOUSE RESTAURANT: 908 Elm, Marysville. You don't have to wear hoopskirts or a top hat to enjoy dining here in the ambience of the Victorian and post-Victorian eras. Oak woodwork, leaded-glass windows, and a tiled fireplace add to the charm. The menu offers original creations and old favorites, and prices are reasonable for such an elegant setting. You can't go wrong with the Chicken Baton Rouge for $8.95! National historic register. Open Tuesday through Thursday 5 to 9 p.m., Friday and Saturday 5 to 10 p.m., and Sunday 11 a.m. to 2 p.m. Phone 913/562-2279.

KOESTER HOUSE MUSEUM:
Broadway and Tenth, Marysville. This large Victorian home, built in 1876, displays period furnishings. The decorative arches of the breezeway behind the house, the summer kitchen, and the carriage house make this tour delightful. The entire block, developed by the Koester family, is listed on the state and national historic registers. Open Tuesday through Saturday 10 a.m. to noon and 1 to 4:30 p.m., and Sunday 1 to 4:30 p.m. Phone 913/562-2417. Admission fee is $2.50 for adults, $1 for children.

HISTORIC COURTHOUSE:
1209 Broadway, Marysville. This 1891 Romanesque Revival building no longer functions as the county courthouse. Once you've taken in the beauty of the red brick with terra cotta and stone trim, go inside and enjoy the many county exhibits. Run your hand along the copper side rails as you go upstairs. Inside the courtroom you're welcome to put on the judge's robe and take a photo! Open Monday through Wednesday 1 to 4 p.m.; Thursday through Saturday 9 a.m. to noon, 1 to 4 p.m; and Sunday 1 to 5 p.m.; $1 donation appreciated. Phone 913/562-5012.

UNION PACIFIC DEPOT:
Alston and Hedrix Streets, Marysville. This blond brick, southwestern-style building with the colorful trim is listed on the national historic register. Still a freight terminal.

MARYSVILLE HISTORIC HOMES:
The Pusch-Randell-Anderson home at 1000 Elm and the Olin Deibert Home on U.S. 77 1/2 mile north of U.S. 36 are both private homes listed on the national register.

BENCH-MARK STUDIO:
The stone house beside the Pizza Hut on east U.S. 36, Marysville. Al and Jean manufacture jewelry that Jean designs and do sculpting and bronze casting as well. Visitors are welcome to watch them at work or browse and buy. They also have a small art gallery with paintings and pottery. Open October through March weekdays 9:30 a.m. to 5:30 p.m. The rest of the year they're usually open Tuesday through Thursday 9:30 a.m. to 5:30 p.m. Call 913/562-3761 first to be sure.

MARYSVILLE ANTIQUE SHOPS:
Westside Antiques, 207 Center; York's Carousel Antiques, 410 Center; Busby Antiques, Tenth and Center.

SANDY'S PANTRY:
911 Broadway, Marysville. Enjoy oriental food and sandwiches in this intriguing limestone building in the historic Koester block. Open Monday through Friday 11 a.m. to 7 p.m. Phone 913/562-2322.

TOLEDO'S DELI:
723 Broadway, Marysville. Tasty soups, salads, and sandwiches here. Open Monday through Friday 9 a.m. to 7 p.m., Saturday 10 a.m. to 2 p.m. Phone 913/562-5049.

HOLLENBERG PONY EXPRESS STATION HISTORICAL MARKER AND BRICK MEMORIAL:
Junction of U.S. 36 and K-148. Good explanation of the Pony Express days.

PONY EXPRESS ANTIQUE MALL:
Junction U.S. 36 and K-148. Open Monday through Saturday 10 a.m. to 6 p.m., Sunday noon to 4 p.m. Phone 913/337-2357.

OKETO HISTORICAL MUSEUM:
Downtown Oketo. 1990 population
116; 1970 133. Built in 1884, this building is on the National Register of
Historic Places and features Indian
artifacts. Phone Warda at 913/744-3516
for a tour.

H A N O V E R

1990 population 696; 1970 793.

**HOLLENBERG PONY EXPRESS
STATION:** From U.S. 36 west of
Marysville 11 miles, take K-148 north,
then go one mile east on K-243, near
Hanover. Said to be the only unaltered
Pony Express station remaining at its
original location. This is where Pony
Express riders slept and changed
horses. G.H. Hollenberg and his wife
also sold supplies, food, and lodging
to travelers on the Oregon-California
Trail . Wagons were repaired here and
animals sold. Pass through low doorways inside and let exhibits tell the
story of a day on the overland trail.
There's a nice shaded area for picnicking and imagining those Pony Express
riders galloping up to the station.
Attend the Pony Express Festival held
the last Sunday of every August.
Station open Tuesday through
Saturday 10 a.m. to 5 p.m. and Sunday
1 to 5 p.m. Donations appreciated.
Phone 913/337-2635.

**ST. JOHN'S CATHOLIC
CHURCH:** Hanover. Look for the
spire. Take an appreciative look inside.

RICKY'S CAFE: West end of North
Street, Hanover. Small-town, country
kind of place. The price is right and
the food is great. Get a 10-ounce steak
for $6.25. Folks come from all over.
Open daily 7:30 a.m. to 11 p.m.,
Sunday 9 a.m. to 2 p.m. Phone
913/337-8903.

**SCHWARTZ GROCERY AND
DEPARTMENT STORE:** South
Church, Hanover. From soup to
shoes, novelties to kitchen utensils,
this old building with the wooden
floors and pressed tin ceilings probably has what you need. Phone
913/337-2212.

BREMEN WELL: Four miles east of
Hollenberg Station, Bremen. More
people work at the Bremen Farmers
Mutual Insurance Company than live
in this unincorporated town. Don't
run into the hand-dug well in the
middle of the street!

W A S H I N G T O N

*1990 population 1,304; 1970 1,584. For
accommodations information call
913/325-2116.*

**WASHINGTON ANTIQUE
SHOPS:** George and Martha's
Antiques, 321 C; Hen House
Collectibles, Fourth and C.

**MOORE-BALLARD BED-AND-
BREAKFAST:** 301 West Second,
Washington. The Dunhams have
poured their heart and soul into reno-
vating this historic Victorian home.
Phone 913/325-3292 for reservations.

**CITY PARK AND FAIR-
GROUNDS:** U.S. 36 and D, Washington. WPA limestone buildings and
a mill creek dam are featured here.
Free RV parking and electrical
hookups. Phone 913/325-2116.

**KANSAS SPECIALTY DOG SER-
VICE.** 124 West Seventh, Washington. Dogs are trained here to assist
people with disabilities. Evening or
weekend group tours of the canine
building and discussion of services are
available, including a video. Free.
Phone 913/325-2256 to plan ahead.

WASHINGTON COUNTY HISTORICAL MUSEUM: 208 Ballard, Washington. Interesting county exhibits on display here. Tells the story of the 150 country schools once located in the county. Open June through September Tuesday, Wednesday, and Friday 1 to 4 p.m.; October through May Sunday 2 to 4 p.m., Thursday 10 a.m. to 3 p.m. Free. Phone 913/325-2198.

WASHINGTON STATE FISHING LAKE: Located 12 miles northwest of Washington. Catch largemouth bass, channel catfish, bluegill, and redear sunfish at this 111-acre lake. Two floating fishing piers.

MORROWVILLE: Cummings City Park, Morrowville. In 1925, two local men invented the bulldozer. A replica is displayed in the city park. 1990 population 173; 1970 201.

WATERVILLE

1990 population 601; 1970 632.

WEAVER HOTEL: 126 South Kansas, Waterville. Listed on the national register, this 1904 hotel is currently closed.

THOMPSON MUSEUM AND INDIAN ART GALLERY: 331 East Commercial, Waterville. Turn-of-the-century furniture and Indian artifacts can be found here. Open Wednesday, Saturday, and Sunday 2 to 4:30 p.m. Phone Ina at 913/785-2654.

POWELL HOUSE: 108 West Commercial, Waterville. This Victorian home, listed on the national register, was built in 1895 by William Fitzgerald. Fitzgerald was credited with building 85 percent of Waterville's houses before 1935. A drive around town will take you by many more Victorian homes.

ROEPKE DELI: U.S. 77, Waterville. The deli section of this processing plant supplies fresh meat for excellent sandwiches. Open weekdays 8 a.m. to 7 p.m., Saturday until 3 p.m. Phone 913/785-2558.

CITY LIBRARY: Northeast side of square, Blue Rapids. 1990 population 1,131; 1970 1,148. This 1877 limestone building on the national register is the oldest continuous library in Kansas.

ALCOVE SPRING: Blue Rapids. About one mile north of Blue River on U.S. 77; just south of gypsum plant, turn west on unsurfaced county road. No signs. Road meanders around some hills before you reach a railroad track. Backtrack about a half-mile to a drive leading east. A large gravestone commemorating Sarah Keyes, an 1846 Oregon Trail casualty, is a checkpoint. Follow the nearby stream to its source, Alcove Spring. A national historic site.

ROUND BARN: Blue Rapids. From K-9 junction with U.S. 77 go 1-1/4 miles east. A well-preserved 1914 round barn, 90 feet in diameter, can be found here. Dave Stump, owner, welcomes lookers. Be considerate on private property. Phone 913/226-7410.

DALE SHIRLEY'S FLOWER GARDEN: One-half mile east of Vermillion on K-9, three miles north on county road. One of the most inspiring stories in Kansas. Why do 7,000 people come to Dale's place every summer? This young man loves to grow flowers, thousands of them, and to share their great beauty with people. He farms by day and plants flowers at night. Best viewing July to frost. Visitors welcome. Phone 913/382-6357. Vermillion 1990 population 113; 1970 191.

SENECA

1990 population 2,027; 1970 2,182.

HAND-DUG WELL: Eleventh and Pioneer, Seneca. This is one of the largest hand-dug wells in the state. A new walkway has been built around the well for viewing. Call 913/336-2294 or stop at the Chamber of Commerce (Sixth and Main) for admittance to walkway. Free.

NEMAHA COUNTY HISTORICAL SOCIETY MUSEUM: Sixth and Nemaha, Seneca. The old county jail now serves as the county museum. Make sure you see the steerhorn table. Open weekdays noon to 4 p.m. Phone 913/336-6366.

1923 SUTZ FIRE ENGINE: Sixth and Main, Seneca. Look inside glass front to see this old fire engine restored to possibly better than original condition!

SAINT MARY'S CHURCH: Located in Saint Benedict (unincorporated). Go west of Seneca one mile on U.S. 36, then four miles north on K-178 to Saint Benedict. This magnificent church building is listed in the National Register of Historic Places. The exterior is rather common looking but the church received the 1982 Kansas Preservation Alliance Award for Excellence in Interior Restoration. Usually open for viewing 8 a.m. to 5:30 p.m.

OTTAWA

1990 population 10,667; 1970 11,036. For information about Ottawa area accommodations call 913/242-1000.

ARCHITECTURAL TOUR: Ottawa. A self-guided auto tour map featuring George Washburn's architecture is available at the Chamber of Commerce, 109 East Second, Ottawa. Phone 913/242-1000. While following the tour, keep your eyes open for the many other beautifully restored homes in Ottawa.

MAIN STREET BAKERY AND SANDWICH SHOP: 306 South Main, Ottawa. The screen door takes you to tasty baked goods and sandwiches on a variety of breads. Open Monday through Friday 4 a.m. to 5:30 p.m., Sunday until 2 p.m. Phone 913/242-9701.

ANTIQUE SHOPS: Ottawa has more than 14 antique shops. Start at Tecumseh Street Antiques, 122 West Tecumseh, and ask about other shops.

OLD DEPOT MUSEUM: West of Main on Tecumseh, Ottawa. Open May through September Saturday and Sunday 1 to 5 p.m. Phone 913/242-8478.

OSAWATOMIE

1990 population 4,590; 1970 4,294. For accommodations information call the Chamber of Commerce, 913/755-4114. Ask for a historical driving tour brochure or pick one up at 526 Main, Osawatomie.

JOHN BROWN MEMORIAL PARK: Tenth and Main, Osawatomie. Shade trees, stone walking bridges, and picnic areas have turned this territorial battleground into a peaceful, relaxing place. Stop at the John Brown statue, cast by the same Paris company that did the Statue of Liberty, and read the inscription. This 20-acre park is a national historic site and was dedicated by President Teddy Roosevelt in 1910.

JOHN BROWN MUSEUM: John Brown Memorial Park, Osawatomie. Follow the red brick street to the museum. Once inside the stone building you'll find a cabin built in 1854 and some John Brown artifacts. Open Tuesday through Saturday 10 a.m. to 5 p.m. and Sundays 1 to 5 p.m. Phone 913/755-4384.

CREAMERY BRIDGE: North Eighth, Osawatomie. See one of only eight Marsh Arch triple-span bridges left in Kansas. One rainbow span of this cement bridge is 140 feet high. Spanning the Marais des Cygnes river, the Creamery Bridge was built in 1930. After crossing the bridge turn left immediately into the fishermens' parking lot. Take the steps down to the river for a good view.

POTTAWATOMIE CREEK BRIDGE: South Sixth, Osawatomie. This Marsh Arch triple-span bridge contains 1,500 cubic yards of concrete. Both bridges are on the National Register of Historic Places.

THE SOLDIERS' MONUMENT: Ninth and Main, Osawatomie. Elm and oak trees shade this monument to those who died in the 1856 Battle of Osawatomie.

THE MILLS HOUSE: 212 North First, Osawatomie. This Queen Anne style house is listed on the national register. Note the inlaid stone on the front siding. The house can be admired only from the outside, but try to imagine the nine fireplaces inside. The home is privately owned and is being restored.

ASYLUM BRIDGE: North First, Osawatomie. Park your car at the barrier and take a good look. This pin-connected reverse Parker truss structure spans the Marais des Cygnes River and is listed on the National Register of Historic Places.

OSAWATOMIE STATE HOSPITAL MAIN BUILDING: Osawatomie. Take U.S. 169 to K-279 and follow signs to the state hospital. Only part of this impressive building remains as an example of the standard design for hospitals in the 19th century. The building is on the National Register of Historic Places. Note the fountain and pillars across the street from the two towers.

CAFE ITALIANO: Downtown Osawatomie. This homey cafe serves Italian plus homestyle food. Open Monday 11 a.m. to 8 p.m., Thursday 11 a.m. to 9 p.m., Friday and Saturday 11 a.m. to 11 p.m. and Sunday 11 a.m. to 9 p.m.

MIDWAY DRIVE-IN: Three miles from Osawatomie on Old U.S. 169. Open Friday, Saturday, and Sunday at dusk. Call 913/755-2325 for show and time.

TROJAN LANES: 212 East Main, Osawatomie. If you think you can keep score manually, this is the bowling alley for you. Brunswick pinsetters and ten 1956 wooden lanes are still used today. Owners Jerry and Shirley Owens are more than happy to take you behind the pins to see how the pinsetters operate. Don't hesistate to ask! Current rate is $1.55 a game, 60 cents for shoes. One free game for out-of-towners. Open Monday through Thursday noon to 10 p.m., Friday and Saturday noon to midnight, Sunday noon to 6 p.m. Phone 913/755-4974.

PAOLA

1990 population 4,698; 1970 4,622. For information call 913/294-4045.

THE BAKERY THREE HAWKS: Ten East Peoria, Paola. Enjoy breakfast pastries and bagels (no doughnuts) with gourmet coffees and teas. The health-conscious person will love the soups, salads, and sandwiches and give in later to cheesecakes, tortes, and three-layer cakes. Open Monday through Friday 7:30 a.m. to 5:30 p.m., Saturday until 3 p.m. Phone 913/294-3161.

PAOLA CULTURAL CENTER:
Wea and Miller, Paola. It's worth stepping inside to see this 1916 auditorium, wooden seats and all. Next to the Ursuline Academy. Call Lani at 913/294-3800.

PARK SQUARE: Center of town,
Paola. Gazebo, fountain, and park benches make this a good place to rest. The city band plays every Thursday night June through August. Concessions available. Call Lani at 913/294-3800 to confirm.

MIAMI COUNTY COURT-
HOUSE: Just south of Paola business district. George Washburn designed this red brick Romanesque Revival courthouse. Spanish-American War memorial inside. Take a look at the courtroom on the second floor.

SWAN RIVER MUSEUM:
105 West Peoria, Paola. This local museum is open Saturday 9 a.m to noon, Monday 1 to 4 p.m., and Thursday 5 to 8 p.m. Phone 913/294-2663.

HILLSDALE LAKE: From K-68 turn
north a few miles west of the Paola exit or go 2-1/2 miles west from Hillsdale. Fishermen, hunters, naturalists, campers, picnickers, and windsurfers love this lake. Call 913/783-4366 for information.

HIDDEN SPRING NATURE
TRAIL: Hillsdale Lake near the visitor center on 255th Street. Trailhead is just west of visitor center. Enjoy 3/4 mile of natural sounds, sights, and smells as this narrow trail takes you through the woods, over streams, and by a snake "condo" and natural spring. This is a must when you're in this area. Pick up a trail brochure at the visitor center. Phone 913/783-4366.

HILLSDALE BANK BAR-B-CUE:
Hillsdale is north of Paola on a county road. Restaurant located at corner of Church and Frisco. The bank in this little town was abandoned in 1930, but the ribs that Greg and Donna Beverlin serve have brought the place back to life. The atmosphere is almost as good as the ribs! A Burlington Northern train also serves as a dining area. Open Thursday and Sunday 11 a.m. to 8 p.m., Friday and Saturday 11 a.m. to 9 p.m. If you're very hungry, go early. This place gets packed! Phone 913/783-4333.

L O U I S B U R G

1990 population 1,964; 1970 1,033. Home of Rabbit Creek gourmet foods.

LOUISBURG CIDER MILL AND
COUNTRY STORE: Four miles west of U.S. 69 on K-68, Louisburg. Step onto the boardwalk and mosey on over to the Lost Trail Saloon, the Old Country Store, or the red barn where you can watch apple cider being made. The western-style saloon, named after the Cider Mill's famous Lost Trail Root Beer, serves delicious hickory smoked ribs. The saloon is open May through December Saturday 11 a.m to 7 p.m. and Sunday 11 a.m. to 5 p.m. Stop at the Country Store and buy some Louisburg Cider Mill apple cider, apple butter, preserves, root beer, or sparkling water. The store is chock full of other Kansas food products too, and is open daily 9 a.m. to 6 p.m. See apple cider being made Labor Day through Thanksgiving. Call 913/837-5202 to confirm.

HOMETOWN PIZZA: First and Broadway, Louisburg. The red brick building, roof awning, and big glass front windows make you want to step inside for pasta, pizza, sandwiches, and salad bar. Open Tuesday through Friday 4 to 10 p.m., Saturday and Sunday 11 a.m. to 11 p.m. Phone 913/837-2211.

BLAIR HOUSE: Fifth and Metcalf, Louisburg. Full menu service or buffet. Open daily 6 a.m. to 8 p.m. Phone 913/837-4419.

CATTLEMAN'S BAR-B-CUE HOUSE: Eighth and Metcalf, Louisburg. Open daily 9:30 a.m. to 9 p.m. Phone 913/837-5361.

S P R I N G   H I L L

1990 population 2,191; 1970 1,186. Spring Hill was a major stop on the underground railroad.

K AND M B-B-Q: 603 North Webster, Spring Hill. The barbecue of this local couple became so popular at fairs that they decided to open their own place. Open Tuesday through Saturday 11 a.m. to 9 p.m., Sunday noon to 6 p.m. Phone 913/686-5145.

G A R D N E R

Annexation in the early 1990s helped the population increase from 1,839 in 1970 to 3,191 in 1990.

THE DOLPHIN SONG: 102 South Elm, Gardner. It was a Meisinger family project to plan the interior design and promote environmental awareness with a careful selection of shop products. Open Tuesday through Saturday 10 a.m. to 5 p.m., Thursday until 8 p.m. Phone 913/856-7513.

THE DOWNTOWNER CAFE: 108 South Elm, Gardner. The men's coffee club takes over in the morning, but you're welcome anytime! Open Monday through Saturday 6 a.m. to 8 p.m. and Sunday until 2 p.m. Phone 913/884-8112.

GARDNER DELI: 213 East Main, Gardner. Get gourmet hamburgers and huge sandwiches here. Home-made soup in the winter. Open Monday through Saturday for lunch. Phone 913/884-8301.

LANESFIELD MUSEUM: Take U.S. 56 to 191st Street, then go 1/2 mile west to Dillie, then one mile north. This one-room schoolhouse, listed on the national register, was also a mail stop on the Santa Fe Trail. A costumed school teacher helps provide a glimpse into the past. Free. Open Tuesday through Sunday 1 to 5 p.m. Phone 913/893-6645.

T O P E K A

1990 population 119,883; 1970 125,011. Topeka is the capital city of Kansas. For accommodations or additional area attraction information call the Topeka Convention and Visitors' Bureau, 1-800/235-1030.

TOPEKA ZOO AND TROPICAL RAIN FOREST: One-quarter mile south of I-70 at the Gage Park Exit in Topeka. Become transported into a world of tropical flora and fauna. Exotic birds abound. Nearby gorillas, lions, hippos, elephants, giraffes, and even barking muntjac deer are showcased. Admission fee. Open every day of the year except Christmas 9:30 a.m. to 4:30 p.m. Phone 913/272-7042.

CAROUSEL IN THE PARK: West side of Gage Park, Topeka. A rare treat. One of fewer than 200 original American carousels remaining, this grand old carousel continues to delight children of all ages. Admission 50 cents. Open every day May through Labor Day 10 a.m. to 5 p.m. Open weekends only in April, September, and October.

GAGE PARK MINI-TRAIN: West of zoo in Gage Park, Topeka. Great fun — a 13-minute ride on a charming red train. Only 50 cents. Visitor hours are the same as for the carousel.

REINSCH ROSE GARDEN: Gage Park, Topeka. Over 350 varieties of roses, 7,000 bushes. Enjoy strolling in this wonderful garden. Normal blooming season is June through October.

KANSAS MUSEUM OF HIS-TORY: 6425 Southwest Sixth, Topeka. Splendid displays make the Kansas story real, including everything from a Pawnee Indian earthen lodge to a 1933 Chevy. A display everyone will love, even though it weighs 110,000 pounds, is the *Cyrus K. Holiday*, an 1880s steam locomotive beautifully restored. The Discovery Place is a hands-on gallery where visitors can touch, feel, smell, hear, manipulate, and even try on artifacts. Free. Open Monday through Saturday 9 a.m. to 4:30 p.m. and Sunday 12:30 to 4 p.m. Phone 913/272-8681.

HISTORIC WARD-MEADE PARK: 124 Northwest Fillmore, Topeka. Five acres of living history in a realistic setting — livery stable, general store, depot, prairie home, log cabin, and a restored 1870 Victorian mansion. Victorian luncheons may be arranged for 12 or more by reservation. Admission fee. Open Tuesday through Friday 10 a.m. to 4 p.m., weekends 1 to 4 p.m. Phone 913/235-0806.

COMBAT AIR MUSEUM: Hangars 602 and 604, Forbes Field south of Topeka on U.S. 75. Airplanes representing every American conflict

since human flight began are here: WWI Jenny, C-47, F-11F Tiger Blue Angel, Beech RU-8D, Super Constellation, Voodoo jets , and more. Admission fee. Open every day 10 a.m. to 4 p.m. Phone 913/862-3303.

KANSAS STATE CAPITOL: Topeka Boulevard and Tenth, Topeka. Kansas was organized as a U.S. territory in 1854. Seven locations served as territorial capitals. On January 29, 1861 Kansas became the 34th state of the Union. By November Topeka had been selected as the capital city. Construction of the capitol was started in 1866 and completed 37 years later in 1903.

CAPITOL TOURS: Originating at the lower level beneath the rotunda, 55-minute guided tours of the capitol are offered every day except Sunday. Starting times are 9, 10, and 11 a.m. and 1 and 3 p.m. The capitol is open every day from 8 a.m. to 5 p.m. On Sunday only the east door is unlocked.

JOHN STEUART CURRY MURALS: Second floor capitol building. Curry, a native Kansan, was commissioned to paint murals on the second level of the capitol telling the Kansas story. The project became clouded in controversy when a certain group maintained that the realism Curry sought to portray presented a negative image of Kansas. Curry was not allowed to finish the central and unifying part of his project. He refused to sign the panels he completed. A dramatic painting depicting John Brown is the most famous section.

HEARTLAND PARK: South of Topeka on U.S. 75. One of the country's newest motor racing complexes. The park features a unique road course and a quarter-mile drag strip. Call 913/862-4781 for schedule.

ELDERBERRY BED-AND-BREAKFAST: 1035 Southwest Fillmore, Topeka. Rich oak woodwork, pocket doors, and beveled glass highlight the elegance of this 1887 Queen Anne home only seven blocks from the capitol. This home received the 1990 Preservation award from Historic Topeka, Inc. Phone Carol or Jerry at 913/235-6309.

THE SUNFLOWER BED-AND-BREAKFAST: 915 Southwest Munson, Topeka. Stained glass windows, medallions, Eastlake style oak fireplaces, and period furnishings make this 1887 Victorian only seven blocks from the capitol a great place to stay. Three rooms, two shared baths. Phone 913/357-7509.

HERITAGE HOUSE, AN HISTORIC INN AND FINE DINING: 3535 Southwest Sixth, Topeka. You'll always remember your luxurious hours here. Thirteen sleeping rooms/suites and baths tastefully decorated give you comfort and relaxation. A European-trained chef prepares delicious gourmet meals. Call Don or Betty Rich for reservations, 913/233-3800.

C.W. PORUBSKY GROCERY AND MEATS: 508 Northeast Sardau, Topeka. This little store and adjoining lunchroom are remnants of "Little Russia." You'll enjoy the homey atmosphere. Lunch is served from 11 a.m. to 2 p.m. Phone 913/234-5788.

SEABROOK TAVERN: From Gage and 21st Streets 1/2 block west. This bar and grill is the home of the largest hamburger in the world — only $16. Eat the whole thing by yourself and it's free! Open weekdays 11:30 a.m. to 1:30 p.m and 5 to 11 p.m. Phone 913/272-9749.

SERENATA FARMS: West edge of Big Springs on U.S. 40 (about eight miles east of Topeka). Recreate the Oregon Trail days here. Trams pulled by classic John Deere tractors take you to Oregon Trail swales, to the springs where travelers refilled water barrels, and to picnic sites. If desired, entertainment includes folk music and native American culture talks. Admission fee. May through October. Please call Marti Newell for tour schedules and details, 913/887-6660.

HOLTON

1990 population 3,196; 1970 3,063. Call 913/364-3963 for accommodations information.

HOLTON: Twenty-six miles north of Topeka on U.S. 75. The 1920 courthouse and a gazebo are in the middle of the square business district. A streetscape renovation project around the square includes period lighting, flowering trees, park benches, and distinctive walkways with personalized engravings of past and present citizens and friends of Holton. Numerous antique, craft, and gift shops on square.

HOTEL JOSEPHINE: Ohio and Fifth, Holton. This red brick corner building has been in continuous operation as a hotel since 1890. A 100-year-old box grand piano and 1890s registry enhance a richly decorated lobby. Guest rooms in this two-story building are decorated individually with antique furniture and have modern bathrooms. Owners George and Marjorie Gantz are knowledgeable about area attractions. Phone 913/364-3151 for reservations.

ROEBKE HOME MUSEUM: 216 New York, Holton. Every room in this two-story house is full of vintage clothing, including an 1880s maroon wedding dress and a 1920 flapper outfit. Meals catered for groups. Hours by appointment. $2 admission fee. Phone 913/364-2087 or 364-2421.

JACKSON COUNTY MUSEUM:

New York and Fourth, Holton. This old plumbing store holds displays about Campbell College, a silk factory once located in Holton, WPA American Costume Figurines, and other local history. Open Friday and Saturday 10 a.m. to 5 p.m., Sunday 2 to 4 p.m. or by appointment. Phone 913/364-2087 or 364-2421.

BUR OAK TREE: Nebraska and Seventh, Holton. The breadth of this 220-year-old gnarled bur oak is astounding. On private property. Ask about it at Hotel Josephine.

SEARS AND ROEBUCK MAIL-ORDER HOUSE: 401 Kansas, Holton. This 2-1/2-story house was ordered from the 1912 Sears and Roebuck catalog! Imagine the pieces arriving for assembly. Private residence.

WPA SWIMMING POOL:
North on Nebraska, Holton. One of the state's largest. Built by WPA workers in 1937 and renovated in 1985.

WILDWOOD: One mile east of Holton on K-16. During the blooming season, enjoy the colors and scents at Faith Newman's flower and herb farm. Find dried flowers like pussy toes, love-lies-a-bleeding, globe amaranth, love-in-the-mist, bells-of-Ireland and more hanging from the shop ceiling. See, buy, or order dried arrangements here. Open Monday through Saturday 9:30 a.m. to 5 p.m. Closed January. Phone 913/364-2877.

NORTHWEST KANSAS

ATWOOD SECTION: Atwood, Bird City, Lenora, Logan, Ludell, McDonald, Norton, Oberlin, St. Francis. *Page 72 to 76.*

COLBY-GOODLAND SECTION: Colby, Goodland, Hill City, Morland, Studley. *Page 63 to 66.*

OAKLEY SECTION: Gove, Monument, Oakley, Park, Quinter, Russell Springs, Sharon Springs, WaKeeney, Wallace, Weskan. *Page 67 to 72.*

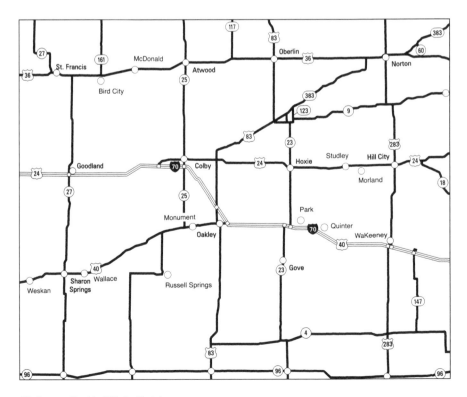

Photo opposite side: Windmill at dawn

Recently some eastern professors have referred to the northwest part of Kansas as the "Buffalo Commons," a region unfit for human habitation. The truth of the matter is that this land's people love it here; most would not move if given the opportunity. The harsh weather and the lonely landscapes test the mettle of prairie denizens, but they face the wind with a smile and say, "This land builds character."

And they are right; the glint in their eyes reflects courage, initiative, pride, and dreams yet to be realized.

To catch the spirit of the west you must visit its people. They use words sparingly, but when they feel your genuine interest and support, you will have gained friends and, of course, useful travel tips. They are proud of their corner of Kansas; take time to discover why.

A few practical suggestions: Once beyond I-70 plan food and fuel stops carefully because service hours may be short in small towns, especially on Sunday. Take winter weather warnings seriously.

GOODLAND

1990 population 4,983; 1970 5,510. Call the Goodland Convention and Visitors' Bureau at 913/899-3515 for additional restaurant and lodging information and area brochures.

MAIN STREET: Goodland. The red bricks on Main were laid by the legendary Jim Brown, who could lay them almost as fast as they could be brought to him — 150 per minute! He laid many of the brick streets in Kansas during the 1920s.

THE HIGH PLAINS MUSEUM: 1717 Cherry, Goodland. Quotes and recordings shed light on exhibits such as the Dust Bowl, the Kidder Massacre, and autocamping in 1910. See the first helicopter and push a button to watch the rotation of the propeller! It's a fun museum. A herbarium is in the works. Open Monday through Saturday 9 a.m. to 5 p.m. (Mountain Time) and Sunday 1 to 4 p.m. Free. Phone 913/899-4595.

CARNEGIE ARTS CENTER: 120 West Twelfth, Goodland. Rotating exhibits prepared by the Goodland Arts Council are on display in this 1912 national historic site. Teddy bears by Linda Foster are for sale here. Open Tuesday through Friday 10 a.m. to 5 p.m. and Sunday 2 to 4 p.m. (MT). Free. Phone 913/899-6422.

SHERMAN COUNTY COURTHOUSE: Broadway and Eighth, Goodland. The art deco tilework on this blond brick building with stone trim gives a pleasing look to the 1931 structure.

PIONEER SCULPTURE: On the courthouse grounds, Goodland. "They Came to Stay" is a powerful statue of a pioneer couple. You can almost see the strain of hard work and love of the land in their eyes.

Pioneer Sculpture, Goodland

HISTORIC TOUR OF GOOD-LAND:
A self-guided historic tour brochure that highlights some of Goodland's architectural diversity is available at the High Plains Museum, or call Marciea at 913/899-3515.

TELEPHONE BUILDING:
Tenth and Main, Goodland. It's certainly worth a drive by to see the art deco tiles on this building.

PUPPET FACTORY:
Seventeenth and Broadway, Goodland. Tours are available in this old grocery-store-warehouse-turned-puppet factory. Phone 913/899-7143.

CRAZY R'S RESTAURANT:
1018 Main, Goodland. Rod is the crazy one with the long hair and a swagger in his walk. But he sure can cook up some great steaks. Open daily 11 a.m. to 11 p.m., closed on Sunday. Phone 913/899-3430.

HEART HAVEN BED-AND-BREAKFAST:
One mile east of Goodland. This beautiful two-story home is for guests only, with bedrooms upstairs and a lounging area downstairs. Stools at the table make it a favorite pastime of guests to sip tea and chat in the kitchen. Outbuildings include the Coo Coo's Nest in the old chicken house. Even the metal chicken coops are filled with handmade crafts, gifts, and collectibles. The Book Bin is filled with used books in the "Lindbergh Bunkhouse." Call Carol or Cecil at 913/899-5171 or 913/899-3114 for reservations or a brochure.

MID-AMERICA CAMP INN:
I-70 exit 17 south, Goodland. Phone 913/899-5431.

SMOKEY GARDENS FOR CAMPING AND FISHING:
Ten miles south and two west of Goodland on the North Fork of the Smoky Hill River. Public primitive camping in a beautiful oasis of trees and grassy area around a pond.

COLBY

1990 population 5,396; 1970 4,658. Call the Colby Convention and Visitors' Bureau at 913/462-7643 for additional restaurant and lodging information and area brochures.

PRAIRIE MUSEUM OF ART AND HISTORY:
1905 South Franklin, Colby. Take exit 53 from I-70. Make no mistake; this is not just another community museum. Colby residents Joe and Nellie Kuska collected artifacts from all over the world. Their distinctive collection of 28,000 items has been turned over to the museum. It includes 16th-century Meissen porcelain, the Sorceress bisque doll, toys, silver, clothing, furniture, and wedding gowns through the decades. The unique building's architect was George Kuska, the son of Joe and Nellie. Open Tuesday through Friday 9 a.m. to 5 p.m., Saturday and Sunday 1 to 5 p.m. Admission fee. Phone 913/462-4590.

MUSEUM COMPLEX:
1905 South Franklin, Colby. At your own pace, explore a furnished 1930s farmhouse, a sod house, a one-room school, and a country church that reflect the lives of early western Kansas settlers.

THE COOPER BARN:
Part of the museum complex. This cattle barn was built in 1936 to house Hereford show cattle. It's 66 feet wide, 114 feet long, and 48 feet high. The barn was moved 16 miles from its original location to the museum complex in 1991.

NORTHWEST KANSAS RESEARCH EXTENSION STATION:
Experimental Road and west U.S. 24, Colby. Visitors are welcome to walk among the labeled gardens,

shrubs, and trees on this 77-year-old farm. Always open.

THOMAS COUNTY COURT-HOUSE: 300 North Court, Colby. A statue of a pioneer woman and baby stands in front of this 1906 courthouse, as does a memorial wall to Thomas County veterans. If you make arrangements, Rosalee will take you on a tour of this national historic site, including a trek up to the attic. Phone 913/462-4500.

BOURQUIN'S OLD DEPOT RESTAURANT: I-70 and Franklin on the frontage road, Colby. The smell of fresh bread, plus crafts, Kansas products, and the potbellied stove create a cozy feeling. The delicious and interesting entrees are a delightful complement to the rustic setting. There are oatmeal pancakes for breakfast and quiche, sandwiches, and soups available for lunch. Fettuccine, lemon chicken, and vegetable stroganoff are among the evening features. The specialty of the house is bread pudding with a Chantilly Cream topping. Summer hours Memorial Day through September are 7 a.m. to 8:30 p.m. daily, Sunday 7 to 10 a.m. Other months open Monday through Saturday 10 a.m. to 5 p.m. Closed January and February. Phone 913/462-3300.

CAMPGROUND: Next to Bourquin's. This grassy area offers 50 campsites and hookups March through December. Phone 913/462-3300.

FIELDS OF FAIR TASTING ROOM: I-70 exit 333 at White's Factory Outlet above White's Landing Restaurant, Colby. Yes, they make wine in Kansas. The vineyard is in Saint George, Kansas, but a tasting room and retail area are here. Try a taste of Prairie Dew or Flint Hills Red. Open daily 9 a.m. to 9 p.m., Sunday noon to 6 p.m. Phone 1-800/732-1984.

GAMBINO'S: 485 North Franklin, Colby. Red brick walls, wooden floor, and tall wooden booths make this a pleasing place to have pizza. Open daily at 11 a.m. Phone 913/462-3347.

M O R L A N D

1990 population 234; 1970 300. Thirteen miles west of Hill City via U.S. 24 and 1/2 mile south on K-85. Give Charlie or Faye Minium a call at 913/627-3165 (daytime) or 913/627-5345 (evening) or stop in at the Citizens State Bank to find out about the Morland-area attractions listed below.

DOWNTOWN MORLAND: For people who like to poke around in old shops, Minium Dry Goods and Acheson Furniture may be for you. At the dry-goods store you will find straw hats, overalls, yarn, quilting material, and more. It will take a dedicated rummager to enjoy Acheson's, but almost anything can be found here. Stores open Monday through Saturday.

EASTSIDE TAVERN/WESTSIDE RESTAURANT: Downtown Morland. Stop here for delicious home cooking and their famous Percy burgers. Some say they may be the largest hamburgers in the state. This is one of the few places where you can rub shoulders with genuine cowboys wearing chaps. Open 9 a.m. to midnight.

PAUL HOUSE BED-AND-BREAKFAST: 208 West Main, Morland. A nice, comfortable place to stay. Alice can inform you about area attractions. Phone 913/627-3875 for reservations.

MORLAND WELDING SHOP: At
the intersection of U.S. 24 and K-85,
Morland. The Morland welding shop
represents two very different worlds.
It looks like and almost is your typical
oil patch and farmer welding shop.
Put aside your apprehensions, walk
in through smoke and sparks, and ask
for David Brown, the owner. You'll
like this friendly young man, and I'm
sure you'll agree he's a metal artist
par excellence. He fashions discarded
gears, shafts, sickles, seemingly any
random objects into aesthetic abstract
facsimiles of old tractors, racers, cars
— beautiful creations. David's wife,
Cynthia, paints this metal art in stunning colors. Usually open Monday
through Saturday 8 a.m. to 6 p.m.
Phone 913/627-5775.

Cottonwood Ranch, Studley

MINIUM QUARRIES: West of
Morland. This fossil dig lies in a
rugged pasture. The Miniums will
need to guide you to this treasure
trove where patient archaeologists dig
up the bones of mastodons, camels,
three-toed horses, and rhinoceroses
that roamed our land in the Miocene
Epoch. Plans are to cover the site with
a building soon. This is special and
the scenery is beautiful, especially in
wildflower season.

ANTELOPE LAKE: From the junction of U.S. 24 and K-85 go 2-1/4
miles west and 1/2 mile north. This
charming lake was a WPA project in
the 1930s. You'll enjoy the drive
around the lake. Good place for bird
watching and fishing or just eating
your picnic lunch. The tranquility of
the prairie land surrounds you here.

COTTONWOOD RANCH: One
mile west of Studley (unincorporated)
on U.S. 24. Also known as the John
Fenton Pratt Ranch. You may visit
this 1880s sheep ranch any time. It is
owned and being restored by the
Kansas State Historical Society. The

flavor of old England is here in the
stone ranch house, the stone sheep
and shearing sheds, and stone fences.
Some special features of the house are
stone corner, window, and door trim
of pink and yellow shades of local
limestone; fish scale shingles under
the gables; turned balustrades on the
veranda; and stained-glass windows.
You're welcome to look around. For
information call curator Don Rowlison
in the evening, 913/627-5866.

**GRAHAM COUNTY OIL MUSE-
UM:** West U.S. 24, Hill City. 1990
population 1,835; 1970 2,071. Exhibits
tell the story of oil in the county. Get
key from the motel across the street or
from the Chamber of Commerce at
409 North Pomeroy. Free. Phone
913/674-5621.

**GRAHAM COUNTY HISTORI-
CAL MUSEUM:** 414 North West,
Hill City, in the public library. Open
weekdays 9 to 4:30 p.m., Saturday
10 a.m. to 4 p.m. Free. Phone
913/674-2722.

OAKLEY

1990 population 2,045; 1970 2,327. For restaurant, lodging, and attractions information in Oakley call Della Beamer, 913/672-4862.

FICK FOSSIL AND HISTORY MUSEUM: 700 West Third, Oakley.

Fossils are plentiful around Oakley, and many fascinating fossils collected by the Ficks and George Sternberg are displayed here. More natural history displays. County exhibits are very well done. Open Monday through Saturday 9:30 a.m. to 5 p.m. and Sunday 2 to 4 p.m. Free. Phone 913/672-4839.

PICNIC IN THE PARK: City Park,

Oakley. One block east of Main at Hudson. Every Friday noon there are local entertainment and food vendors. Last Friday in May through second Friday in July. Phone 913/672-4862.

YELLOW BRICK ROAD:

112 Center in front of the Daylight Donut Shop, Oakley. Would you like your name engraved on this yellow brick road? It's a great gift idea. Phone Della 913/672-4862 to order your personalized piece of the sidewalk.

OAKLEY LIVESTOCK BARN:

205 South Freeman, Oakley. Take a seat in the bleachers and watch the cattle paraded in and auctioned off. Cattle sale every Saturday afternoon. Diner open on sale day. Phone 913/672-4100 for other special sales.

OAKLEY MUNICIPAL GOLF COURSE: Southwest side of Oakley

next to U.S. 83 bypass and U.S. 40. New trees have been planted, making this nine-hole course more difficult! Grass greens. Green fee. Phone 913/672-3081.

COLONIAL STEAKHOUSE:

Junction of U.S. 83 and I-70, Oakley. Good food in a comfortable atmosphere. Open daily 6 a.m. to 11 p.m. Phone 913/672-4720.

PRAIRIE DOG TOWN: Junction

of I-70 and U.S. 83, Oakley. See 200 Kansas animals including buffalo, rattlesnakes, and a five-legged cow. Pet and feed some animals. Admission fee. Open daily 9 a.m. to 8 p.m. Memorial Day through Labor Day. Phone 913/672-4994.

OLD GLORY ANTIQUES:

Junction of U.S. 83 and I-70, Oakley. Look for this depot full of antiques near Camp Inn and Colonial Steakhouse. Open daily 9 a.m. to 5 p.m. Phone 913/672-4833.

CAMP INN: Junction of U.S. 83 and

I-70, Oakley. RV and tent campers have access to a swimming pool, miniature golf course, shower area, self-service laundry, game room, grocery, and gift shop. Phone 913/672-3538.

EL RANCHITO: Monument (unin-

corporated) on U.S. 40 nine miles west of Oakley. Come here only if you're in search of a dining adventure. There will be no sign outside, just look for a particle-board door and chipped paint. Nothing fancy inside either, just great Mexican food. Customers come from all over scrambling for the few booths and counter space. Open Tuesday through Friday noon to 8 p.m. Phone 913/672-3731.

MOUNT SUNFLOWER: Weskan.

Three miles west of Weskan, 11 miles north, 9/10 mile west, and 3/10 mile north. You'll cross a cattle guard to get to the highest point in Kansas, elevation 4,039 feet. No mountains or hills here, just a peaceful spot in a pasture where you can see forever across the High Plains. Though the Ed Harold family designed the Mount

Mount Sunflower, Weskan

Sunflower sculpture to mark the highest point in Kansas, they really created a tribute to the spirit of western Kansas. The most inspiring time to visit this homemade monument is at sunset or sunrise.

SHARON SPRINGS

1990 population 872; 1970 1,012. Home of the Rattlesnake Roundup, the only one in Kansas. Held annually the first weekend in May. For information about the roundup, other area attractions, or accommodations call Brenda Beringer, 913/852-4935.

THE GENERAL STORE: 212 North Main, Sharon Springs. The pressed tin walls and broad check-out counter are a good backdrop for the bulk spices, nuts, flour, popcorn kernels, cheese, and meats. Most of the food products come from Kansas towns like Moundridge, Marienthal, Concordia, and Dodge City. Buttons and fabrics also sold here. Open daily 9:30 a.m. to 5:30 p.m. Closed Sunday. Phone 913/852-4256.

SHARON SPRINGS GOLF COURSE: K-27 at south edge of Sharon Springs. Watch out for the rattlesnakes on this nine-hole course with sand greens.

TOWN OF WALLACE: Make sure you get off U.S. 40 and drive down Main Street in Wallace. This historic town is trying to stay alive. 1990 population 75; 1970 112.

CLARK-ROBIDOUX HOUSE: In the northwest corner of Wallace you'll find an 1880 white house built in the Gothic Revival style. Robidoux was an influential Wallace businessman. Private property.

SECTION HOUSE: Southwest side of Wallace. Railroad superintendents and Union Pacific telegraphers lived in this post rock structure built in 1879. Attempts are being made to place this house on the national historic register.

FORT WALLACE MUSEUM: Just east of Wallace on U.S. 40. The museum tells the history of the fort and the county. We recommend starting at the museum, then going out to the site of the fort. Note the photos of Wallace and the fort. The Weskan depot and Pond Creek Station are also on museum grounds. A historical marker tells about Fort Wallace. Open May through September daily 9 a.m. to 5 p.m., Sunday 1 to 5 p.m. Donations appreciated. Phone 913/891-3564.

FORT WALLACE CEMETERY: Take first road south of museum, then go east and follow the signs to the cemetery. A monument commemorates the soldiers that gave their lives defending the fort. Wooden grave markers give the names, ages, and causes of death of many people who lived in early Wallace or were passing through. One man was run over by a wagon, another by a railroad car, another was hanged by vigilantes. Other gravestones tell grim stories of diphtheria and typhoid fever epidemics and the 1874 massacre of a German family.

FORT WALLACE: Once located across from the Fort Wallace cemetery. Nothing remains of Fort Wallace today. The fort was the last in a chain of four on the 700-hundred-mile trail from the Missouri River to Denver. In the spring of 1886, a storm destroyed homesteads throughout the area. Settlers used materials from the abandoned fort to reconstruct their homesteads.

SCENIC DRIVE: Whether you take the county road from Wallace east to Russell Springs or U.S. 40 northeast and then K-25 south to Russell Springs, you'll see the beautiful rolling hills and reddish bluffs of the Smoky Hill River valley.

R U S S E L L   S P R I N G S

1990 population 29; 1970 83. Russell Springs is the Cow Chip Capital of Kansas. This was the Logan County seat until 1963. After months of heated negotiation, the Kansas Supreme Court allowed an election won by three votes to decide the question, and the seat moved to Oakley.

BUTTERFIELD TRAIL HISTORICAL MUSEUM: Russell Springs. The museum is housed in the former Logan County courthouse and sits atop the Butterfield Trail. Exhibits depict early life in the county. Open May through September from 10 a.m. to 5 p.m. Tuesday through Saturday, Sunday 1 to 5 p.m. Phone 913/751-4242. Nearly a thousand horses and riders start the annual Butterfield Trail ride here the first weekend in June.

SCENIC DRIVE: The unpaved county road east of Russell Springs stairsteps southeast to U.S. 83, marking the change from red outcroppings to chalk

formations in the Smoky Hill River valley. On one stretch of road, red outcroppings to the west and chalk formations to the east signify the dividing line between the High Plains and Smoky Hills geologic regions.

KEYSTONE GALLERY: Twenty-six miles south of Oakley on U.S. 83. Chuck Bonner and Barbara Shelton have converted a 1917 limestone church into a studio and gallery for Chuck's art and souvenirs. See Chuck's Late Cretaceous Period mural and displays of fossils found in the area. This is a great place to ask questions about the many natural area attractions, including nearby Monument Rocks. Buffalo can sometimes be seen in a field next to the gallery. Open daily during the spring and summer and according to the weather the rest of the year. Phone 316/872-2762.

MONUMENT ROCKS OR CHALK PYRAMIDS: Twenty miles south of Oakley on U.S. 83, east four miles, then two miles south. You'll have no regrets about going out of your way to see this National Natural Landmark. You can climb on and

Chalk Pyramids, Gove County

Cobra Rock in the Castle Rock badlands, Gove County

touch these amazing geologic features standing alone on the prairie. The natural doors and windows in the chalk formations create great photo opportunities. These sediments, buried for millons of years, are part of the amazing geological diversity of Kansas. Some of the pyramids have already crumbled to ruin. See them while you can. Phone Della at 913/672-4862 or Chuck and Barbara at 913/872-2762 for information.

GOVE: The town of Gove, population 148, is the county seat, complete with courthouse and county offices for the Soil Conservation District and Social and Rehabilitation Services. Many other buildings are abandoned in this two-block downtown. 1990 population 103; 1970 172.

PARK CHURCH: I-70 Park exit. Stop in Park to see the beautiful architecture of the Catholic church. 1990 population 150; 1970 178.

Q-INN RESTAURANT: Exit 107 from I-70, Quinter. 1990 population 945; 1970 930. The setting is basic but the food and service are excellent. Buffalo meat is featured and comes in the form of chili, stew, burgers, or steaks. It's highly recommended that you top off your meal with one of the pies. In season, the strawberry pie is the ultimate choice. Open daily 6:30 a.m. to 9 p.m. Phone 913/754-3820.

CASTLE ROCK: Fifteen miles south of the Quinter I-70 exit, 4-1/2 miles east, then north across a cattle guard for a mile in a pasture. A dramatic product of Smoky Hill chalk formation erosion. Castle Rock and the nearby Badlands are sedimentary remnants of an ancient ocean. Fossil remains of sharks' teeth, clams, and fish may be found in the chalk. This is private property; please treat it respectfully. Phone Tom for information during the day at 913/754-3651.

WAKEENEY

1990 population 2,161; 1970 2,334. 305 miles east of Denver, 305 miles west of Kansas City on I-70. Pharmacist James Cleland says, tongue-in-cheek, "At one time Denver, Kansas City, and WaKeeney were the same size. But our city fathers by careful planning have managed to keep WaKeeney's population down, thereby avoiding problems the big cities face." For information on area attractions or accommodations call Cindy at 913/743-5785.

JIM'S BAKERY AND DELI: North Main, WaKeeney. Stop in for bakery items like apple and cherry turnovers or a loaf of bread. At mealtime, choose from soups, salads, or sandwiches on a variety of homemade breads. Open weekdays 10 a.m. to 6 p.m., Saturday 8 a.m. to 4 p.m. Phone 913/743-2670.

CLELAND DRUG SODA FOUNTAIN: 221 Main, WaKeeney. This modern drug store has a 1950s soda fountain with about a dozen swivel stools. If you have any questions about the history or geology of the area ask Jim, the pharmacist and owner. Open weekdays 9 a.m. to 6 p.m., Saturday until 5 p.m. Phone 913/743-6321.

GIBSON PHARMACY SODA FOUNTAIN: 125 North Main, WaKeeney. This is probably the only two-soda-fountain town in the state! This remodeled 1940s fountain is open weekdays 8:30 a.m. to 6:30 p.m., Saturday 9 a.m. to 5 p.m. Phone 913/743-5753.

ELK DREAMER GALLERY: 202 South First, WaKeeney. A surprise; after absorbing the intriguing facade, enter and see the fine selections in this commercial art gallery.

Open Monday through Saturday 10 a.m. to 5 p.m. Phone 913/743-2408.

TREGO COUNTY MUSEUM: Fairgrounds east side of WaKeeney along U.S. 283. An interesting county museum concentrating on the pioneer era. Free. Open daily 1:30 to 4 p.m. Closed Monday. Phone 913/743-2964.

THISTLE HILL BED-AND-BREAKFAST: Southwest of WaKeeney. Four guest rooms in a beautiful cedar farm home offer relaxation and prairie exploration in a 60-acre prairie-wildflower restoration garden. Breakfast, with homemade everything, is the first thing you'll go home and tell about. Call Dave and Mary Hendricks for reservations and directions. Phone 913/743-2644.

CEDAR BLUFF RESERVOIR: Southern Trego County on K-147. Sandy beaches, picnicking, and camping facilities. One of the highest concentrations of deer in Kansas. The reservoir was designed in 1951 to retain 6,900 surface acres of water, but water depletion and farming practices have reduced it to about 1,500 acres.

Elk Dreamer Gallery, WaKeeney

For information call the Cedar Bluff Reservoir office at 913/726-3212.

CEDAR BLUFFS: A remote area in the Cedar Bluff Wildlife area. A fantastic panorama of bluffs 150 feet above the Smoky Hill River. Roads leading to the bluffs are rough and difficult to follow, but it's worth the effort for the hardy. Please obtain a map at the Cedar Bluff Reservoir office before you attempt the drive.

THRESHING MACHINE CANYON TRAIL: The two-mile trail begins in the North Shore area of Cedar Bluff State Park. In 1867 a party of Brigham Young followers, transporting a threshing machine to Salt Lake City along the Butterfield Overland Dispatch Route, were attacked by Indians and killed and their threshing machine burned. You can get more information at the park office.

SAINT FRANCIS

1990 population 1,495; 1970 1,725. For lodging, restaurant, and attractions information in the Saint Francis area call Teri, 913/332-2961.

THE BREAKS: Exit Saint Francis north on Benton Street and travel about 15 miles north. The deep ravines, cliffs, and box canyons of this golden-eagle country are especially overwhelming during wildflower season. Upon leaving the city limits, you'll pass fields of wheat, corn, soybeans, sunflowers, and pinto beans; you'll pass cattle grazing and areas of wild plum and chokecherry; and then, all of a sudden, this Kansas wonder will be upon you. A drive around the south rim of the breaks is being worked on, but the county road will give you a good glimpse also. Call Tobe Zweygardt (913/332-2809) or Milton Lambe (913/332-3119) for

information about the best route north, or call the Chamber of Commerce (913/332-2961) for a map.

CHERRY CREEK ENCAMPMENT SITE: 1-3/4 miles north of Saint Francis on K-27. See this personal tribute to the Cheyenne survivors of the Sand Creek Massacre. They came here to regroup and recuperate after the massacre, and other Plains tribes met the Cheyenne here to plan retaliation.

CHEYENNE COUNTY MARKERS: There are 21 disks marking old post office sites in the county, 21 marking cemeteries, and 78 marking sites of one-room schoolhouses.

WASHINGTON STREET: Downtown Saint Francis. The brick sidewalks and old-fashioned street lights provide a friendly atmosphere downtown.

CHEYENNE COUNTY MUSEUM: U.S. 36, Saint Francis. A county history timeline and exhibits that portray county life, plant and wildflower displays, photos and much more inform the public about the area. A 1914 church with a working Reed Organ is part of the museum complex. Open Monday through Friday 1 to 4 p.m. Donations appreciated. Phone 913/332-2504.

CITY PARK: U.S. 36. Excellent camping site with electricity, showers, bathrooms, dump station, and picnic area. Free.

DAIRY KING: U.S. 36 and Quincy, Saint Francis. Ice cream and hamburgers. Open daily 11 a.m. to 9 p.m. April through September.

DUSTY FARMER: U.S. 36, Saint Francis. Full menu of American and Vietnamese food, salad bar. See extensive collection of miniature tractors. Open daily 6:30 a.m. to 10 p.m. Phone 913/332-2231.

TRI-STATE MARKER: At the corner of Kansas, Nebraska, and Colorado. Best thing to do is call the Saint Francis Chamber of Commerce for a map to this open-range mailbox. Phone 913/332-2961.

HISTORICAL MARKER: Eleven miles north of U.S. 36 on K-161. (About six miles north the countryside changes dramatically.) The historical marker and iron sculptures made by Tobe Zweygardt tell about a nearby U.S. Cavalry campsite. The dedication to make such a memorial is almost as impressive as its historical significance.

RUSTY R CAFE: Downtown Bird City. 1990 population 467; 1970 671. A 1920 corner bank building and drug store now house this local cafe. A family or small group can have fun sitting at the counter in the middle of the dining area. Open Monday through Saturday 7 a.m to 9 p.m. Phone 913/734-2681.

AZTEC SALES: South of U.S. 36 at Bird City. Antiques and collectibles. Open Monday through Friday in the summer. Phone 913/734-2711.

BIRD CITY LIBRARY: Downtown Bird City. The stone used for this building makes it unique.

MCDONALD GROCERY: Downtown McDonald. 1990 population 184; 1970 269. Go on in and buy something; help keep these small-town markets alive! Used-to-be apartments above and underground stores below. White benches out front under the awning are a good place to relax. Open Monday through Friday 8 a.m. to 5:30 p.m. Phone Lois at 913/538-2528 or 538-2206.

FROSTY MUG: Downtown McDonald. The renovated first floor in this old brick hotel serves as a pool hall and short-order restaurant. Watch out for the saloon girl falling down the steps. Open Monday through Saturday for lunch and supper. Phone 913/538-2505.

SCENIC DRIVE: Enjoy the draws and bluffs between McDonald and Atwood on U.S. 36. People in the area are used to the scenery, but those who don't drive here regularly are intrigued.

ATWOOD

1990 population 1,388; 1970 1,658. For information about Atwood lodging, restaurants, and area attractions call 913/626-9630.

ATWOOD LAKE AND WALKING TRAILS: U.S. 36 on west edge of Atwood. A mile of walking trail between the lakes has benches and lamp posts along the way. The drive around the lake takes you through a tunnel of cottonwood trees. A historical marker just beyond the covered walking bridge tells about frontier days in Rawlins County.

THE OL' DEPOT: Northwest side of Atwood Lake. Twenty-five local crafters stuff this old Atwood depot full of crafts, antiques, and collectibles clear to the attic. Open Thursday through Saturday 10 a.m. to 6 p.m. and Sunday noon to 6 p.m. Phone 913/626-3114.

RAWLINS COUNTY MUSEUM: 308 State, Atwood. A Rudolph Wendelin (artist/creator of Smoky the Bear) county historical mural warms you up to the museum as soon as you walk in. Other highlights are a model of Atwood in the late 1800s and a Governor Hayden display. Open Monday through Friday 9 a.m. to 4 p.m. and Saturday 1 to 4 p.m. Phone 913/626-3885.

RAWLINS COUNTY COURT- HOUSE: A Pete Felten buffalo sculpture stands in front of this 1907 Romanesque Revival building.

JAYHAWK THEATER: 420 Main, Atwood. The mountain scene ceiling border painted in 1910 when the theater opened has been spruced up recently, but the original painting can be seen backstage. Call Sheila or Marcille at the Chamber of Commerce (913/626-9630) for a tour. Movies shown Friday and Saturday night and Sunday afternoon and evening. Call 913/626-9462 for movie listings.

ATWOOD COUNTRY CLUB GOLF COURSE: North of town. Out-of-towners must pay green fee to use this course. Nine holes, grass greens, no carts. Phone 913/626-9542.

THE FLOWER PATCH BED- AND-BREAKFAST: 610 Main, Atwood. Before you even get to the front door, the herbarium makes you feel good about being there. A gift shop with herbs, dried flowers, and herbal jams and jellies tells you what Karen Gatlin likes to do. Two upstairs bedrooms have private baths, and breakfast is served on the patio by the gardens. Guests are welcome to use the pool. Phone 913/626-3780.

COUNTRY CORNER BED-AND- BREAKFAST: South K-25, Atwood. Families are welcome in this large two-story home. Take a walk in the country or relax by the fireplace. Phone 913/626-9516.

HOME ON THE RANGE BED- AND-BREAKFAST: Rural Atwood. Hunters or those hunting for country relaxation will enjoy a stay at the Heussman's ranch. Phone 913/626-9309.

THE HOLSTE HOMESTEAD BED-AND-BREAKFAST: Rural Ludell. Ideal place for a family interested in seeing a dairy operation and playing in a farm playhouse! Guests stay on one floor, the Holste family on another. The front porch is a great place to relax. Phone Ruth or Harlan at 913/626-3522.

THE PORK PALACE BED-AND- BREAKFAST: Rural Ludell. Ted and Gertie invite you to their place in the country. Phone 913/626-9223.

OBERLIN

1990 population 2,197; 1970 2,291. For information about accommodations and area attractions call the Chamber of Commerce at 913/475-3441.

PETRO-PAL: U.S. 36, Oberlin. Good place to get gasoline, pick up free tourism brochures, and ask questions about area attractions. Open 8 a.m. to 11 p.m. daily. Phone 913/475-2609.

MAIN STREET: Oberlin. The wide, red brick streets, lamp globes, and attractive awnings make downtown Oberlin a pleasant place to shop.

ADDLEMAN DRUG STORE: 137 South Penn, Oberlin. Fonda Farr, the curator at the local museum, promises that the cherry limeades and malts at this old-fashioned soda fountain are the best around. Though the drug store has modernized over the years, the black marble counter and back bar with mirrors are part of the original building. Open Monday through Saturday 8:30 a.m. to 5:30 p.m. Phone 913/475-2661.

DECATUR COUNTY MUSEUM AND LAST INDIAN RAID MUSEUM: 258 South Penn, Oberlin. The last Indian raid in Decatur County occurred in 1878. The museum relates both sides of the story and tells what led up to the raid. Besides

Indian artifacts, the museum has a massive collection of county exhibits in period rooms. The outdoor courtyard is flanked by a depot, jail, sod house, and country school. Open June, July, and August Tuesday through Saturday 9 a.m. to 5 p.m. and Sunday 1:30 to 4 p.m. September through November open 10 a.m. to 4 p.m. Closed for the noon hour. Admission fee. Phone 913/475-2712.

NATIONAL HISTORIC SITE: Hall and Penn, Oberlin. Current plans are to convert the old Bank of Oberlin, built in 1886, into a bed-and-breakfast and public dining area! It's expected to open in the spring of 1995. The building has recently been registered as a national historic site. The ceilings, 16 feet high on the first floor, are made of wood wainscoting. When 1995 rolls around get on the phone and call Gary Anderson (913/475-2905) for a reservation.

GATEWAY CENTER: U.S. 36 and U.S. 83 junction, Oberlin. This state-of-the-art multipurpose facility hosts everything from trade shows to concerts. In the theater you won't find a bad seat. There are plans to build an outdoor amphitheater and a nature trail that will run under the highway and connect with downtown Oberlin. Congratulations to the people of Oberlin for supporting such a tremendous asset to the city. Call 913/475-2400 for performance information.

PIONEER FAMILY SCULPTURE: Ash and Penn, Oberlin. This is a Pete Felten creation.

DECATUR COUNTY COURT-HOUSE: East side of business district, Oberlin. Built in the modern eclectic style with brick and stone trim and completed in 1927.

ANTIQUE SHOPS: Wood Shed Antiques and Collectibles, 156 South Penn, Oberlin. Open daily 9 a.m. to 5 p.m. Closed Sunday. Phone 913/475-3922. Times Past, 104 South Rodehaver, Oberlin. Open daily 9 a.m. to 5 p.m. and Saturday 9 a.m. to 3 p.m. Phone 913/475-3516. Past Meets Present, U.S. 36, Oberlin. Open daily 10 a.m. to 5:30 p.m. Closed Sunday. Phone 913/475-3535.

N O R T O N

1990 population 3,017; 1970 3,627. For accommodations and information call the Chamber of Commerce, 913/877-2501.

GALLERY OF ALSO RANS: 105 West Main, Norton, in First State Bank mezzanine. This gallery of large black-and-white photographs is a tribute to the men who ran for president and lost! Dates clear back to Thomas Jefferson who, in his first attempt to become president, lost to John Adams. Biographies included. Open weekdays 9 a.m. to 3 p.m., Saturday 9 to 11:30 a.m. Free. Phone 913/877-3341.

STATION 15: Norton City Park. A replica of an 1850s stagecoach depot can be found here.

VISITORS' INFORMATION CENTER: On U.S. 36 in Norton. Open in the summer only.

SEBELIUS LAKE AND PRAIRIE DOG STATE PARK: Located on Prairie Dog Creek about three miles southwest of Norton. For camping and boating enthusiasts, boat ramps, camping and picnic sites, showers, electrical hookups, and trailer dump stations are available. Added attractions in the state park are an adobe house on its original site, a one-room school, and, you guessed it, a prairie dog town in Prairie Dog Park. The adobe house illustrates the poignant loneliness of pioneer life on the prairie. For more area information call the Norton Convention and Visitors' Bureau, 913/877-2501. State park permit required.

LOGAN

1990 population 633; 1970 760.

DANE G. HANSEN MUSEUM:

110 West Main, Logan. Imagine the Smithsonian in Kansas. The Dane G. Hansen Museum annually sponsors five to seven traveling exhibits from the Smithsonian Institution. The museum also sponsors exhibits from the Kansas Arts Commission and various other mid-America art organizations. Built in memory of the Hansen family, the museum and surrounding plaza bring new cultural and social opportunities into this part of Kansas. Priority is given to purchasing and displaying Kansas art. A true cultural jewel worth visiting. Open Monday through Saturday 9 a.m. to noon and 1 to 4 p.m., Sundays and holidays 1 to 5 p.m. Phone 913/689-4846.

CHURCH OF THE TRANSFIGU-RATION: 210 Washington, Logan.

Registered with the Kansas State Historical Society. The church was built in 1890 of native limestone quarried north of Logan. It is now a museum. Pick up the key at the Dane Hansen Museum.

PRIDE OF THE PRAIRIE: Just

west of the Hansen Plaza, Logan. Here is a change of pace, a local locker plant where you can pick up smoked sausages, other meat products, and smoked cheeses. This type of shop is fast disappearing from the Kansas scene. Phone 913/689-4288.

THE BARBEAU HOUSE BED-AND-BREAKFAST: 210 Washing-

ton, Lenora (15 miles south and six miles west of Norton). Perhaps the best restored and period-furnished Victorian-Queen Anne house in the state. Crowded streets are no problem. Features are an oak hand-worked staircase, etched glass exterior doors, and "spirit of Christmas" antique collection. Call hosts Lelia and Brad Hall for reservations at 913/567-4886. Lenora 1990 population 329; 1970 439.

SOUTH CENTRAL KANSAS

GREAT BEND SECTION: Alden, Burdett, Ellinwood, Great Bend, Hoisington, Larned, Lyons, Pawnee Rock. *Page 77 to 81.*

HUTCHINSON SECTION: Abbyville, Arlington, Buhler, Hudson, Hutchinson, Kinsley, Macksville, Nickerson, Partridge, Pleasantview, Plevna, Pretty Prairie, St. John, Stafford, Sylvia, Yoder. *Page 81 to 89.*

MCPHERSON SECTION: Canton, Galva, Inman, Lindsborg, McPherson, Marquette. *Page 89 to 94.*

MEDICINE LODGE SECTION: Anthony, Argonia, Belvidere, Coldwater, Freeport, Harper, Kiowa, Lake City, Medicine Lodge, Protection, Sun City, Wilmore. *Page 94 to 98.*

NEWTON SECTION: Durham, Goessel, Halstead, Hesston, Hillsboro, Kechi, Marion, Moundridge, Newton, Peabody, Sedgwick, Walton. *Page 98 to 108.*

PRATT SECTION: Adams, Cheney, Cunningham, Greensburg, Haviland, Isabel, Kingman, Mullinville, Nashville, Norwich, Pratt, Rago, Sawyer, Spivey, Waterloo, Zenda. *Page 108 to 111.*

WELLINGTON SECTION: Belle Plaine, Caldwell, Conway Springs, Mulvane, Oxford, Wellington. *Page 111 to 113.*

WICHITA SECTION: Haysville, Wichita. *Page 113 to 118.*

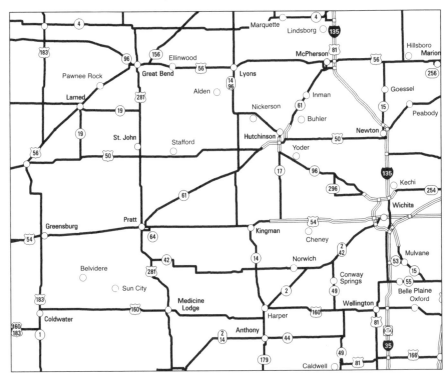

Photo opposite side: Kansas Sampler Festival, Penner Farm, Inman

SOUTH CENTRAL KANSAS

South central Kansas is a region of contrasts. Wichita, the largest city in Kansas, represents the urban extreme — a state university — an intercontinental airport, large factories, and sophisticated cultural facilities. Tiny Freeport, at the other extreme, hangs on to its name with a population of eight.

In between the extremes are a delightful and colorful mix of people, places, and happenings. The Yoder Amish drive buggies to church while the horsey set in Andover plays polo. In Sumner County a wheat farmer proudly tools along in a 300 horsepower, air-conditioned, eight-wheeled John Deere tractor, and in the suburbs a banker pulls on white gloves and proudly mounts his 18-horsepower garden tractor. Lindsborg features Handel's Messiah, LaCrosse features barbed wire, and Greensburg is proud of its well.

There is something special for everyone in south central Kansas. Nature lovers enjoy a mix of wildflowers and buffalo near Canton; they thrill to thousands and thousands of shorebirds migrating through refuges in Stafford and Barton counties; they relax in the serene beauty of Wichita's Botanica or Belle Plaine's Bartlett Arboretum.

There are places so wild and remote in Barber and Comanche counties that there may be hidden places unseen by the human eye. At the same time virtually every square inch in the wheat belt has been turned and scrutinized annually for a century. Historic tracks of the Santa Fe and Chisholm trails have long since been erased by plows. Now giant grain combines harvest food for the world where once wagon wheels rolled.

Two south central Kansas events, the Kansas State Fair in Hutchinson early in September and the Kansas Sampler Festival near Inman the first weekend in October, offer an overview of the state and its riches. Either event will help you plan your Kansas mini-vacation.

GREAT BEND

1990 population 15,427; 1970 16,133. For additional accommodations, restaurant, and area attractions information call 316/792-2401.

BRIT SPAUGH PARK AND ZOO: Entrance is just north of Main and Nineteenth, Great Bend. It's big enough to have a good variety of animals but small enough not to wear you out! One section of the zoo has a variety of bears, foxes, a timber wolf, a puma, a golden eagle , and much more. The surroundings look very pleasant for the animals, with big shade trees literally forming a roof over some of the cages. The other section has zebras, elks, bison, llamas, and a variety of deer. Native Kansas animals like the coyote, pronghorn, and prairie dog can be seen here plus wild turkeys, barn owls, turkey vultures, and quail. Ponds are full of ducks and geese. Open daily 8 a.m. to 5 p.m. Free. In the park are lots of playground equipment, a public swimming pool, and many picnicking sites.

KANSAS OIL AND GAS HALL OF FAME AND MUSEUM: West Tenth, Great Bend. Look for the derrick out front. The intent is to honor deserving people in the business and to educate the public, especially about environmental concerns. Displays include a petroleum products room, a geology room, a drilling exhibit, and a number of scale models. Additional displays are in the planning stages. Open Wednesday and Saturday

1 to 5 p.m. Free. Phone Danny Biggs (316/793-5742) for an appointment.

BARTON COUNTY HISTORICAL SOCIETY MUSEUM AND VILLAGE: South of the Arkansas River bridge on U.S. 281, Great Bend. Museum fans will have a heyday. Even if you don't usually like museums, you may surprise yourself. Follow the red brick sidewalk to the village buildings consisting of an 1873 stone house and a turn-of-the-century schoolhouse, church, blacksmith shop, post office, Waupin windmill, and Santa Fe depot, plus two metal buildings full of pioneer and antique farm implements and other artifacts. Suitcases crowd the benches in the depot; a 1916 map of the United States hangs in the school; and you can ring the bell in the church and take a drink from the windmill pump. Open mid-April to mid-November Tuesday through Sunday 1 to 5 p.m. Free. Phone 316/793-5125.

SHAVERS ART GALLERY: Fine Arts Building, southeast corner of Barton County Community College, Great Bend. This new gallery houses excellent traveling exhibits, local exhibits in all media, and occasional historical exhibits. Open weekdays and Sunday 1 to 4 p.m. during the school year. Hours may soon expand. Phone Norma Ward at 316/792-9242 to check schedule or to make a tour appointment.

WALNUT BROOK BED-AND-BREAKFAST: Choose comfort inside and partake of a memorable breakfast, or stay in an 18-foot teepee outside with breakfast served by the campfire! The country surroundings are surpassed only by the hospitality of Janet and Mike Hammeke and their boys, Tim and Danny. You're welcome to use the pool, sauna, hot tub, and fireplace in season. Horse-and-carriage rides for an additional charge. Murder mysteries every third Friday and western entertainment bi-monthly for the public. Phone 316/792-5900.

RALPH WALLACE RESTAURANT: 1203 Main, Great Bend. Famous for its smorgasbord. Menu service also. Open daily 11 a.m. to 9 p.m. Phone 316/793-6162.

TWELFTH STREET RESTAURANT: 1203 Main, Great Bend. Enter on Twelfth Street side. Excellent pasta, steak, seafood, and cocktails here. Open Monday through Saturday from 4:30 p.m. until the last person leaves. Phone 316/793-6162.

CAROLYN'S CORNER CAFE: 2020 Forest, Great Bend. Get homemade food in this pleasing atmosphere. Open Monday through Saturday 6 a.m. to 4 p.m., Thursday until 9 p.m. Phone 316/792-2072.

GRANNY'S KITCHEN: Tenth and Pine, Great Bend. Good place to mix with the locals for homemade food. Open 6 a.m. to 2 p.m. Tuesday through Saturday, Sunday 7 a.m. to 2 p.m. Phone 316/792-8344.

KIOWA KITCHEN MEXICAN RESTAURANT: East of Great Bend on K-156. The weathered wood siding and porch make this an inviting restaurant. Open Tuesday through Saturday 11:30 a.m. to 9:30 p.m. Phone 316/793-9855.

FORT ZARAH STATE HISTORICAL MARKER: A couple of miles east of Great Bend on K-156. Fort Zarah stood here from 1864 to 1869 to protect wagon trains and guard settlers from Indian attacks.

CHEYENNE BOTTOMS: Northeast of Great Bend on K-156. An estimated 45 percent of North America's shorebirds stop here in the spring. The bottoms are a critical habitat for the endangered whooping crane, peregrine falcon, bald eagle, piping plover, and least tern. Surfaced roads make it possible to get up close in your car. Phone 316/793-7730 for more information.

HOISINGTON

1990 population 3,182; 1970 3,710.

AMY JO'S RESTAURANT:
118 East First, Hoisington. Get some great homemade food in this pleasant and homey atmosphere. Open Monday through Friday 6 a.m. to 8 p.m., Sunday 7 a.m. to 1:30 p.m. Phone 316/653-4707.

PARK WALKING TRAIL: Just off
U.S. 281 northwest of the Hoisington business district. This 1-1/4 mile sidewalk trail meanders through the city park.

ELLINWOOD

1990 population 2,329; 1970 2,416.

UNDERGROUND TUNNELS:
Downtown Ellinwood. Speculation has it that limestone-lined basements were built some time before a disastrous fire in 1880. A number of businesses occupied the basements for a time. Many interesting stories still circulate about activities that occured in these underground passages after the public stairways were closed. Ah, if only those walls could talk. Small admission fee. Feel the mystery in the air and call for a guided group tour 316/564-2199, 564-2218, or 564-2339.

BILL STARR ANTIQUES: Main
and U.S. 96, Ellinwood. This old hotel was built in 1894. Most of the antiques can be found in the Sunflower Dining Room. Open Monday

through Saturday 9 a.m. to 5 p.m. and Sunday noon to 5 p.m. Phone 316/564-2400.

OUR MOTHER'S TREASURE:
Downtown Ellinwood. Antiques, collectibles, and flea market items. Open Thursday through Saturday 9:30 a.m. to 5:30 p.m. Phone 316/564-2396. More antiques can be found in the Showcase across the street.

WAXY'S RESTAURANT:
Downtown Ellinwood. Enjoy local atmosphere weekdays 6 a.m. to 8 p.m., Sunday 7 a.m. to 2 p.m. Daily noon buffet, bierocks Wednesday noon. Phone 316/564-2566.

LYONS

1990 population 3,688; 1970 4,355.

CORONADO-QUIVIRA MUSE-
UM: 105 West Lyon, Lyons. Former Secretary of the Interior Stewart Udall considered it the best Coronado museum in the Southwest. A replica Quiviran Indian Lodge, a Stan Herd mural, and Coronado and Santa Fe Trail artifacts make this museum a must. Admission fee. Open daily 9 a.m. to 5 p.m., Sunday 1 to 5 p.m., closed holidays. Phone 316/257-3941.

STORYBOOK SCULPTURE: In
front of the museum. A heartwarming life-size bronze sculpture of a mother reading a storybook to her children. The sculptor was George Lundeen from Nebraska.

RALPH'S RUTS: Four miles west
and 3/4 mile north of Chase. You'll see a small gate near a D.A.R. Santa Fe Trail marker. Looking east you'll see swales about six feet wide. Contrary to expectation the old Santa Fe Trail shows up as weathered swales rather than parallel wagon ruts. At points in this pasture you will find

seven parallel swales. Wagon trains here usually drove four wagons abreast. Ralph Hathaway, owner of the pasture, usually takes time to share his expert knowledge of Santa Fe Trail lore if you call him in advance at 316/938-2504.

SANTA FE TRAIL POINTS OF INTEREST: A map drawn by Ralph Hathaway details other trail points of interest between the Little Arkansas River crossing and the town of Ellinwood. Get the map at the Coronado Museum or from Mr. Hathaway. Cow Creek Crossing, Buffalo Bill Mathewson's well, the Plum Buttes Massacre site, and Gunsight Notch are among the places you'll want to see.

BUFFALO BILL MATHEWSON'S WELL: Four miles west on U.S. 56 and one mile south of Lyons. Buffalo Bill operated a road ranch nearby, but only the hand dug well remains.

FATHER PADILLA CROSS: Three miles west of Lyons on U.S. 56. A large cross in memory of Father Padilla, who accompanied Coronado on his 1542 journey into the land of the Quivira Indians.

OZ PARACHUTE CLUB: At the airport west of Lyons on U.S. 56. Would you like to watch parachute jumpers? It happens every weekend at the airport, weather permitting. Phone 316/257-5002 for information.

HOLLINGER'S ANTIQUES: 304 East Avenue North, Lyons. A large and very well-organized offering of antiques and collectibles in an old lumber yard. Open Monday through Friday 9:30 a.m. to 5 p.m., Sunday 1 to 5 p.m. Phone 1-800/536-3711.

RICE COUNTY COURTHOUSE: Downtown Lyons. Completed in 1911, this Romanesque Revival courthouse is a real showcase.

SANDHILL PRAIRIE FARM: Four miles south of Lyons on K-14, then nine miles east on Saxman Road. August through October is a good time to come out, pick some apples, do some bird-watching, and enjoy the Williamson farm. Phone 316/897-6631 for daily times.

ALDEN

1990 population 182; 1970 238.

PRAIRIE FLOWER CRAFTS: Downtown Alden. Three old red brick buildings with tin awnings prepare you for the wooden floor inside but not for the incredible selection of gifts, crafts, silk flowers, cards, baskets, and one of the largest stocks of fabric in Kansas. People come from all over the state for this experience. Open Monday through Saturday 10 a.m. to 4:30 p.m. Phone 316/534-3551. Ask here about the depot museum.

THE VILLAGE CAFE: Downtown Alden. Get great food at this community-owned restaurant. Open weekdays 6:30 a.m. to 4 p.m., Sunday 11 a.m. to 1:30 p.m. Phone 316/534-3165.

PAWNEE ROCK

1990 population 367; 1970 442.

PAWNEE ROCK LANDMARK: Signs on Pawnee Rock's main street will direct you to the winding path that will take you to the top of Pawnee Rock (not the town but the historic landmark). From the top of the rock try to imagine teams of oxen pulling wagons across the prairie, or maybe Plains Indians and buffalo will come to mind. The rock's elevation was much higher until the 1870s when settlers and railroad companies used the stone for building material.

DOROTHY'S ANTIQUES: U.S. 56 at Pawnee Rock. This intriguing antique shop is usually open Monday through Saturday afternoons. Check to be sure, 316/982-4323.

L A R N E D

1990 population 4,490; 1970 4,567. For area accommodations and information call 1-800/747-6919.

SANTA FE TRAIL CENTER: Two miles west of Larned on K-156. Life-size exhibits tell the story of the Santa Fe Trail and its environment. Excellent for children. Admission fee. Open daily 9 a.m. to 5 p.m. Closed Monday Labor Day through Memorial Day. Phone 316/285-2054.

FORT LARNED NATIONAL HISTORIC SITE: Six miles west of Larned on K-156. Major Santa Fe Trail and Indian Wars military outpost. Admission fee. Open daily 8 a.m. to 5 p.m. Phone 316/285-6911.

PRAIRIE JUNCTION: 320 Broadway (U.S. 56), Larned. This wonderfully restored depot serves soups, salads, and sandwiches for lunch and a creative poultry, seafood, Italian, Mexican, and steak menu for evening meals. Open Monday through Friday 11 a.m. to 9 p.m., Saturday 5 to 10 p.m., and Sunday 11 a.m. to 2 p.m. Phone 316/285-6939.

NANNIE LAROSE ANTIQUES: 421 Broadway, Larned. Soft hues of pink, mauve, and cranberry, Victorian decor, and the subtle aroma of herbs invite you to look at dried floral bouquets, cut glass, antique furniture, herbs, and vintage clothing. Open daily 10:30 a.m. to 5:30 p.m. Sunday by appointment. Phone 316/285-6577.

MEMORIES RESTORED: Seven miles west of Larned on K-156, then three miles north on a gravel road. Fine antiques, quality restoration, wheat weaving, antique light fixtures, Kansas art, and more. Open Monday through Saturday 9 a.m. to 6 p.m. Call Vicki Dipman, 316/285-3478.

CENTRAL STATES SCOUT MUSEUM: 815 Broadway, Larned. Former scouts especially will want to take a nostalgic trip down these aisles. Open April through October weekdays 9 a.m. to 5 p.m., weekends 9 a.m. to 9 p.m. $1 admission. Phone 316/285-6427.

HISTORICAL MARKER: South of Burdett on K-156. This marker tells about a local Burdett man, Dr. Clyde Tombaugh, who discovered the planet Plut... 248;...

H U T C H I N S O N

1990 population 39,308; 1970 36,885. Located in the Arkansas River valley (non-Kansans say "Arkansaw"). North and east of Hutchinson scenic sandhills lie between the Arkansas and the Little Arkansas rivers. Hutchinson is the home of the Kansas State Fair and the national junior college basketball tournament. Huge grain terminals and salt mines are dominant features. For area information and accommodations call 316/662-3391.

KANSAS COSMOSPHERE AND SPACE CENTER: 1100 North Plum, Hutchinson. World-class Omnimax Theater entertainment, nationally recognized Hall of Space Museum, and Discovery Workshops rivaled only by the Smithsonian National Air and Space museum. Young and old will enjoy it. Included in this complex is a state-of-the-art planetarium. Admission fee. Open Monday through Friday 9 a.m. to 9 p.m., Saturday 10 a.m. to 9 p.m., and Sunday noon to 9 p.m.

For Omnimax and planetarium show times and reservations call 1-800/397-0330 or 316/662-2305.

BOWMAN HOUSE BED-AND-BREAKFAST: 1500 North Main, Hutchinson. Antiques, pocket doors, and massive oak woodwork adorn this 1909 home with a huge wrap-around porch. Ping-pong and pool tables downstairs. Private baths in both guest rooms, and the former nanny's room is a great place for the kids! Guests are within walking distance of downtown, an ice cream parlor, and the Kansas Cosmosphere. Phone 316/663-5824.

MIDWEST FEED COMPANY: 14 West B, Hutchinson. A thriving feed store like they used to be. You'll like the atmosphere, the bird feeders and barrels of birdfeed, baby chicks in season, garden care products, and more. Open Monday through Friday 7:30 a.m. to 5:30 p.m., Saturday till noon. Phone 316/665-8041.

MORTON'S INTERIORS: 405 North Washington, Hutchinson. Mike Livingston calls the art he creates ethnic furniture. Stop in and you'll see how his furniture reflects a culture or a period. Open Monday through Friday 9 a.m. to 5 p.m. and by appointment on Saturday. Phone 316/662-2781.

SMITH'S MARKET: 211 South Main, Hutchinson. The bright colors and sweet savor of fruit and vegetables make you feel as if you're in a garden even more so when you see Hutchinson artist Pat Potucek's lovely bucolic mural on the west wall. Can you resist the bins of bulk candy? Open Monday through Saturday 7 a.m. to 6 p.m. Phone 316/662-6761.

RENO COUNTY MUSEUM: 100 South Walnut, Hutchinson. Four galleries of exhibits reflecting life in

Reno County. "101 Children's Place" is a hands-on display for children. Free admission. Open Tuesday through Saturday 10 a.m. to 4:30 p.m., Sunday noon to 4:30 p.m. Phone 316/662-1184

UNION EQUITY TERMINAL ELEVATOR "J": 816 North Halstead, Hutchinson. One of the largest grain terminals in the world, 67 feet short of one-half mile. Holds enough wheat for 1.3 billion loaves of bread. View and photograph from adjacent safe parking areas only.

CAREY PARK: South end Main, Hutchinson. Lovely shaded drives, lighted pathways, swimming pool, and great playgrounds for children.

HUTCHINSON ZOO: Northeast corner of Carey Park, Hutchinson. A delightful oasis of natural flora and fauna. Open 10 a.m. to 4:45 p.m. Free.

ANCHOR INN RESTAURANT: 126 South Main, Hutchinson. Some say this is the best Mexican food in Kansas. Open daily lunch and supper hours. Closes at 6 p.m. on Sunday. Phone 316/669-0311.

PABLO'S: 101 North Main, Hutchinson. Perfect for a light lunch — sandwiches, pasta, and salad bar. Lots of old advertising signs on the wall. Open Monday through Saturday 11 a.m. to 4 p.m., Sunday 11 a.m. to 2 p.m. Phone 316/663-1717.

FRAESE DRUG SODA FOUNTAIN: 100 North Main in the Wiley Building, Hutchinson. Why not follow up your sandwich at Pablo's with a soda or sundae? Open Monday through Friday 8 a.m to 5 p.m., Saturday 8:30 a.m. to 3 p.m. Phone 316/662-4477.

GIORGIO'S: 1401 East 11th, Hutchinson. This fine Italian eatery was decorated by Wynona Mason of

Hunter's Leigh Bed-and-Breakfast, Salina. Open daily 11 a.m. to 9 p.m. Phone 316/663-8966.

PRIME THYME RESTAURANT: 2803 North Main, Hutchinson. This is a good place for steaks, seafood, chicken, and salads. Open daily 11 a.m. to 10 p.m., Saturday closed at 9 p.m. Phone 316/663-8037.

SAND HILLS STATE PARK: Two miles north of Hutchinson on K-61 to 56th Street. Park your car and hike miles of trails across sand dunes covered with prairie grasses, wild flowers, sand hill plums and groves of cottonwoods. Free entry. Always open.

DILLON NATURE CENTER: A quarter mile east of K-61 on 30th, Hutchinson. North side of the road. An interpretive center, wooded trails, and a pond populated with ducks and geese make this a good place for birdwatching, fishing, and picnicking. Enjoy the new education and discovery building. Open during daylight hours. Phone 316/663-7411 for information and programming.

FOX THEATRE: 20 East First, Hutchinson. Listed on the national register, this 1931 building is one of the finest examples of theater art deco in the central United States. It's being restored to reopen as a cinema and performing arts center. Phone Martha Slater (316/662-9262) for group tours or schedule of events.

FLAG THEATER: 310 North Main, Hutchinson. This 1936 newly-renovated theater is home to area children's theater and other theatrical and musical monthly family programming. The Flag, with the only festival stage complex in the state, also has monthly melodramas. Call to rent a balcony for your group! Admission fee. Phone 316/662-7469 for information.

AMISH COMMUNITIES NEAR HUTCHINSON: The predominantly Amish communities of Pleasantview and Yoder represent a unique way of life some of us connect with grandfather's farm. The Amish understand our interest in their ways, but they do not appreciate being treated as a curiosity. Please respect them and their privacy. Since the Amish have religious scruples about personal photographs, please don't photograph them. You may take pictures of their farmsteads, buggies, horses, and shops. They welcome you to their shops and love to engage in conversation and trade.

YODER HARDWARE AND LUMBER: Downtown Yoder (unincorporated). Kerosene lamps, wicks, chimneys, horseshoes, and horse collars will strike your eye as you enter. These are not antiques, they are new items used every day by customers. Open Monday through Friday 8 a.m. to 5 p.m., Saturday 8 a.m. to noon. Phone 316/465-2277.

KOFFAHAUS: Downtown Yoder. Locally crafted originals, quilts, wood carvings, and wheat weaving. Open Monday through Friday 9 a.m. to 5 p.m., Saturday 9 a.m. to 4 p.m. Phone 316/465-2475.

YODER FURNITURE FACTORY: Junction of K-96 and Yoder Road, Yoder. Fine heirloom solid-wood furniture is handcrafted here. Open Monday through Friday 9 a.m. to 5 p.m., Saturday 10 a.m. to 5 p.m. Phone 316/465-3344.

DUTCH MILL BAKERY: Yoder Road and Red Rock Road, Yoder. As you enter you are greeted by the aroma of fresh baked breads, cinnamon rolls, cookies, pies, cakes, and cobblers. Open Monday through

Friday 8 a.m. to 5 p.m., Saturday until noon. Phone 316/465-2314.

AND COUSINS MAKE THREE:
1-1/4 miles north of Yoder. The shop almost looks a bit gaudy painted up with bright flowers, but once you enter the doors you'll see tasteful wood crafted items made by owner Ann Thornburg's husband, Dale, plus dolls, baskets, quilts, and much more. Open Monday through Saturday 9:30 a.m. to 5 p.m. Phone 316/662-8472.

And Cousins Make Three, Yoder

THE HOME PLACE:
1-1/2 miles north of Yoder. A whole barn crammed with antiques — furniture, glassware, tools, toys and farm implements. A great excuse to enjoy the ambience of a working farm and an old barn full of nostalgia. Carol, Ray, and Jenny would love to have you stop in. Open Tuesday through Saturday 10 a.m. to 5 p.m. Phone 316/662-1579.

COUNTRY VARIETY STORE:
1-3/4 miles east of Yoder on Red Rock Road. This little farm store is where you may buy the beautiful fabrics, threads, and notions that the Amish wear. Straw hats too. Open

8 a.m. to 5 p.m., closed Sunday and Wednesday. No phone.

YODER CAFE:
West of Yoder on K-96. You may see buggies parked here. Good food, great pies. Open Monday through Saturday 6 a.m. to 8 p.m. Phone 316/465-3612.

KOCHENHAUS:
Rural Yoder. Homestyle cooking in an Amish home for groups of 12 to 30. Write for evening meal reservations and directions, 8612 South Obee Road, Haven, Kansas 67543.

COUNTRY TEA ROOM:
Rural Yoder. Luncheons are served in an Amish home to groups of eight to 28. Soup or salad, sandwiches, and dessert. For reservations and directions write to 6414 South Halstead, Hutchinson, Kansas 67501.

OLD NAVAL AIR STATION:
One mile west and 3/4 mile south of Yoder. An old hangar, abandoned runways, and high wire fences are remnants of the World War II Hutchinson Naval Air Station. Giant four-engine Liberator bombers trained here.

WHOLE EARTH FARMS:
24510 Willison Road, Mount Hope (about 1/2 mile north of Cheney Reservoir on the Buhler-Haven Road). What a colorful surprise — flowers, scented geraniums, herbs, everlastings. Those special plants for the discriminating gardener are here. Open April and May 10 a.m. to 7 p.m. Closed on Thursday. Call Sandy Shepherd at 316/445-2565.

PLEASANTVIEW

Five miles southwest of Hutchinson on U.S. 50 and K-61. The retail focus of the Dutch, Amish, and Mennonite traditions is here. The shops reflect the values, integrity, and quality inherent in the community.

DUTCH KITCHEN: Pleasantview. Great country food, great country atmosphere. Open Monday through Saturday 6 a.m. to 8 p.m., closed Sundays and holidays. Phone 316/662-2554.

STUTZMAN'S GREENHOUSE AND GARDEN CENTER: Pleasantview. A dazzling array of color greets you as you enter. In season anyone will appreciate the beauty in these vast greenhouses. Open Monday through Saturday 8 a.m. to 6 p.m. during the growing season. Phone 316/662-0559.

GLENN'S BULK FOOD SHOPPE AND GOSPEL BOOKSTORE: Pleasantview. Food for body and soul. A great idea — basic foods and health foods purchased in bulk and sold to you in quantities you want. Open Monday through Saturday 9 a.m. to 6 p.m. Phone 316/662-2875.

COUNTRY HOME FURNISHINGS: Pleasantview. High-quality oak furniture, mostly handcrafted by local artisans. Open Monday through Saturday 9:30 a.m. to 5 p.m. Phone 316/665-1161.

NICKERSON

1990 population 1,137; 1970 1,187.

HEDRICK'S EXOTIC ANIMAL FARM: Southeast side of Nickerson on U.S. 96. This is the place to see giraffes, camels, kangaroos, llamas , ostriches, and zebras. Drive down the lane that cuts through the middle of the farm or stop at the fence and say hello to the animals. They like to eat fingers, so watch out! Phone 316/422-3296 for group tours.

HEDRICK'S BED-AND-BREAKFAST: Located on exotic animal farm. Each of the rooms is decorated in honor of one of the animals, with murals painted by local artists. The giraffe room has a seven-foot-high canopy bed, the zebra room has black-and-white striped bedspreads. The bed-and-breakfast is in the shape of a horseshoe, and in the hollow of the shoe you can see kangaroos! Each room has access to an outside deck and affords a view of the animals. Phone 316/422-3296.

BUHLER

1990 population 1,277; 1970 1,019. Buhler is one of the host cities of the Kansas Sampler Festival.

LAVON'S BAKERY AND BBQ: One block east of Second and Main, Buhler. A homey little place serving sandwiches, barbecued meats, bakery goodies, and ethnic foods from bierocks, and Italian pockets to enchiladas. Small dining area inside or out. Open Wednesday, Thursday, and Friday 11 a.m. to 6:30 p.m. Phone 316/543-2411.

COUNTRYSIDE DINING: 7305 North Buhler Road, Buhler. Serving brunches, luncheons, and dinners to groups and buses with food prepared just for you. By reservation only. Phone 316/543-2760.

ADRIAN'S A TO Z: Downtown Buhler. Gifts, collectibles, furniture, and warm hospitality. Don't forget, LaVern says Adrian's A to Z is the glider rocker capital of Buhler! Open Monday through Friday 10 a.m. to 5 p.m., Saturday 10 a.m. to 4 p.m. Phone 316/543-6488.

BARTEL CABINET SHOP: 211 North Main, Buhler. Custom-made furniture that will please the most discerning eye. Groups may arrange shop tours by reservation. Display rooms open to the public. Open weekdays 8 a.m. to 4:30 p.m. Phone 316/543-6767.

CAL-MAINE FOODS, INC.:

South Main, Buhler. Here's a chance to see your sunny-side-up or over-easy coming in from farms near Buhler, processed and packaged for you. About 65,000 dozen eggs move through here daily. You are welcome if you make an appointment in advance. Call John Miller or Gary Tatro at 316/543-2272.

ARLINGTON

1990 population 457; 1970 503.

CAROLYN'S ESSENHAUS:

104 East Main, Arlington. The fresh breakfast rolls and doughnuts taste great with the free coffee, the meals are homemade, and the pies are excellent, especially the Sour Cream Raisin! You'll get daily specials, verenike on Friday evening, Mexican on Tuesday evening. Open Monday through Saturday 6 a.m. to 8 p.m. Phone 316/538-4711. Ask here about Cooper's Antiques and Ike Neufeld's hand-carved farm scenes.

PRETTY PRAIRIE

1990 population 601; 1970 561.

D&J GROCERY: Downtown Pretty Prairie. It's another small-town grocery trying to stay alive. Note the pressed tin ceilings. Darrell plans to line shelves above the groceries with antiques. Ask him for a tour of the theater. Phone 316/459-6611.

1936 PRETTY PRAIRIE CIVIC THEATER: Downtown Pretty

Prairie. The building dates back to 1888 and the wooden chairs date back to the theater opening. Movies are shown every Friday night in the spring and for special groups. An "Our Gang" short feature always precedes the main attraction because Little Rascal Alfalfa lived in Pretty Prairie for two years. The original advertising canvas drop is still used. See Darrell at the grocery for more information.

THE COUNTRY CAFE: Downtown Pretty Prairie. Open Tuesday through Saturday 11 a.m. to 8 p.m., Sunday 11 a.m. to 2 p.m. Phone 316/459-6681.

SKATING RINK: Downtown Pretty Prairie. This wooden-floored skating rink is open every Saturday night. Admission fee. Phone 316/459-6908.

U.S. 50 ALMOST GHOST TOWNS: West of Hutchinson on

U.S. 50. Take time to get off the main highway and drive through the almost-deserted main streets of Partridge, Abbyville, Plevna, and Sylvia. If you're hungry when you get to Partridge, we recommend the Partridge Cafe.

PLEVNA

1990 population 117; 1970 124.

PLEVNA GENERAL STORE:

Downtown Plevna. No matter how far out of the way it is, make the effort to come here. Listed on the national register, this store is like a museum except that you're allowed to touch and buy things. The wall shelves are stocked with groceries, dry goods, and antiques. There's a walk-in porcelain cooler, and you won't be able to resist sitting on the wooden chairs at the wooden counter and ordering a sandwich or talking with Charlie. This general store has run almost continuously since 1880. Open weekdays 8 a.m. to 6 p.m., Saturday until 4 p.m. Phone 316/286-5655.

STAFFORD

1990 population 1,344; 1970 1,414.

HENDERSON HOUSE BED-AND-BREAKFAST: 518 West Stafford, Stafford. If you want elegance, comfort, and privacy this is the perfect place. The house is a 1903 neo-classical style with a wrap-around porch. The angled rooms, ball-and-spindle fretwork, and leaded-glass windows highlight the beauty of this home. The cozy bedrooms are upstairs and have private baths. A hostess will come over to get you situated. The wicker porch swing on the screened-in porch is a great place to curl up and read a book. Tandem and single bicycles available. Phone 316/234-6048 or 316/682-5803.

WEIDE HOUSE: 302 North Green, Stafford. Enjoy a two-room suite here in another renovated Victorian home. Phone 316/234-6048 or 316/682-5803.

CURTIS CAFE: 104 South Main, Stafford. It's fun to sit at the counter here and ask questions about the jigsaw puzzles that fill almost every inch of wall space! Conversation is good and so are the daily specials. Chicken and noodles on Tuesday! If you like homemade pies or bread pudding with vanilla sauce, it's no puzzle — you should come here. Open daily 5:30 a.m. to 4 p.m. Closed Sunday at 2 p.m. Phone 316/234-5644.

REMEMBER WHEN: 100 North Main, Stafford. The tall glass double doors lead you to Christmas decorations and other items made by local crafters and artists. Open Tuesday through Saturday 10 a.m. to 5 p.m.

and Sunday 1 to 5 p.m. Phone 316/234-5017.

STAFFORD COUNTY MUSEUM: Broadway and Main, Stafford. From early family photographs to military uniforms worn by county men, this is the place to acquaint yourself with county history. You'll even find out where the phrase "sleep tight" came from. Open Monday through Thursday 1:30 to 3:30 p.m. Donations appreciated. Phone 316/234-5664.

ELROY'S PIZZA: Main Street, Stafford. When the locals brag about the pizza you know it must be good. The dough is made fresh every day, and toppings include jalapeno peppers, pineapple, sauerkraut, barbecue, plus all the regulars. Open Tuesday through Thursday 3 to 9 p.m., Friday and Saturday 11 a.m. to 10 p.m., and Sunday 4 to 9 p.m. Phone 316/234-5408.

ELROY'S II: 113 South Main, Stafford. Once you get past all the toy trains and dolls you'll find the best treat of all, a working soda fountain. Though the wooden back bar is gone, the black cows, green rivers, and other ice cream delectables still taste pretty great. Open Tuesday through Saturday 9 a.m. to 6 p.m. Phone 316/234-6994.

QUIVIRA WILDLIFE REFUGE: Six miles north of the railroad crossing on North Main in Stafford to four-way stop, then six miles east to Quivira Refuge sign, then one mile north. The refuge consists of 21,820 acres including a 362-acre remnant of original prairie with hundred-year-old cottonwoods. Fifteen miles of canals and 25 miles of dikes provide nearly 5,000 acres of managed wetlands and marshes. Spring and fall are the best times to see migratory birds. It is not unusual for over a half-million birds to use Quivira as a staging area during spring migration. You might see bald or golden eagles during the winter. Free. Phone the refuge manager at 316/486-2393 for more information and bird chart. No camping here.

SAINT JOHN
1990 population 1,357; 1970 1,477.

CEDAR MINE FURNITURE:
114 North Main, Saint John. What a treat! Tim will probably be at work constructing furniture from white cedar logs, but go on in amidst the cedar chips and aroma and flag Tim down for a mini-tour. Open Monday through Friday 8 a.m. to 5 p.m. Phone 316/549-3254 or 549-3282 to make sure Tim is there.

LEGEND FINE ARTS: South side of square, Saint John. It's unusual to find a collection of furniture and art like this in Kansas. Also find works from Prairie Print Makers charter members Herschel Logan and Birger Sandzen. Irregular hours. Phone 316/549-3877.

WHITE PICKET FENCE: First and Santa Fe, Saint John. When is the last time you saw a white picket fence?

STAFFORD COUNTY PARK ON THE SQUARE: Saint John. On a warm spring day the fountain, flower barrels, and benches make this park a wonderful place for a short respite. Red brick streets surround the square.

HUDSON
1990 population 159; 1970 181.

WHEATLAND CAFE: Downtown Hudson. They say that Darrel Bauer serves more plates at the Sunday buffet than there are people in the town.

With 150 people living in Hudson you know that this is a popular eatery for out-of-towners. The meat is fresh and the chicken-fried steaks and pan-fried chicken are hand-breaded. Mexican buffet and BBQ ribs on Friday evening. Don't expect fancy decor in this 1914 building, just excellent food. Tuesday through Saturday 9 a.m. to 8 p.m., Sunday 11 a.m. to 2 p.m. Phone 316/458-4761.

ANTIQUE AND COLLECTIBLE SHOPS: Downtown Hudson. After you maneuver your car to a stop between the shade trees, you may want to take a minute to sit on the long white bench in front of the Shark's Nestt and soak in the scene before you go antiquing. The hours at the two shops are erratic, but one is usually open during the noon hour. Phone Shark's Nestt, 316/458-4383; Treasure Inn, 316/458-4201.

STAFFORD COUNTY FLOUR MILL: Hudson, just head toward the elevators. This is the home of Hudson Cream Flour, and Al is willing to give group tours. He shows a film, takes you through the mill, and shows you where and how they package the flour. You'll leave with a sack of flour and a better understanding of the milling process. Call Al Brensing at 316/458-4121.

CITY PARK BAND SHELL: East of downtown Macksville. This band shell, built in 1939, is made up of rocks from 48 U.S. states. Nice place for a picnic. Macksville 1990 population 488; 1970 484.

KINSLEY
1990 population 1,875; 1970 2,212.

EDWARDS COUNTY MUSEUM: U.S. 56 west side of Kinsley. This museum is a great asset to the community of Kinsley. You'll find period furnishings in this sod house and numerous county exhibits. Open May through September daily 10 a.m. to 5 p.m., Sunday 1:30 to 5:30 p.m. Donations appreciated. Phone 316/659-2420.

HISTORICAL MARKER: East of Kinsley on U.S. 50 a marker tells about the Battle of Coon Creek.

MCPHERSON

1990 population 12,422; 1970 10,851. Oil production and refining, flour milling, and manufacturing (pharmaceuticals, plastic pipe, fiberglass insulation) are major industries. For area information and accommodations call 316/241-3303.

AMERICAN DREAM SAFARI: Originates in McPherson. Capture the adventure of T.W. Pierson's guided classic car tours to points of interest in Kansas and the United States. Tad is also working on innovative Kansas wheat truck tours. Phone 316/241-5656 for information about personalized tours.

ANTIQUE AUTO RESTORA- TION: McPherson College Campus, Templeton Hall at Baer and Euclid, McPherson. Watch restoration in progress, see prize-winning cars — Pierce Arrow, Maxwell, Knight, Studebaker. Visitors welcome during school term weekdays, 8 a.m. to 3:30 p.m. For guided tour call Jim Willems, 316/241-0731. For group and weekend tours call 316/241-0731 and ask for the Publicity Department.

MCPHERSON MUSEUM: 1130 East Euclid, McPherson, in the restored 1920s Vaniman home. County pioneer, archaeological, cultural artifacts. Open 1 to 5 p.m. daily, closed Monday. Phone 316/241-5977.

MCPHERSON COUNTY COURT- HOUSE: 100 block North Maple, McPherson. Romanesque Revival style, circa 1894, listed on the national register. Statue of county's namesake, Civil War General James McPherson, is located in adjoining Memorial Park.

MCPHERSON OPERA HOUSE: 200 block South Main, McPherson. Listed in the National Register of Historic Places. Drive by only until restoration is complete. For information call Jackie Engel, 316/241-2193.

CRANBERRY HOUSE BED- AND-BREAKFAST: 303 South Walnut, McPherson. This renovated 1906 house is a beauty with shiny hardwood floors, lots of windows, a screened-in porch, and a balcony upstairs overlooking the flower gardens. The Wisteria Room, in shades of plum, teal, and blue, has a jacuzzi and private bath. Tree-lined Walnut Street is a good place to walk and view many old homes in excellent condition. For bed-and-breakfast reservations call Marg at 316/241-3331.

MAIN STREET DELI: 108 South Main, McPherson. The deli food selection tastes great in this renovated building with its orginals columns. Photos on the wall depict McPherson County days gone by. All the breads are made on the premises. The soup in a bread bowl is excellent. Open Monday through Saturday 8:30 a.m. to 8 p.m. Phone 316/241-1888.

SOMETHING SPECIAL: 106 South Main, McPherson. Fine country and Victorian gifts in an old bank building with wooden floors and pressed tin ceilings. Open Monday through Saturday 10 a.m. to 5:30 p.m., Wednesday noon to 5:30 p.m. Phone 316/241-1125.

BELLI BROTHERS MUSIC SER- VICES: 110 South Main, McPherson. A great place for model train enthusiasts — HO scale transition era featuring mainline passenger trains of many roads and N scale focusing on modern Kansas rolling stock. Yes, they also sell and service musical instruments. Open Monday through Saturday 9 a.m. to 4:30 p.m. Phone 316/241-5557.

KREHBIEL'S COUNTRY STORE: From Kansas Avenue and Centennial in McPherson go 2-1/2 miles north and 1/4 mile east. Specialty meats processed here from Kansas beef and pork plus Kansas food products. Open Monday through Saturday 9 a.m. to 5 p.m. Phone 316/241-0103.

CULVER'S FISH FARM: Three miles west of McPherson on U.S. 56, then 1/4 mile north and 1/2 mile west. The largest fish hatchery west of the Mississippi Delta. Call for information, 316/241-5200.

MCPHERSON VALLEY WETLANDS: Five miles west of McPherson on U.S. 56. A visitors' center is being developed here by the Kansas Department of Wildlife and Parks to interpret this partial restoration of a chain of lakes and marshes reaching across McPherson County. Call Todd Pesch, manager, for information. Phone 316/241-7669 or 241-3946.

THE QUILT BARN: U.S. 56 and Mulberry, Galva. Features Quilt Barn collection by Richard Enns — quilts, wall hangings, fabrics, classes, and demonstrations. Open Monday through Saturday 9:30 a.m. to 5:30 p.m. Call Debra at 316/654-3400. Galva 1990 population 651; 1970 522.

CANTON

1990 population 794; 1970 893.

MAXWELL GAME RESERVE: Six miles north of Canton, west one mile. See buffalo, elk, deer, and wild-

flowers. Adjacent McPherson County State Lake affords camping, hiking, and fishing. Call 316/628-4592 for information.

CHERYL'S CAFE: 128 North Main, Canton. Good food available Monday and Tuesday 6:30 a.m. to 3 p.m., Wednesday through Saturday 6:30 a.m. to 8 p.m., Sunday 11:30 a.m. to 2 p.m. Phone 316/628-4900.

LINDSBORG

1990 population 3,076; 1970 2,764. Stop at the Chamber of Commerce (104 East Lincoln) for information about Swedish cultural events, craft shops, food, and lodging. Open weekdays 9 a.m. to 4 p.m. (closed for lunch). Phone 913/227-3706.

BRUNSWICK HOTEL RESTAURANT: 202 South Main, Lindsborg. Settle into this renovated old hotel for a first-class meal. Open Tuesday through Friday for lunch and dinner, Saturday 5 to 9 p.m., Sunday 11 a.m. to 1:30 p.m. Phone 913/227-2903.

SWEDISH CROWN RESTAURANT: 121 North Main, Lindsborg. Try the Swedish meatballs covered in the chef's secret sauce with parsley potatoes! Other Swedish cuisine also on the menu. Swedish smorgasbord on Saturday. Swedish folk art contributes to decor. Open for lunch and dinner daily. Phone 913/227-2076 for reservations.

SWEDISH COUNTRY INN BED-AND-BREAKFAST: 112 West Lincoln, Lindsborg. The dusty blue carpet and quilts against the white pine furniture make for a charming Scandinavian ambience. Bright and cheery, bicycles provided to guests for touring around town, smorgasbord breakfast. Phone 913/227-2985 for reservations.

SMOKY VALLEY BED-AND-BREAKFAST: Second and State, Lindsborg. Each room has a private bath, TV, and VCR. The suite includes an antique woodburning fireplace and whirlpool bath. Just a short walking distance from downtown. Phone 1-800/532-4407 or 913/227-4460.

BIRGER SANDZEN MEMORIAL GALLERY: 401 North First, Lindsborg. Study Sandzen's brilliant pastel-colored oil paintings from a distance, then go up close and watch the transformation. This gallery has a formal atmosphere with a courtyard fountain. It houses many Sandzen lithographs and crayon drawings. Roving exhibits from other artists are also featured. Open 1 to 5 p.m. Wednesday through Sunday. Admission fee. Phone 913/227-2220.

FORSBERG GALLERY: 125 North Main, Lindsborg. Artist Maleta Forsberg has many originals and prints on sale in this Old-World styled gallery with a light and airy ambience. Here 120 other Kansas artists show and sell sculptures, woodcuts, jewelry, ceramics, paper, prints, and more. Open 9 a.m. to 5:30 p.m. Monday through Saturday and Sunday noon to 5 p.m. Phone 913/227-3307.

THE HITCHING POST: 205 South Jackson, Lindsborg. Frank Reese flew out of his saddle once when a steer ran into his horse, so he made a bronze sculpture to tell the story. His attention to detail brings the many statues of western lore to life. You'll talk about this place for a long time. The studio is open when he's home. Come by and just ring the doorbell. Phone 913/227-2774.

ANTON PEARSON WOOD-CARVING STUDIO: 505 South Main, Lindsborg. Follow the path through the garden to a rustic studio filled with Anton Pearson's character woodcarvings best known for their depictions of immigrants' lives. Anton has passed away, but son-in-law Norman Malm has carried on the woodcarving tradition. Norman adds humor to his characters, as shown by the gigantic grasshopper being fought off by a farmer with his pitchfork. If you need help with household or farmyard chores ask about his Swedish Tomtes! Unless Norman is at coffee or fishing, the studio is open. Phone 913/227-2695.

HEMSLOJD: 201 North Main, Lindsborg. The Swedish translation of *hemslojd* is "home factory," and you'll feel like you've stepped into one here. Smell the sugar pine wood shavings as you watch the Swedish folk art Dala horses being cut out with a tracing lathe and put together. Then watch as the flower-patterned saddle is painted on. See craftsmen at work Monday through Saturday 9 a.m. to 5:30 p.m. Gift shop also open Sunday 12:30 to 4:30 p.m. Phone 913/227-2053.

PRAIRIE WOODS: 134 North Main, Lindsborg. You won't find a nail in Gene Applequist's picnic table on display. See his other sugar pine Swedish peasant style furniture. Note the fingerprint design on some pieces. Several artists have their work for sale here, and one artist can usually be found at work. Open 10 a.m. to 5 p.m. Monday through Saturday; 1 to 5 p.m. on Sunday. Phone 913/227-3927.

KONSTVERK GALLERY: 131 Harrison, Lindsborg. See and buy Birger Sandzen prints, Lester Raymer oils, Phil Epp acrylics, and other artists' work. Ask Rick or Marilyn Nelson for a tour of Lester Raymer's Red Barn Studio. Open 10 a.m. to 5 p.m.

Tuesday through Saturday, Sunday 1 to 5 p.m. Phone 913/227-2998.

THE KITCHEN SHOP: 113 North Main, Lindsborg. The stained-glass windows and recessed entrance invite you to turn the knob on the tall narrow double doors and enter a long-ago time brought back by Ray and Vicki Kahmeyer. Their store is full of gourmet specialties and tasteful modern kitchen accessories including Ray's hand-crafted pottery. Antique kitchen utensils line shelves high above the wooden floor. Open Monday through Saturday 10 a.m. to 5 p.m. Phone 913/227-3990.

PRESSER HALL: Bethany College Campus, Lindsborg. Attend any musical occasion here so that you can hear the splendor of the pipe organ. The most well-known event performed here is Handel's *Messiah.* Call the Chamber at 913/227-3706 for information.

McPHERSON COUNTY OLD MILL MUSEUM AND COMPLEX: 120 Mill, Lindsborg. Plan to spend hours here exploring the renovated Smoky Valley Roller Mill, the first McPherson County Courthouse, the depot, blacksmith shop, Swedish Pavilion used at the World's Fair, antique farm equipment, and the many county exhibits. Open April through October Tuesday through Saturday 9:30 a.m. to 5 p.m. and Sunday 1 to 5 p.m.; November through March daily 1 to 5 p.m. Closed Mondays. Phone 913/227-3595.

REO ANTIQUE AUTO MUSE-UM: Corner of Harrison and Lincoln, Lindsborg. The brass trim, big silver grilles, wooden spokes, starting cranks, and rumble seats of cars like the 1929 REO Flying Cloud Deluxe Coupe, 1907 Cadillac Runabout, 1911 Model T Ford, and 1922 Hupmobile

Vehicle from Reo Antique Auto Museum, Lindsborg

are displayed in a renovated 1920s vintage service station and annex. Open April through October daily 9:30 a.m. to 5 p.m. and Sunday 1 to 5 p.m.; November through March daily 10 a.m. to 3 p.m., Sunday 1 to 3 p.m. Admission fee. Phone 913/227-3252.

CORONADO HEIGHTS: Two miles north, one mile west of Lindsborg. This hill and lookout provide an expansive view of the Smoky Valley. It's quite likely that Coronado's scouts used this hill as a lookout.

MALM'S SMOKY VALLEY PLAZA: Junction of U.S. 81 and K-4, Lindsborg. One hundred campsites around two man-made lakes accommodate RVs or tents. Dump station, laundry facility, showers. Restaurant for campers in 100-year-old renovated barn. Phone 913/227-2932.

MARQUETTE

Nine miles west of Lindsborg on K-4. 1990 population 593; 1970 578. Vintage downtown buildings, circa 1887-1912, have been restored to their original Victorian charm and are listed on the Kansas Register of Historic Places. This small town is the place to enjoy early Kansas architecture — front facades with recessed entries, cast-iron columns, and pressed tin fronts. Pressed tin friezes have been painted in original colors reflecting Swedish influence.

CITY SUNDRIES: Downtown Marquette. Step up to the 1901 marble soda fountain and order a peanut eclair. Original bentwood chairs, ice cream tables, stained-glass back bar, and curved glass display cases. Owner Sandra Meyers will be happy to give you additional Marquette information. Open every day from 9 a.m. till mid-evening. Phone 913/546-2584.

LARSON PIPE ORGAN COMPANY: Downtown Marquette. Follow the musical notes into Brion Larson's pipe organ factory. They build and rebuild church organs here. You are welcome to stop in. Phone 913/546-2779.

HANSON-LINDFORS HOME: 211 East Fifth, Marquette. This 16-room house built in 1888 is listed on the national register. It's been authentically restored and furnished with period antiques. Adjoining is a furnished pioneer cabin built in 1871. For an appointment to visit this private home call Allen or Laurie Lindfors at 913/546-2348.

INMAN

1990 population 1,035; 1970 836. Inman is one of the host cities for the annual Kansas Sampler Festival. For area information call 316/585-2389.

STAN HERD MURAL: Main Street, south of bank, Inman. An outstanding mural depicting early-20th-century

Inman by the eminent Kansas artist Stan Herd. A view from inside the bank gives the work a three-dimensional effect. See it any time. Buy some homemade sausage at nearby Larry's Market.

INMAN'S MCCORMICK-DEERING DAYS MUSEUM: Main and Center, Inman. A museum that commemorates the era when McCormick-Deering tractors and binders were widely used. See exhibits of domestic, railroad, agricultural, milling, and cultural artifacts of the early 1900s. Special features are a working model HO railroad, cast-iron toy implements, McCormick tractors, and a Model T Ford. Open April through October Thursday and Friday 1 to 5 p.m., Saturday 9 a.m. to 5 p.m., and Sunday 1 to 4 p.m. Phone 316/585-2626 or 316/585-2226.

INMAN HISTORICAL COMPLEX: North Main Street, Inman. The site features a restored 1906 Inman Telephone office and a Rock Island depot. Across the street is the Inman Library now housed in a restored limestone 1893 Odd Fellows Hall.

CHICKEN HOUSE MUSEUM: Rural Inman. An old chicken house and round top full of I.H., John Deere, Cushman, and Maytag one-cylinder engines; pump jacks; drag saws; seeders; cherry pitters; old hand tools; and much more. Edward Martens says that he and his wife, Billie Jean, love to share these artifacts and converse about old times with people who value nostalgic treasures. Call 316/585-6691 for an appointment to see this private collection.

MAIN STREET FLORAL AND CRAFT: 200 South Main, Inman. The striking scent of potpourri invites you in to browse among dried floral arrangements and other hand-crafted items. Open 11 a.m. to 4 p.m. Phone 316/585-2247.

RUTHIE'S CAFE: Main Street, Inman. This local cafe is especially crowded on Thursday for the vereni-ke! Arrive before noon. Open Monday through Friday 6:30 a.m. to 4 p.m., Saturday 6:30 a.m. to 2 p.m., Sunday 11 a.m. to 1:30 p.m. Open Thursday evening till 8 p.m. Phone 316/585-6925.

JANTZ'S ANTIQUES: Highway K-61, Inman. Furniture, collectibles, antiques, dolls, and more. Open Tuesday through Friday 10 a.m. to 5 p.m. Phone 316/585-2325 or 585-2186.

STONE CORRAL ON THE SANTA FE TRAIL: From Inman go eight miles west, five miles north, and west to the Little Arkansas River. You will need a guide here to help you find a huge live cottonwood tree that was a trail landmark, the trail river crossing, and the site of the stone corral. Call Willmer Ekholm in advance for details and guidance. Phone 316/489-6487.

LAKE INMAN: Three miles east and one mile north of Inman. The largest natural lake in Kansas.

KANSAS SAMPLER CENTER: Three miles south and 1-3/4 miles east of Inman on Arapaho Road. This is the home of the Kansas Sampler Foundation which is dedicated to preserving the rural culture of Kansas. In the Sharon Schmidt building, audio/visual shows and displays feature "samples" of Kansas's diverse culture and attractions. Kansas books, gifts, and food products are sold in the lobby. The lobby features timbers from the turn-of-the-century Balzer barn. To see a Kansas slide show call 316/585-2389 in advance.

Meals or snacks available for larger groups.

KANSAS SAMPLER FESTIVAL: Held on the Penner Farm, three miles south and 1-3/4 miles east of Inman. The festival, held annually the first Saturday and Sunday in October, is a "sampler" of what there is to see and do in Kansas. Over 150 exhibitors display in tents set up amid trees and prairie on the Penner farm. Enjoy Kansas slide shows, stage acts, ethnic food, stump-speaking, surrey rides, and much more. Admission fee. Phone 316/585-2389 or 585-2374.

MEDICINE LODGE

1990 population 2,453; 1970 2,545. Geographically the famous Red Hills and the High Plains offer typical Kansas contrasts. Dramatic red sandstone, shale mesas, buttes set off by green grass, and invading cedars provide lovely vistas west of Medicine Lodge. Even the High Plains here belie the "Kansas is flat" misapprehension with unusual Cheyenne Sandstone formations near Belvidere. The line between the Red Hills and the High Plains is perhaps most explicit about ten miles east of Coldwater on U.S. 160.

Pickup trucks parked at cafes during the morning coffee hour usually tell a lot about a region. If there are flatbed four-wheelers, expect to see ranchers. Gritty-looking 4x4s with an assortment of cans and tools indicate oil-field swampers. Fancy 4x4s are usually driven by wheat and milo farmers. You'll see all three in this area. For area information call 316/886-3417.

MEDICINE LODGE PEACE TREATY PAGEANT: A treaty promising peace for the Indian tribes was signed near present-day Medicine Lodge in 1867. This treaty is

commemorated by the Medicine
Lodge Peace Treaty Pageant every
three years on the last weekend in
September. The next pageant is
scheduled for 1994. Call 316/886-9815
for details.

**SAGEBRUSH GALLERY OF
WESTERN ART:** 115 East Kansas,
Medicine Lodge. Earl Kuhn's watercolors of western landscape and livestock are extraordinary. Open daily
9 a.m. to 5 p.m. unless at an art show.
Call first, 316/886-5163.

STOCKADE MUSEUM: 209 West
Fowler (U.S. 160), Medicine Lodge.
The museum is enclosed by a replica
frontier stockade. Open daily 1 to
5 p.m. Phone 316/886-3417.

CARRIE NATION HOME: Just
west of Stockade Museum, Medicine
Lodge. See the place this tempestuous
temperance crusader called home.
Open Wednesday through Sunday
1 to 5 p.m. Phone 316/886-3553.

BETTY'S ANTIQUES: 315 North
Main, Medicine Lodge. A few teddy
bears (2,250 to be exact) and 420 Santa
Clauses share this home with Betty.
The bears are for viewing; antiques
are for sale. Hours are irregular. Call
316/886-5284 to make sure she'll be
there.

**HEREFORD HOUSE RESTAU-
RANT:** Junction of U.S. 160 and 281,
Medicine Lodge. Full menu and buf-
fets. Large enough to accommodate
groups. Open daily 6 a.m. to 8 p.m.,
Sunday 9 a.m. to 3 p.m. Closed
Monday. Phone 316/886-5634.

**LAKE CITY/SUN CITY RED
HILLS TOUR:** Take U.S. 160 west
out of Medicine Lodge. You'll soon
see striking red mesas and buttes.
After about 13 miles take the Lake
City turnoff going north. From Lake
City, go west to Sun City, then south

to U.S. 160, then finish the loop by
going back to the Lake City turnoff.
This is a rewarding trip for scenery
lovers, especially in the green months.
A low sun, morning or evening, will
enhance the red colors and offer shad-
ow contrasts. Some of the roads are
not passable when wet.

LAKE CITY: A charming Main
Street that simply died. A few residences still exist in this unincorporated town.

SUN CITY: 1990 population 88; 1970
119. A lively ghost town with quite a
bit of traffic passing through. Only
the post office and a few residences
show activity.

HATHAWAY'S: Downtown Sun
City. Locally known as Busters, this
bar and grill can take care of anyone's
hankering for a good hamburger.
Buster, owner of this place for 48
years, is a character you won't forget.
Open Monday through Saturday
9 a.m. to 6 p.m. Phone 316/248-3256.

BELVIDERE: Unincorporated. This
is the metropolitan center for the area
— two stores in town here. Stop at the
Medicine River General Store for
sandwiches, cowboy supplies, and a
bittersweet look at the past. Usually
open weekdays 10 a.m. to 6 p.m. Call
316/862-5689 for details. Also visit
the nearby Trails End Junk Shop for a
great collection of antiques. Usually
open daily 8 a.m. to 6 p.m. Phone
316/862-5603.

**KANSAS COWBOY CAMP-
OUTS:** Gyp Hills near Belvidere.
Whether you want to feel like a cowboy for the weekend or just enjoy the
unique atmosphere of the Gyp (Red)
Hills, this Kansas adventure might be
for you. You'll sleep in a cowboy
teepee, eat chuck-wagon meals, saddle up your horse and ride through
the hills and wildflowers, fish or

swim in the pond, and enjoy campfire entertainment. You can even learn how to rope steers! Get more information on this weekend adventure by calling Fay at 316/862-5689. Family rates available.

STAN HERD MURAL: Wilmore on the grain elevator. Wilmore 1990 population 78; 1970 96.

THE RANCH HOUSE CAFE: Downtown Wilmore. Eat good food with the local citizens. Open daily 6 a.m. to 2 p.m., Tuesday 6 a.m. to 8 p.m., closed Sunday. Phone 316/738-4386.

COLDWATER

1990 population 939; 1970 1,016.

STAN HERD MURAL: West Main, Coldwater. A mural near the museum juxtaposes pioneer farming and modern grain elevators.

COMANCHE COUNTY MUSEUM: West Main, Coldwater. Small county museum with county pioneer artifacts including several Model T Fords. Open June through August Tuesday and Thursday 2 to 4 p.m. or call Rachel Booth for an appointment, 316/582-2513.

CLARA'S SCHOOL HOUSE: South U.S. 183, Coldwater. Antiques and collectibles are displayed in this 1885 brick schoolhouse. Open Thursday, Friday, and Saturday 10 a.m. to 6 p.m. and Sunday 2 to 6 p.m.

COMANCHE RESTAURANT: South U.S. 183, Coldwater. Large enough to serve tour buses. Open daily breakfast to 8 p.m. Large groups should call in advance, 316/582-2767.

CAMP LARK: 2-1/2 miles south of Coldwater, one mile west, 3/4 mile north. A restaurant out in the country in the beautiful setting of an old

church campground. Open Monday, Wednesday, Thursday, Friday 5 to 10 p.m., Saturday 11 a.m. to 10 p.m., Sunday 7 a.m. to 10 p.m. Cabins are available. Phone 316/582-2276.

PROTECTION

1990 population 625; 1970 673.

STAN HERD MURAL: Pine and Broadway, Protection. This is Stan Herd's home town. Look up on a wall to see a scene typical of the 1930s on the High Plains — a farmer pulling a oneway with a McCormick-Deering tractor.

MARIA'S FILLING STATION: Pine and Broadway, Protection. A nice, clean little cafe for lunch and supper. Open Monday to Saturday 9 a. m. to 8 p.m., closed at 2 p.m. on Tuesday. Sunday chicken dinner carry-out only. Phone 316/622-4552.

KIOWA

1990 population 1,160; 1970 1,414. Almost at the Oklahoma border in southeast Barber County. Combines everywhere, wheat trucks, cattle trucks — this is farm country. No glitz and glamour in Kiowa; the attraction here is the reality of farm life. Have coffee at the Horseshoe Cafe and catch the flavor of the conversation. Carrie Nation came to Kiowa in 1900, destroying saloons right and left.

In the spring and again in the fall when combines and trucks are poised and ready for harvest, it's not too difficult to imagine horses, wagons, buggies, and even bicycles lined up a hundred years ago for the fabulous land rush into the Cherokee Strip.

KIOWA HISTORICAL SOCIETY MUSEUM: 107 North Seventh, Kiowa. Kiowa area exhibits, in this old red brick city hall, feature Carrie Nation and the Cherokee Strip Land Rush. Open daily 1 to 5 p.m. Closed Sunday. Free.

ANTHONY

1990 population 2,516; 1970 2,653.

HISTORICAL MUSEUM OF ANTHONY: West Main Street, Anthony. A very good portrayal of early Harper County life housed in a classic brick Santa Fe depot. Outside display of Case steam tractor, Woods Brothers thresher, and other farm implements. Open Thursday, Friday, and Saturday 9 a.m. to 5 p.m. Call 316/842-3852 for special appointments.

ANTHONY FLEA MARKET: Corner of Bluff and Main, Anthony. Open Friday noon to 7 p.m., Saturday and Sunday 9 a.m. to 5 p.m. Phone 316/842-3490.

STARVIEW DRIVE-IN THEATER: North of Anthony on K-14. These outdoor drive-ins are an endangered species. Shows dependent on weather and season. Phone 316/842-3207.

NELSON'S RESTAURANT: 725 West Main, Anthony. Any traveler will feel comfortable here. Groups and buses welcome. Open Monday through Saturday 6 a.m. to 8 p.m. Closed Sunday and holidays. Phone 316/842-5225.

HARPER

1990 population 1,735; 1970 1,665.

ROUND BARN: From north end of Central Street, Harper, go 3/4 mile east, then 1/2 mile west. This is private property; you may drive onto the yard to snap photos. Please, no smoking near old wooden structures. The

other and larger famous round barn near Harper is collapsing.

Round barn, Harper

RED BARN: Main Street, Harper. A venerable barn used for community activities. For an inside look and a lot of Harper area lore call Dollie Mathes, 316/896-2490.

RUNNEYMEAD CHURCH: Eleventh and Pine, Harper. Circa 1889. The church was originally built in the short-lived town of Runneymead, which was populated by wealthy English and Irish playboys. This church and one grave are the only tangible reminders of a social experiment that failed. For a tour call Edith McIntire, 316/896-2824, or Gail Bellar, 316/896-2304.

HARPER HISTORICAL MUSEUM: 804 East Twelfth, Harper. Small local-interest museum open summer months on Saturday and Sunday 1 to 5 p.m. For special tours call Edith McIntire, 316/896-2824, or Gail Bellar, 316/896-2304.

GIFTS, CRAFTS, ANTIQUES: Three small shops in Harper. Country Blessings, 1403 Central; Creative Crossings, 913 Central; and Uniques and Antiques, 914 Central. All are closed on Sunday.

FREEPORT: Northeast of Anthony on county road. Claims to be the smallest incorporated city in the United States, with eight voting-age citizens. Stop at the Garvey elevator for information.

ARGONIA

1990 population 529; 1970 591.

SALTER HOUSE: Osage and West, Argonia. This was the home of Susanna Madora Salter, the first woman mayor in the United States, elected in 1887. The house is furnished with pieces from that period. Next door the former Mayfield church houses artifacts from this area. Open Sunday afternoons in summer. Call Ruth Harper for details, 316/435-6733.

NEWTON

1990 population 16,700; 1970 15,439. Stop in at the Newton Convention and Visitors' Bureau and admire the American Renaissance architecture in this renovated building. Jacque or Tammy can help plan your Newton tour or inform you about area accommodations. Ask for the excellent self-guided Newton Historical Driving Tour brochure. Phone 316/283-7555.

THE HAWK HOUSE BED-AND-BREAKFAST: 307 West Broadway, Newton. Lon and Carol Buller welcome guests to their turn-of-the-century home. This three-story house features a massive oak stairway, oak floors, stained glass, and french doors. Call 316/283-2045 to make reservations.

OLD MILL RESTAURANT: 301 North Main, Newton. You'll find a more formal atmosphere in this beautifully restored flour mill. Open

Monday through Friday 11:30 a.m. to 2 p.m. and 5 to 9 p.m., Saturday 5 to 9 p.m., Sunday 11:30 a.m. to 2 p.m. Phone 316/283-3510.

THE BREAD BASKET: 219 North Main, Newton. This is the ideal place for soup, salad, and sandwich. Check out the blackboard menu and order at the counter. Get your own drinks in the back room. Soup specialties are green bean and ham, chicken borscht, cream of potato , and a thick chicken and noodle. Yum! Loaves of home-made bread for sale, too. Treat yourself to verenike and German buffet on Friday and Saturday. Open Tuesday through Thursday 6:30 a.m. to 2 p.m., Friday and Saturday 6:30 a.m. to 8 p.m. Breakfast buffet on Saturday. Phone 316/283-3811.

LEN AND FLO'S KITCHEN: 714 North Main, Newton. Walk up to the counter and place your order in this friendly ol' place full of local flavor. All sandwiches served on home-made buns. Verenike, borscht, and zwieback served Thursdays at noon. Open 7 a.m. to 3 p.m. Phone 316/283-3650.

D BARN: West of Meridian 1-3/4 miles on 24th, Newton. This 70-year-old hay barn was converted into a house 11 years ago. Now it's a restaurant. Take a drive into the country for a four-course meal of chicken on Thursday evening, barbecue on Friday, and steak on Saturday evening. Reservations only; call 316/283-6653.

VOTH POTTERY: 417 North Main, Newton. Once inside, you'll know you've stepped into an artist's world. Either you'll find Brian at work on his high-temperature stoneware and functional pottery or he'll be sipping his coffee and in the mood to visit with customers. Open Tuesday through Friday 10 a.m. to 6 p.m. and

Saturday 10 a.m. to 5 p.m. Phone 316/283-8078.

CARRIAGE FACTORY GALLERY: 128 East Sixth, Newton. This onetime carriage factory now houses original artwork by area artists. The watercolor, oil, and pastel paintings are available for viewing or sale along with Rollin Karg hand-blown glass. Open Tuesday through Saturday 11 a.m. to 4 p.m. and Sunday 1 to 4 p.m. Donations appreciated. Phone 316/284-2749.

NATIONAL SOCIETY OF TOLE AND DECORATIVE PAINTERS: 414 North Main at Newton Station, Newton. Go up two flights of stairs. Visitors are invited to explore the variety of decorative painting in the hallways and offices. Open Monday through Friday 8 a.m. to 5 p.m. Best to call for tour appointment. Phone 316/283-9665.

HIGH STREET COMPANY: 315 North High, Newton. Found on a side street east of Main, this lone red brick building with the porch awning and many storefront windows was once a flourishing neighborhood grocery. There are wooden floors, antique ceiling lights, bins of colored soap, hanging rugs, baskets, dried flowers, glass jars filled with swizzle sticks and French white lights. Many unique gift items. Open Monday through Friday 10 a.m. to 5:30 p.m., Saturday until 4 p.m. Phone 316/283-1080.

THE ROAD RUNNER ANTIQUE MALL: 415 North Main, Newton. A high stone wall on one side and a brick wall on the other serve as background for the furniture and vintage clothing featured in this long and narrow old building. Make sure you go up to the store loft. Open daily

10 a.m. to 6 p.m., Sunday 1 to 5 p.m. Phone 316/283-6001.

ANDERSON'S BOOKS, GIFTS, AND OFFICE SUPPLIES: 627 Main, Newton. Oh, if only this creaky wooden floor could talk. We'd hear plenty of stories about this 100-year-old family business. Open Monday through Saturday 9 a.m. to 5:30 p.m. Open till 8:30 p.m. on Thursday. Phone 316/283-3570.

GOOD EARTH GENERAL STORE: 1809 North Main, Newton. This white house by the big cedar tree is the place to buy bulk foods, spices, teas, and coffees as well as gift items. Open 10 a.m. to 6 p.m. Monday through Friday, Saturday until 5 p.m. Phone 316/283-8626.

KAUFFMAN MUSEUM: North Main and 27th, North Newton. Warning: Do not leave Newton without visiting this award-winning museum. The displays depicting Mennonite migration, life on the Kansas prairie, and Mennonite influence are superb. Quotes add significance to each exhibit. A prairie reconstruction project in front of the museum helps bring the story to life. Open Tuesday through Friday 9:30 a.m. to 4:30 p.m., Saturday and Sunday 1:30 to 4:30 p.m. Admission fee. Phone 316/283-1612.

MENNONITE SETTLER STATUE: Athletic Park, West First and Grandview, Newton. This 17-foot limestone statue of a Mennonite farmer is unusual because Mennonites have generally considered a stone marker a more appropriate way to pay tribute. This statue was dedicated in 1942.

WARKENTIN HOUSE: 211 East First, Newton. The original owner, Bernhard Warkentin, was largely responsible for Mennonite migration to Kansas, the Kansas milling industry, and the introduction of Turkey

Red Wheat. The leatherette wainscoting, ball-and-spindle fretwork, and dentil block design are just a few of the details to look for in this grand house built in 1887. Open April, May, and September through December, 1 to 4:30 p.m. Saturday and Sunday; June through August, 1 to 4:30 p.m. Tuesday through Sunday. Admission fee. Call Pat at 316/283-0812 or Gladys at 316/283-1699 for tour appointments. They'll be glad to open for your convenience.

THE NEAL HOUSE: 301 East Fourth, Newton. This Victorian Italianate home, built in 1875, is on the state and national historic registers. Private property.

THE S.A. BROWN HOUSE: 302 West Sixth, Newton. This house, built in 1878, is on the national historic register. Note the round turret, four types of shingles, and wraparound porch. Private property.

THE GRANARY: Bethel College Campus, North Newton. Take the drive past the tennis courts until you come to a yellow metal building. See wheat-weaving done here and ask the friendly folks to show you the bundles and bundles of wheat hanging from back room ceiling racks. Wheat-weaving products available for sale here. Open 9 a.m. to noon and 1 to 3 p.m. during school year. Irregular summer hours. Phone 316/283-3940.

BETHEL COLLEGE ADMINIS-TRATION BUILDING: Bethel College Campus, North Newton. Bethel was the first Mennonite College in the nation. Listed on the the national register.

CHISHOLM TRAIL MARKER: Bethel College Campus, North Newton. This informative marker is in front of the Fine Arts Center.

SAND CREEK TRAIL: This 2-1/2-mile one-way bike and walking path runs parallel to Sand Creek from Athletic Park at West First to Centennial Park.

MID-KANSAS RV PARK: Junction I-135 and K-15, North Newton. Electrical hookups, dump station. Open daily 7 a.m. to 8 p.m., Sunday 1 t o 7 p.m. Call 316/283-5530.

WALTON MUSEUM: Downtown Walton. 1990 population 226; 1970 211. This little white clapboard house was the first building in Walton and now displays early Walton photos and artifacts. Free. Phone 316/837-3252 or 837-3481.

PEABODY

1990 population 1,349; 1970 1,368. Peabody boasts many red brick side streets and beautifully restored 1880s buildings in the downtown district. A monument to the Mennonite migration is found in the city park on South Walnut. Call Julie at 316/983-2175.

MAYESVILLE MERCANTILE: 111 Walnut, Peabody. The recessed entrance with iron pillars, prism glass above the door, and a fancy screen door will entice you to enter this newly registered national historic site. This old grocery store is chock full of antiques, wooden barrels, crocks, bird cages, kerosene lamps, and more. Antique kitchen wares and tools hang from the ceiling and walls; the old cooler room is full of vintage hats and clothing; the produce cooler now holds jewelry; and the old-fashioned meat counter stores frozen lamb and cheese curds! In the summer herbs and plants abound. Open Monday through Saturday 10 a.m. to 5 p.m. and Sunday 2 to 5 p.m. Phone 316/983-2210.

PHOENIX DRY GOODS:
103 North Walnut, Peabody. Appropriately named after the mythical bird that rose from its ashes, this 1884 building was renovated after a 1990 fire and now radiates turn-of-the-century charm. Western wear, blue jeans, and dress clothes look more inviting above the shiny wooden original floors and under old-fashioned hanging ceiling lights. Open 10 a.m. to 5 p.m. Monday through Saturday, open till 7 p.m. on Thursday; Sunday 1 to 5 p.m. Phone 316/983-2340.

TUMBLEWEED ANTIQUES:
101 North Walnut, Peabody. Once you lay your eyes on this handsome 1884 corner building you'll be itching to see the inside. Marilyn Payne specializes in vintage quilts (1880s to 1930s) and mid-1800s handcrafted furniture. Fine antiques. Her summer hours are Tuesday through Sunday 11 a.m. to 5 p.m. Winter hours are Tuesday, Thursday, Friday 11 a.m. to 4 p.m. Call 316/983-2765 for appointment. Shop phone is 316/983-2200.

PEABODY DRIVING AND WALKING TOUR:
Pick brochure up at city office or most downtown businesses. More than 50 downtown businesses, historic homes, and points of interest are described in this informative brochure. Take special note of the Heath/Berns home at 404 North Walnut (private property) and the facade of the 1922 Sunflower Theater on Main Street. Write Julie Irish, City Hall, Peabody, Kansas 66866 or call 316/983-2174 to obtain a brochure prior to visit.

KORNER KITCHEN:
Corner of Walnut and Second, Peabody. This striking 1886 limestone building with stone arches and angled front entrance was originally the Kansas State Bank. Basic fare served here. Open Monday through Saturday 6 a.m. to 1:30 p.m. Phone 316/983-2307.

WORLD WAR II POW CAMP:
Vine and Second, Peabody. Built as the Eyestone Garage in 1919, it housed the Motor Inn Hotel on the second floor. In World War II this red brick building served as a prisoner-of-war camp.

JONES SHEEP FARM BED-AND-BREAKFAST:
Drive south out of town on Maple Street, unpaved road. This 1930s farm home is plain and simple. No phone or TV here but privacy, screened-in porch, nearby sheep pasture, and unpaved roads for walking make this a peaceful getaway. Marilyn delivers her famous breakfasts in a basket and lets you eat at your own pace. Call 316/983-2815 or write RR 2, Peabody, Kansas 66866 for a brochure.

PEABODY HISTORICAL MUSEUM:
106 East Division, Peabody. This building was the first free public library in Kansas. The three homey rooms are filled with town and county history. The Poe Doll collection is a feature. Take a look at the photo showing downtown in 1879 . Open Memorial Day through Labor Day Thursday through Sunday 1 to 4 p.m. Phone Gwen Gaines 316/983-2391.

THE MORGAN HOUSE:
212 North Walnut, Peabody. This two-story Queen Anne cottage was built in 1881 and is currently being restored.

MARION

1990 population 1,906; 1970 2,052. Named after Revolutionary War General Francis Marion and founded in 1860. Limestone buildings date back to 1877 and create a rustic look in this town at the base of the Flint Hills. For area accommo-

*dations and information call Peggy at
316/382-3703.*

COPPER SHED: Five miles south of
Main from Third Street, then 1-1/2
miles west of Marion. Ern Hett has a
barn full of copper prairie art and
sculptures that integrate such things
as barbed wire, saw blades, sickle
guards, and horseshoes. Fascinating!
Daughter Julie displays her crafts
here, too. Open Monday through
Friday 10 a.m. to 5 p.m. A call to
316/382-2041 is appreciated first.
Weekend hours can be arranged.

WILLIE'S WOOLIES: Two miles
east of Marion on K-256, four miles
south, and 1/8 mile west. Earlene and
Willard work on these quality crafts
year round. The stuffed animals made
from sheep pelts, wool, or wool fabric
are displayed throughout the living
room and will no doubt win your
heart. Phone 316/382-2054 for an
appointment.

SPRING BRANCH POTTERY:
Two miles west of Third and Main,
Marion. If the low-water bridge is tra-
versable then it's a clear shot to Paula
Barta's kiln and potter's wheel. See
pottery at all stages. Buy if you wish.
Paula is usually there, call to be sure.
Phone 316/382-2827.

FLINT HILLS CLAY WORKS:
126 West Main, Marion. Shelves and
shelves with wheel-thrown stoneware
pottery made on the premises. Opportunity to see potters at work. Get
Marion and Kansas pottery souvenirs
here. Open Monday through Friday
9 a.m. to 5 p.m., Saturday 9 to 3 p.m.
Phone 316/382-3620.

FLINT HILLS GOLD: 210 East
Main, Marion. Look at hundreds of
wax ring patterns and design your
own ring. Many earrings and rings
for sale made at the store. Open 9 a.m.

to 5 p.m. Monday through Thursday
and Saturday 9 a.m. to noon. Phone
316/382-2544.

WALKING TRAIL: Central Park on
East Main, Marion. Take a 15-minute
walk along Luta Creek under Chinese
elm and cottonwood trees. Gas lights
show the way after dusk. Children
will enjoy the old-time merry-go-
round and other play equipment in
the park. Bring your horseshoes!

KINGFISHER'S INN: East of
Marion on K-256, then follow signs to
county lake. The pan-fried chicken,
charbroiled steaks, and Italian food
taste extra delicious in this peaceful
setting overlooking the lake. Open
Wednesday through Saturday 11 a.m.
to 2 p.m. and 5 to 9 p.m., Sunday
11 a.m. to 9 p.m. Phone 316/382-3755.

MARION COUNTY LAKE: Two
miles east of Marion on K-256 and
two miles south on Airport Road.
Northern pike, largemouth bass, wall-
eye, and bluegill are among the kinds
of fish stocked in this spring-fed lake.
Fish inside or outside at the heated
fishing dock. Over 40 electric and
water hookups for camping. Call lake
office at 316/382-3240.

MARION RESERVOIR: Five miles
west of Marion. Five parks at the reservoir contain 167 camping sites. Hiking,
swimming, windsurfing, and boating,
too. Family atmosphere promoted.
Phone 316/283-2101 for information.

JUDGE RIGGS GRAVESTONE:
Marion cemetery, northeast corner of
town. Judge Reuben Riggs (1810-
1873), the first judge in Sedgwick
County, died in a blizzard on the way
to a buffalo hunt. A limestone tree
stump with lace, lilies, a scroll, and a
message mark his resting spot.

ELGIN HOUSE APARTMENTS:
Third and Santa Fe, Marion. Hopi

flora crab and holly trees welcome you to this limestone building listed on the national register. Imagine elegant ladies and their dapper escorts arriving on the red brick streets for the governor's balls given here by Governor Hoch (1904-1908).

MARION HISTORICAL MUSUEM: East Main, Marion. The stained-glass window, shiny wooden ceiling, and bapistry of this old Baptist Church are the backdrop for this collection of Marion artifacts. Open in the summer Tuesday through Satur-day 10 a.m. to noon and 1 to 5 p.m. Donations appreciated. Phone 316/382-2287 or 382-3432.

MARION CAFE: 214 East Main, Marion. Open Tuesday through Thursday 6 a.m. to 4 p.m., Friday 6 a.m. to 8 p.m. for Mexican food night, Saturday 6 a.m. to 2 p.m. and 5 to 8 p.m., Sunday 11 a.m. to 2 p.m. Phone 316/382-8997.

STONE CITY CAFE: 211 East Main, Marion. Open Monday through Saturday 6 a.m. to 2 p.m. and Monday through Thursday night 5 to 8 p.m. Phone 316/382-2656.

COUNTRY DREAMS BED-AND-BREAKFAST: From the seven-mile marker on K-150 (Marion to Elmdale road) go three miles north on rock road. Experience the Flint Hills — longhorn cattle, lovely lake, peace and quiet miles from a highway — in a modern ranch home. Five rooms with private baths. Call Kent and Alice for reservations, 316/382-2250.

HILLSBORO

1990 population 2,704; 1970 2,730. For area information or accommodations call Pam at 316/947-3506.

OLDE TOWNE RESTAURANT: 126 North Main, Hillsboro. Atmos-

phere just oozes out of the thick stone walls, pressed tin ceiling, primitives hanging on the wall, and wood floors sculpted by a century of footsteps. If you look close you'll find a sliding barn door and egg crate ceilings in various rooms. The house specials are verenike and sausage, bierocks, and German sausage sandwiches. Other entrees include whitefish, chicken, and steak. Enjoy a Sunday buffet in the rustic red brick basement. Open Monday through Wednesday 10 a.m. to 2 p.m., Thursday through Saturday 10 a.m. to 9 p.m., and Sunday 11:30 a.m. to 2 p.m. The soda fountain is open Monday through Saturday 3 to 10 p.m. Phone 316/947-5446.

REIMER ANTIQUE CAR MUSEUM: 201 South Main, Hillsboro. Albert Reimer collects old cars and his son Melvin helps restore them. Oohs and ahs and reminiscing are allowed as you check out the light green 1951 Lincoln Cosmopolitan convertible with big whitewall tires, the rare 1941 Lincoln business coupe, a 1912 Depot Hack, and a 1928 Lin-coln Phaeton with dual windshields. Call the chamber at 316/947-3506 or go next door to 205 Main and Pete Klassen will give you a tour. No admission fee.

PIONEER ADOBE HOUSE MUSEUM: 501 South Ash, Hillsboro. Enter through the white picket fence. The thick walls of this house were built from dirt and grass or straw in 1876. What will you see inside? Oh, the *klena shtov,* the *feashtov,* the *keack,* and if you go down the *gaank* you'll exit the house and enter the attached barn. You'll find out about Mennonite history and the European migration. The barn is full of pioneer farm tools and equipment. Open Tuesday through Saturday 9 a.m. to noon and 1:30 to 4:30 p.m., Sundays and holidays 1:30 to

4:30 p.m.; or call for appointment 316/947-3775 or 316/947-3506. Small admission fee.

FRIESEN DUTCH WINDMILL: Beside Pioneer Adobe House Museum, Hillsboro. This is an exact-size replica of a structure built by Jacob Friesen in 1876 in Gnadenau Village. Dovetails and pins and square nails are being used in construction. Note the millstones inside.

MEMORIAL PARK: Beside Pioneer Adobe House Museum, Hillsboro. Swimming pool, playground equipment, and miniature Statue of Liberty are found here. Camper hookups. Phone 316/947-3162.

SCHAEFFLER HOUSE: 312 East Grand, Hillsboro. In 1887, a German Lutheran immigrant family founded the Schaeffler Mercantile Company and in 1909 built this house accented with a cupola. Phone 316/947-3775 or 316/947-3506 for tour.

A NOSTALGIC BED-AND-BREAKFAST PLACE: 310 South Main, Hillsboro. This house, built in 1915, has slanted ceilings upstairs, so watch your head! Shared bath for the two guest rooms. Make sure you spend some time on the porch swing. Breakfast in the little porch area in summer. Phone Don or Mildred at 316/947-3519 for reservations.

DURHAM

1990 population 119; 1970 143.

O'DELL FARM AND WILD-FLOWER TOURS: 2-1/2 miles west of Durham, one mile north and 1/4 miles east. During wildflower season, usually May or June, Della and Owen invite groups to their farm for tours of the prairie wildflowers. They also have made their pigeon barn and

100-year-old barn into museums of sorts. Meals are served out of the wash house. A campfire adds the finishing touch. Groups only. Admission fee. Phone 316/732-3255.

BLACKSMITH SHOP: Downtown Durham. Tom Donahue's desire was to preserve this part of Durham's history, and he has gone to great lengths to restore the blacksmith shop. The lineshaft, forge, and tools will be authentic, and his hope is for it to be an operational blacksmithy someday. The renovation is still in progress. Call Tom at 316/732-2665 (day) or 316/732-3511 (night) to check on the progress and availability of group tours.

GOESSEL

1990 population 506; 1970 386.

SOD HOUSE STAINED GLASS WORKS: Turn east at K-15 and Goessel. Del Paulsen has prepared this 116-year-old sod house, the outbuildings, and the grounds for group tours. Only an artist could transform a rickety old farmstead into this kind of picture. His stained-glass studio is in the barn. Learn about the history, learn about the artist. Minimum group size is 10. Phone 316/367-8485.

BASE'S EXOTIC ANIMALS: From Goessel's Main Street, go 3/4 mile south on State, or from K-15 follow signs west to Coon Creek Buffalo. Not only is this a charming two home farmstead, it's a delightful sanctuary for exotic animals! Mountain lions, African lynxes, wallabies, pygmy goats, emus, potbellied pigs, foxes, monkeys, cockatoos and more look very comfortable here with buffalo in a nearby pasture. The llama wanders around on a leash and is very affectionate. Spring is an especially memo-

Llama from Base's exotic animal farm, Goessel

rable time on the Base farm with many baby animals being born. The old filling station recently brought to the farm houses Angela Base's dried flowers and beadwork! You're welcome to share the excitement of this menagerie, but call 316/367-8299 first.

BEAR PAW TRADERS: Rural Goessel. Keven Hiebert brings the pre-1840 period to life with his reproductions of mountain man weapons, tools, handmade knives, tomahawks, saddles, beadwork, teepees, and cooking utensils. His shop, a metal building, is fascinating inside. See his collection of fur traders' traps and firearms and his taxidermy and tanning work. Keven also farms, so make an appointment to take this step back in time. Phone 316/367-2639 or 367-8445.

MENNONITE HERITAGE MUSEUM COMPLEX: 200 North Poplar, Goessel. This museum complex tells the story of Mennonite migration to Kansas, emphasizing agriculture and daily life. Open May through September Tuesday through Friday 10 a.m. to 5 p.m. and weekends 1 to 5 p.m. Other months open daily 1 to 4 p.m. Closed in January. Admission fee. Phone 316/367-8200.

ALEXANDERWOHL MENNONITE CHURCH: Just north of Goessel on K-15. Step inside to admire the three-sided balcony and other features. The historical marker just south of the church tells the story of the Mennonites in Kansas. Phone 316/367-8192.

BARNSTORMERS RESTAURANT: K-15 and Main, Goessel. Enjoy chicken, steaks, pork chops, homemade pies and more in a barn-like setting. German buffet on Saturday night. Open Tuesday through Saturday 11 a.m. to 8 p.m., Sunday 11 a.m. to 2 p.m. Phone 316/367-2566.

TATTERED ROSE ANTIQUES: Across from Barnstormers. This antique shop is open by appointment. Phone 316/367-8257.

HISTORICAL MARKER: 5-1/2 miles west of Goessel on K-15 is a marker that tells about the Chisholm Trail, the Cherokee Trail, and the Black Beaver Trail.

MOUNDRIDGE

1990 population 1,531; 1970 1,271.

COUNTRY KITCHEN: 114 South Christian, Moundridge. German buffet every Saturday evening 5 to 9 p.m. Open daily 6 a.m. to 9 p.m., Sunday 8 a.m. to 2 p.m. Phone 316/345-6459.

HISTORICAL MARKER: Four miles west and 1/4 mile north of Moundridge. This historical marker is a memorial to the Swiss Mennonite congregation that migrated to America in 1874.

HOPEFIELD MENNONITE CHURCH: Four miles west, 1/2 mile north, and 1/2 mile east of Moundridge. This church was built in 1882. A nearby memorial tells the story of the Swiss-German Mennonite migration from Volhynia, Russia, to the United States in 1874. An immigrant house once stood at this site.

HESSTON

1990 population 3,012; 1970 1,926.

DYCK ARBORETUM OF THE PLAINS: West Hickory (south side of town, west of Hickory Homes), Hesston. Kansas wildflowers — woodland and prairie — an island garden, a bird-watching area, and a pinetum are features in this wonderful place dedicated to "fostering an appreciation of the natural beauty of Kansas." Open daily dawn to dusk. For guided group tours call Jim Locklear at 316/327-8127.

MIXING BOWL: 108 West Randall, Hesston. It smells like Mom's kitchen on baking day in here. Choose from cinnamon rolls, caramel pecan rolls, honey wheat bread, and other goods baked daily (except Monday). Open Monday 7 a.m. to 3 p.m., Tuesday through Friday 4 a.m. to 5:30 p.m., and Saturday 4 a.m. to 2 p.m. Phone 316/327-2377.

COTTONWOOD GROVE CAMP-GROUND: Just east of Hesston exit on I-135. This grassy and shady area offers water and electric hookups, dump station, showers, and laundry service. Phone 316/327-4173.

HESSTON GOLF COURSE: This is an excellent 18-hole golf course. Green fee required. Phone 316/327-2331.

HALSTEAD

1990 population 2,015; 1970 1,716.

NEE MURRAY WAY BED-AND-BREAKFAST: 220 West Third, Halstead. This Victorian home offers a variety of possibilities. One room on the second floor has a fireplace, and

those celebrating special occasions will enjoy having a private meal served on a sitting porch that adjoins their second-floor room. Kids will have fun in the third-floor dormer! Kathy and Dru also serve evening meals by reservation. Phone 316/835-2027.

HERITAGE INN BED-AND-BREAKFAST: 300 Main, Halstead. Each quaint room has a private bath, cable TV, and small refrigerator and is furnished with antiques. This three-story brown brick hotel with the green canopy entrance has served people since 1922. Breakfast served in the hotel cafe. Phone 316/835-2118.

HERITAGE INN RESTAURANT: 300 Main, Halstead. Steaks, teriyaki chicken, and a variety of fish dishes served Thursday through Saturday 6 to 9 p.m. Open for breakfast and lunch Tuesday through Saturday 7 a.m. to 1:30 p.m. Phone 316/835-2118.

FRONTIER MEATS: 135 Main, Halstead. This attractive red brick building with limestone arches is where you can pick up a jar of canned buffalo, buffalo jerky, or buffalo sticks for the road. In the summer on Mondays look for the covered wagon out front serving buffalo burgers and other specials. Open Monday through Friday 9 a.m. to 5:30 p.m., Saturday 9 a.m. to 1 p.m. Phone 316/835-2155.

HALSTEAD HARDWARE: 208 Main, Halstead. Enter the store with the green iron columns. A screen door takes you to adjoining rooms full of antiques and hardware items. Open Monday through Saturday 9 a.m. to 6 p.m. Phone 316/835-2356.

KANSAS LEARNING CENTER FOR HEALTH: 505 Main, Halstead. Make sure you make the acquaintance of Valeda, the transparent talking woman, and Charlie Bones, the

skeleton. An excellent series of exhibits explain the birth process and interactive displays make it easier to understand the functioning of our ears, eyes, teeth, nose, heart, lungs, and more. Admission fee. Open Monday through Friday 8:30 a.m. to 4:30 p.m. and Sunday 1 to 5 p.m. Phone 316/835-2662.

SUSPENSION BRIDGE: In the city park, just beyond the city limit on the northeast side of Halstead. A stroll across the walking bridge suspended above the Little Arkansas River is fun for all ages.

CITY CEMETERY: North of Halstead on K-89. The founder of Halstead's Hertzler Clinic, Dr. Arthur Hertzler, built a reputation as a research surgeon and author. At the cemetery you'll see a tribute to the Horse and Buggy Doctor and a short poem inscribed on Agnes Hertzler's gravestone that is worth stopping to see.

WARKENTIN HOUSE AND BARN: 140 East North, Halstead. This homestead belonged to Bernhard Warkentin. A barn and carriage house are included on the property. Drive by or phone 316/835-3373 for tour.

THE FANTASTIC WORLD OF GOURMET CHOCOLATE: One mile west of Halstead on Southwest 36 (Sixth Street in Halstead). Yum, yum, yum... Tour a chocolate factory: view a slide presentation, watch chocolate being made, and enjoy delicious samples. Nominal admission. Please call for an appointment, 316/835-3730.

HARVEY COUNTY WEST PARK: West of Halstead 1-1/2 miles, then six miles north. To begin hiking the 2-1/2 mile nature trail, cross the swinging bridge over the creek. Cottonwoods, sand hills, a natural lake, and lots of grassy area make this an exceptional park for picnicking, fishing, camping, swimming, and fun. Boat rental available at West Park Bait Shop.

S E D G W I C K

1990 population 1,438; 1970 1,083.

THE INN AT SEDGWICK: One mile east and 1-3/4 miles north of Sedgwick. Enjoy cocktails and candlelight five course dinners by the fireside or in the secret garden. Hostess Lou Cox's specialty is beef tenderloin with Madeira wine sauce, but you can choose from four entrees. Gentlemen are required to wear ties. Dinners average $25. Call for reservations one month in advance. Phone 316/772-5418.

THE COTTAGE: Adjoining the Inn at Sedgwick. A charming get-away place to spend the night. At dawn the sun reaches across the wheat fields through lovely french doors to greet you. Private bath, no phone, self-serve breakfast. Phone 316/772-5418.

CHAIN-SAW ART: 404 East Fourth, Sedgwick. Drive by to see wooden bears climbing trees and other intriguing wooden figures carved with a chain saw by Jerry Mosiman. See more chain saw art a half block south of Fourth and Jackson.

LEON'S MARKET: 435 Commercial, Sedgwick. It's kind of fun to walk around in this old grocery store with wooden floors. Open Monday through Saturday 8 a.m. to 6 p.m.

K E C H I

1990 population 517; 1970 229.

ANTIQUES: Throughout Kechi. The business district in this town of just over 500 consists mostly of antique shops, 17 of them to be exact! You can't go wrong here if you're looking for a day full of antiquing in one town. Most shops are open Wednesday through Saturday 11 a.m. to 5 p.m. and Sunday 1 to 5 p.m. Phone 316/744-9287 or 744-1337 for more information.

FREEMAN FINE ARTS: 128 East Kechi, Kechi. Usually open on weekends. Phone 316/744-3200.

KARG ART GLASS: 4535 East 61st North, Kechi. You're invited to watch the glassblowers color and then mold hot, pliable glass into sculptures, vases, perfume bottles and other decorative pieces until 3 p.m. on Monday, Tuesday, Thursday, and Friday. The lobby is full of beautiful decorative pieces, vases, paperweights, perfume bottles, and more. Open Monday through Saturday 10 a.m. to 4:30 p.m. and Sunday 1 to 4:30 p.m. Phone 316/744-2442.

KECHI PLAYHOUSE: Corner of North Oliver and Kechi, Kechi. Performances in this old church take place Thursday through Saturday at 8 p.m. and Sunday at 2:30 p.m. June through November. $6.50 admission. Phone 316/744-2152 for reservations.

THE COUNTRY KITCHEN CAFE: Woodlawn and K-254, Kechi. Basic setting, friendly service, and excellent homemade food. Lebanese food served on Thursday from 11 a.m. to 8 p.m. Open Monday through Friday 9 a.m. to 8 p.m., Saturday 7 a.m. to 8 p.m. Phone 316/744-9252.

PRATT

1990 population 6,687; 1970 6,736. Pratt, home of the Miss Kansas Pageant, has a wide, red brick main street lined with a thriving business district. Pratt was vic-

torious after county-seat wars with nearby Saratoga and Iuka nearly a century ago. Just under 200 people live in Iuka, north of Pratt. The tree that stood by the school is the only remnant of Saratoga. It can be seen in a field east of the Wildlife Museum and Aquarium. For additional information on accommodations and area attractions call Jeanette at 316/672-5501 .

KANSAS WILDLIFE AND PARKS WILDLIFE MUSEUM AND AQUARIUM: Two miles east, one mile south of Pratt. Tall cottonwoods surround this 100-year-old, two-story red brick building. The green-tiled hexagonal aquarium holds 12 tanks of Kansas fish and turtles. Watch them being fed around 2 p.m. daily. See diaramas of Kansas animals and displays of birds, bird eggs, butterflies, and grasses. Use ink stamps to make tracks of nine different Kansas animals. Open seven days a week year-round 8 a.m. to 5 p.m. Free. Phone 316/672-5911.

LEMON PARK: South end of Pine, Pratt. Cottonwood, cypress, pine, sycamore, and more contribute to the beauty of this large wooded park. Marshy area with cattails, ball park, walking path, lamp posts, benches, playground equipment, and picnic area makes this a wonderful place to stop and relax. Note the sculptures cut out of tree stumps!

THE BARRON THEATER: Downtown Pratt. The art deco ceilings and lights in this 1930s theater are original. The neon marquee out front draws attention to the beautiful building. Four movies a night, seven days a week. Phone 316/672-3031.

R.R. CREATIONS: 209 South Main, Pratt. Detailed wooden replicas of special buildings are made by R.R. Creations. The "Open Window" collection is special because each building has one window open. Once you see these wooden blocks you'll leave wanting the depot or old schoolhouse in your town to be the next "Open Window" creation. Phone 316/672-3610.

SIGNS BY DESIGN: 621 South Main, Pratt. Glue chipping is an old art form and Terry Ricketts does it beautifully. Stop in here to see his beautiful custom glass designs and gold inlay work. Phone 316/672-3486. Open 10 a.m. to 5 p.m. Monday through Friday.

PRATT COUNTY HISTORICAL MUSEUM: 212 South Ninnescah, Pratt. Nineteen different stores make up an early 1900s Main Street display in this converted lumberyard. See what a dentist's office, general store, and art studio looked like then. Period rooms also show interesting sights like the washing machine on the back porch, the cookstove in the kitchen, and more. Open Tuesday through Sunday 2 to 4 p.m. Donations appreciated. Phone 316/672-7874.

HOUSE AT FIFTH AND OAK: 520 South Oak, Pratt. This 1901 Queen Anne home has been recently renovated and now sports 14 different colors of paint. The widow's walk and ornate trim give a passerby plenty to gawk at. Private residence.

MAYHEW'S RESTAURANT AND EVERGREEN MOTEL AND RV SITES: West side of Pratt on U.S. 54. Maples and pines provide satisfying setting here. Motel rooms all look out to courtyard. Old-fashioned five-headed lamp posts add charm. Phone 316/672-6431.

HOT AND COLD WATER TOWERS: North Main, Pratt. This unique water system is an engineering marvel.

HAVILAND: U.S. 54. 1990 population 624; 1970 705. This small town is home to Barclay College, formerly called Friends Bible College. Located north end of Main Street. Phone 316/862-5252.

GREENSBURG

1990 population 1,792; 1970 1,907.

THE BIG WELL: 315 South Sycamore, Greensburg. By the time you descend four flights of stairs you will have a much greater appreciation for the work it took to hand-dig this 109-foot-deep well. The wooden platform at the cool, damp bottom is a place to look up and marvel at this structure built stone by stone in a perfectly formed 32-foot diameter. Built in 1888 to supply water for the town, the well is open daily from 9 a.m. to 6 p.m. Enjoy the gift shop and ask questions here about other places to visit in Greensburg. Admission fee. Phone 316/723-2261.

FRAN'S ANTIQUES: 222 South Sycamore, Greensburg. Old church full of antiques. If closed go next door to 308 South Sycamore and find Fran. Phone 316/723-2466 or 316/723-3020.

THE LOFT: Grove and U.S. 54, Greensburg. You'll find antiques and handcrafted items in this turn-of-the-century church. Open Tuesday, Wednesday, and Saturday 9:30 a.m. to 5 p.m., Sunday 1 to 5 p.m. Phone 316/723-3387.

PEDLAR'S DINING ESTABLISHMENT AND GIFT SHOP: 220 South Main, Greensburg. Fun place to eat with plants and balloons all around. Lunch buffet is always available. Go upstairs in this 1910 hotel and check out the country wreaths and Christmas crafts that are available for sale in the numerous old bedrooms. Open Monday through Friday 9 a.m. to 8 p.m. and Sunday 11 a.m. to 2 p.m. Phone 316/723-3403.

HUNTER DRUG: 121 South Main, Greensburg. People like to come in here on hot days, sit on the red swivel stools at the old-fashioned soda fountain and let the cherry limeades, 400s, and ceiling fans cool them off. Open Monday through Friday 8 a.m. to 6 p.m. and Saturday 8 a.m. to 3 p.m. Phone 316/723-2331.

TWILIGHT THEATER: Downtown Greensburg. Take in a modern movie in an old-time theater on Friday, Saturday, or Sunday evening. Phone 316/723-2445 for information.

FIRST STATE BANK: Main and Florida Streets, Greensburg. Stop a minute and appreciate the outside appearance of this red brick building listed on the State Register of Historic Places.

LAMKIN MUSEUM: 419 West Morton, Greensburg. In 1959, Walt Lamkin, now 76, started this personal collection of horseshoes, bells, bitters bottles, barbed wire, animal traps, trivets, irons, insulators, lemon squeezers, bridles, bits, and pocket knives. He has a Kansas license plate for every year except 1913. Bibles in 34 different languages and 70 cameras. Walt and his wife Sally welcome serious museum-goers. Donations appreciated. Phone 316/723-2409.

KIOWA COUNTY STATE LAKE: Take a left at end of North Bay, Greensburg. Wooden piers out into this man-made lake add pleasure for fishing, sunning, or just listening to the waves. Blue herons can be seen here.

MULLINVILLE ROUND BARN: 3-1/2 miles south and 1-1/2 miles west of Mullinville. The local historical society has recently purchased this rare round barn. It may be moved eventually to U.S. 54 near Mullinville. 1990 population 289; 1970 376.

CUNNINGHAM JAIL: Located behind depot museum on U.S. 54, Cunningham. Spending time in this jail should have cured any wrongdoer. 1990 population 535; 1970 483.

KINGMAN

1990 population 3,196; 1970 3,622.

EAGLE THEATER: Downtown Kingman. Look for the orange, baby blue, and white marquee on this brown brick building with mansard roof. Movies shown every Friday, Saturday, and Sunday evening at 7:30 p.m. Go early enough to see and appreciate the neon lights, original seats, and interesting lines and patterns of the wall and ceiling paintings. Phone 316/532-5232.

RIVERSIDE PARK: South edge of Kingman on K-14. Big cottonwoods provide the backdrop for this park on the South Ninnescah River. Playground equipment and swimming pool.

FORBIDDEN FRUIT CAFE: Located in block just south of museum on Main Street, Kingman. Early Kingman County photos and soothing colors makes eating here a pleasure. Open Monday through Saturday 11 a.m. to 2 p.m. and 5 to 9 p.m. and Sunday 8 a.m. to 1 p.m. Closed on Wednesday. Phone 1-800/498-5654.

KEN'S DELI DALI: South Main, Kingman. A favorite local spot for breakfast and lunch. Phone 316/532-5739.

KINGMAN COUNTY MUSEUM: 400 North Main, Kingman. Built as a city office and fire station in 1888, this national historic site is the only Kansas building with a cotton-hose-drying tower still intact. The tower rises 80 feet above this brick and limestone building. Many county exhibits can also be seen here. Open every Friday 9 a.m. to 4 p.m. or call 316/532-2627 or 532-5274 for an appointment.

KINGMAN POST OFFICE: North Main, Kingman. Step inside this national historic site and take a look at the WPA mural of the county Cattleman's Picnic.

KINGMAN STATE FISHING LAKE: Seven miles west of Kingman on U.S. 54. Towering cottonwoods escort you down a sandy lane to the lake. This is a great place for a picnic under the huge trees or on one of the floating piers. Good fishing and primitive camping here.

HISTORICAL MARKER: Continue several miles west of Kingman State Lake on U.S. 54. A small buffalo herd helps you appreciate the story of the plains buffalo.

WILDLIFE AREA: About 16 miles west of Kingman on U.S. 54 turn south into a designated wildlife area. Follow adventure on this sandy trail to its end at the South Fork Ninnescah River.

COUNTRY CELLAR: One-fourth mile north of U.S. 54 and K-17, Waterloo (six miles east of Kingman). What a lovely farm — charming flower beds, lofty trees, and bobwhite calling. In the house Charles and Donna Hardesty display ceramics and crafts they make — dolls, bunnies, and ever so many Santas. Open by appointment only. Phone 316/297-3055. Waterloo is unincorporated.

SOUDERS HISTORICAL FARM AND MUSEUM: One-half mile west of Cheney Road and MacArthur Road, Cheney. Floyd and Norma Souders have collected rural memo-

ries going back to their youth eighty years ago and set them into restored and recreated buildings surrounded by prairie grasses and trees. Open by appointment only. Donations appreciated. Phone 316/542-3573 or 542-3296. Cheney 1990 population 1,560; 1970 1,160.

LAKE AFTON OBSERVATORY: West on U.S. 54 three miles past Goddard, then three miles south and one mile east. One large telescope and several smaller ones are available to the public and two staff members are on duty to tell you what to look for. Open summer Friday through Sunday 9 to 11 p.m., rest of year Friday and Saturday 8 to 10 p.m. Small admission fee. Phone 316/689-3191 or 794-8995 to check hours. No reservations required.

K-42 DRIVE: Take this drive located southwest of Wichita. You'll start in Norwich (population 455) then continue through Adams (unincorporated), Rago (unincorporated), Spivey (population 88), Zenda (population 96), Nashville (population 118), Isabel (population 104), and Sawyer (population 183). Take a slow drive down each of these main streets. This trip will make you stop and think.

WELLINGTON

1990 population 8,411; 1970 8,072. For additional information about Wellington area accommodations and attractions call Vivian at 316/326-7466.

CHISHOLM TRAIL MUSEUM: 502 North Washington, Wellington. Three floors and 42 rooms filled with Sumner County artifacts. Open Saturday and Sunday 1 to 4 p.m. Phone 316/326-3820.

OXFORD

1990 population 1,143; 1970 1,113.

OXFORD'S OLD MILL RESTAURANT: Six blocks north on Sumner Street, three blocks east on Cottonwood, and 1/2 mile north on Old Mill Road, Oxford. If you park in the upper parking lot you'll enjoy a tremendous view of the old mill, which is listed on the national historic register, as you descend the stairs. Once inside the dining area you'll be charmed by the wooden beams, the cedar fragrance, and the stone walls. The food is prepared and served in an elegant way as a contrast to the rustic setting. Take time to walk the nature trail and explore the generator room and mill race. Open Thursday through Saturday 11 a.m. to 2 p.m. and 5 to 9 p.m. and Sunday 11 a.m. to 3 p.m. Phone 316/455-3456 for reservations.

STUMPWATER: 218 West Main, Oxford. The atmosphere is basic, but this is a great place for Cajun seafood, snow crab, oysters on the half shell, crawfish, alligator (!), charbroiled buffalo, charbroiled steaks, prime rib, and more! Open Monday through Saturday 10 a. m. to 2 p.m. and 5 to 8 p.m., Friday and Saturday until 9 p.m. Phone 316/455-3518.

CARRIAGE HOUSE CRAFTS 100: 100 Michigan, Oxford. Quaint little place full of antiques, collectibles, locally made crafts, and gifts. Open Thursday through Saturday 10 a.m. to 5 p.m., Sunday 1 to 5 p.m. Closed January through March. Phone 316/455-2457.

BUFFALO PASTURE: 2-1/2 miles north of U.S. 160 and the bank, Oxford. Keep your eyes open right before the bridge for part of Tom Price's 250-head buffalo herd. During the week stop at the Price Farms office, 605 West Main, Oxford, and ask Tom about the best place to see the buffalo. Look at some of the buffalo art he is collecting. Buffalo meat is available for sale here. Phone 316/455-2207 or 316/455-3676.

BELLE PLAINE

1990 population 1,649; 1970 1,553.

BARTLETT ARBORETUM: K-55 and Line, Belle Plaine. One of the most mature arboretums in the Midwest, this oasis of splendor features tulips and pansies in the spring and chrysanthemums in the fall. Between those two seasons, beauty is sustained with perennials, annuals, shrubs, and wonderful trees like the 100-foot-tall southern loblolly pines, tunnels of cottonwoods, plus a gazebo, formal gardens, and a footbridge over the lake. Bring your camera! Open April through November 15th. Admission fee. Phone 316/488-3451.

MULVANE

1990 population 4,674; 1970 3,185.

MULVANE HISTORICAL MUSEUM: 300 West Main, Mulvane. Exhibits inside this 1910 Santa Fe depot tell about the city's early days and include a dollhouse replica of a Mulvane home. A 1940s caboose and 100-year-old jail sit outside the museum. Open Tuesday through Saturday 10 a.m. to 3 p.m. Closed mid-December until May. Donations appreciated. Phone 316/777-0506.

MULVANE ANTIQUE STORES: Time's Past Antiques, 105 West Main, and Good Ol' Days Antique Mall, 219 West Main. Open daily 10 a.m. to 6 p.m., Sunday 1 to 5 p.m. Closed

Tuesday. Phone 316/777-1565 and 777-0756.

CONWAY SPRINGS

1990 population 1,384; 1970 1,153. A nice little town with a live spring in the center of the park. Nearby is a band shell waiting for a band concert.

THE SODA SHOPPE: 203 West Spring, Conway Springs. Scheduled to open April 1994, this is as authentic a soda fountain as you'll find — a 6,000-pound Italian marble bar, an 1892 oak back bar, a German silver fountain with 16 pumps, and soda jerks trained to perform with a flair. Open Friday, Saturday, and Sunday 11 a.m. to 8 p.m. Call Judy Harper at 316/456-2234.

CALDWELL

1990 population 1,351; 1970 1,540. Caldwell rolls out the red carpet for visitors in spite of its rough-and-tumble history. Cattle being driven to Abilene, Newton, and Wichita on the Chisholm Trail entered Kansas here. Brass markers guide visitors to points of interest. For area accommodations call 316/845-2708 or 845-2145.

HISTORICAL MARKER: Located south of Caldwell on U.S. 81. This marker tells about Caldwell and the Chisholm Trail.

PHILLIPS WILDERNESS PHOTOGRAPHY: 23 South Main, Caldwell. Charles Phillips, a world-reknowned wilderness photographer, picked this Caldwell building for his lab. Many of his enlarged prints can be seen through the large storefront windows. Look for the incredible detail. If they aren't printing, tours of the lab are possible. Open Monday

through Friday 8 a.m. to 5 p.m. Phone 316/845-2991.

HARVEST HOME RESTAURANT: 118 South Main, Caldwell. The word here is that the homemade chicken fried steaks are so big you can hardly eat them. Open Tuesday through Saturday 6 a.m. to 9 p.m., Sunday 6 a.m. to 1 p.m., noon buffet. Phone 316/845-2360.

SAINT MARTIN'S CHURCH: Caldwell. It's unusual to see this Spanish Mission architecture in Kansas. The church was built in 1924.

THE BURESH BANK BUILDING: Downtown Caldwell. This 1880s limestone structure was once three stories high but the top story was removed to provide building material for another building.

BORDER QUEEN MUSEUM: Six blocks west of Main on Central, Caldwell. An interesting museum featuring the cattle drives, Wyatt Earp, mammoth tusks, and pioneer items. Open on special occasions. Call Dr. J.E. Turner for an appointment to see the museum, 316/845-2454, or call Don at 316/845-2246.

CALDWELL POST OFFICE: Downtown Caldwell. This 1930s building is listed on the national register. Inside is a Kenneth Evertt mural, *Cowboys Driving Cattle.*

WICHITA

1990 population 304,011; 1970 276,554. The Wichita Convention and Visitors' Bureau at 100 South Main, Wichita, can provide you with area brochures and information about food, lodging, and entertainment. Phone 316/265-2800. Call 316/262-7474 for recorded messages about daily entertainment in Wichita including performances at Crown Uptown Dinner Theater and Century II.

OLD TOWN: In the 400-900 block area of East Douglas, Wichita. Many old buildings and warehouses in this area are being renovated into exciting shops, restaurants, and businesses. From antique shops and galleries to a player piano company, this is one part of town you won't want to miss. For an Old Town brochure listing restaurants and retail shops call 316/268-1130.

TAKE THE TROLLEY: Trolleys were last seen in Wichita in June 1935. Now they're back, and if you're downtown between 11 a.m. and 2 p.m. during the week look for the Lunch Express Trolley to take you to area restaurants. The trolley comes by every ten minutes. Small fee. Phone 316/265-7221.

OLD MILL TASTY SHOP: 604 East Douglas, Wichita. This is one of the grandest of the state's working soda fountains with its wooden back bar and mirrors, long marble counter, stools, and brass foot rail. Booths and tables available too. Great stop for an ice cream treat or meal. Open Monday through Friday 11 a.m. to 3 p.m., Friday and Saturday 5:30 to 9:30 p.m., Saturday 8 a.m. to 9:30 p.m. Phone 316/264-6500.

OLD TOWN BARBEQUE AND CHILI FACTORY: 111 North Washington, Old Town, Wichita. The chili and barbecue brisket, ribs, and links taste terrific in another superbly renovated Old Town building. Phone 316/269-4000.

LARKSPUR RESTAURANT AND GRILL: 904 East Douglas, Old Town, Wichita. The lunch and dinner menu features west coast cuisine — which means the food is baked with herbs, is served with light sauces, and is good for you. But the decadent desserts cancel out the healthful entrees! Open

Calif cuisine (handwritten)

Monday through Saturday. Phone 316/262-5275.

CACTUS CAFE BAR AND GRILL: 126 North Mosley, Old Town, Wichita. Southwestern cuisine is featured here. Phone 316/267-1995.

RIVER CITY BREWERY: 150 North Mosley, Old Town, Wichita. The food in this restaurant is as unique as the locally made beer. A rustic setting has been created here with the brewery on display. Phone 316/263-BREW.

good beer (handwritten)

HEROES SPORTS BAR AND DELI: 117 North Mosley, Old Town, Wichita. This is the place in Old Town to gather with your friends and watch Kansas teams or national match-ups on the big screen. Game or no game, the hearty appetizers, salads, burgers, and sandwiches will certainly grab your attention. Phone 316/264-4376.

fun, games, okay gru but pricey (handwritten)

PASTA MILL: 8008 East Douglas, Old Town, Wichita. This favorite Wichita eatery has been around awhile. The pasta is fresh, the sauce is made from scratch, and the bread sticks are hand-rolled. Phone 316/269-3858.

CHICAGO CAB COMPANY: 118 North Mead, Old Town, Wichita. Dance in Old Town Thursday through Saturday night. Phone 316/265-7544.

WICHITA FARM AND ART MARKET: 835 East First, Wichita. From May through October enjoy this open-air market of fresh produce and arts and crafts. Open Tuesday 8 a.m. to 5 p.m., Thursday noon to 8 p.m., Saturday 7 a.m. to 6 p.m. Phone 316/262-3555.

BOTANICA, THE WICHITA GARDENS: 701 Amidon, Wichita. Enjoy a slow and thoughtful stroll through the beauty and diversity of these gardens. Lunch available on Wednesday and Friday April through October or bring a picnic lunch. Open daily 10 a.m. to 5 p.m., Sunday 1 to 5 p.m. Closed on weekends January through March. Admission fee. Phone 316/264-0448.

SEDGWICK COUNTY ZOO AND BOTANICAL GARDENS:

5555 Zoo Boulevard, exit 10 from I-235, Wichita. A large zoo with animals from across the world in "native" habitat enclosures. A special feature is a Kansas prairie populated with indigenous flora and fauna including grizzly bears. There are also a petting zoo, a tropical rain forest, a darkened herpetarium for nocturnal animals, and boat rides. Admission fee. Open daily in the summer 10 a.m. to 6 p.m., winter 10 a.m. to 5 p.m. Phone 316/942-2212. *fun zoo*

Pontoon boats at the Sedgwick County Zoo, Wichita

yuck - what a waste

OLD COWTOWN MUSEUM:

1871 Sim Park Drive, Wichita. Buildings and grounds resemble a town in the 1870s. Living history re-enactments take place during summer weekends. Open March through October daily 10 a.m. to 5 p.m., Sunday noon to 5 p.m. Remainder of the year open weekends noon to 5 p.m. Admission fee. Phone 316/264-6398 for recorded message about current schedule. Call 316/269-0900 for information about Empire House Restaurant and melodrama.

KANSAS WILDLIFE EXHIBIT IN CENTRAL RIVERSIDE PARK:

Nims and Murdock, Wichita. A small zoo, including racoons, foxes, beavers, and birds, is a nice addition to this roomy park along the Arkansas River. Always open. Free.

RIVERSIDE PARK RENTALS:

551 Nims, Wichita. Paddle boats, canoes, fun cycles, and roller blades available for rent by the Riverside Tennis Courts. Open weekends March through October (depending on the weather). Steve usually opens Saturday at 10 a.m., Sunday at noon. Call the recording at 316/262-1098 for the schedule.

STROUD'S: 3661 North Hillside, Wichita. Stroud's is an old favorite in Kansas City, Missouri but new to Wichita. You'll feel right at home eating the house specialty, pan-fried chicken, in this country atmosphere. Open Monday through Thursday 4 to 9:30 p.m., Friday 11 a.m. to 10:30 p.m., Saturday 2 to 10:30 p.m., Sunday 11 a.m. to 9:30 p.m. Phone 316/838-2454. *LOTS of food, good*

CHISHOLM CREEK PARK NATURE TRAIL: 3238 North Oliver, Wichita. Yes, even the big city of Wichita has parks that surround you with nature and take you away from the hustle and bustle. This 238-acre park boasts a 1-1/2-mile paved nature trail. Interpretive signs explain the various habitat areas. Trails take you through grasslands and woods, and bridges take you across streams. Picnic shelters, grills, restrooms.

PAWNEE PRAIRIE PARK:

Wichita, 1/4 mile west of Maize Road on U.S. 54 to Lark. Take Lark one mile south, then go east on Pawnee for 1/2 mile. Rustic nature trail. Another entrance is at Tyler and Harry.

WICHITA-SEDGWICK COUNTY HISTORICAL MUSEUM:

204 South Main, Wichita. The museum is housed in the old city hall building and is an exhibit of its own. Beautiful limestone, stained-glass windows. Museum displays are a fascinating depiction of how Wichita progressed. Open Tuesday through Friday 11 a.m. to 4 p.m., weekends 1 to 5 p.m. Admission fee. Phone 316/265-9314.

WICHITA OMNISPHERE AND SCIENCE CENTER:

220 South Main, Wichita. Planetarium shows and science demonstrations. Open Tuesday through Friday 8 a.m. to 5 p.m. and weekends 1 to 5 p.m. Admission fee. Phone 316/264-3174 for show times.

CHILDREN'S MUSEUM OF WICHITA:

435 South Water, Wichita. Kids will love this place! Sit on a saddle, get yourself out of a maze, hear your voice echo, go into a room of mirrors or a courtroom, try on a firefighter's suit, much more! Puppet show and science shows on Saturday. Open Tuesday through Friday 9 a.m. to 5 p.m. and weekends 1 to 5 p.m. Admission fee. Phone 316/267-2281.

KANSAS AVIATION MUSEUM:

3350 South George Washington Boulevard. The story of the "Air Capital of the World" is told in this art deco structure, the former Wichita Air Terminal. Open Tuesday through [...] urday [...]3-9242.

FIRST NATIONAL BLACK HISTORICAL SOCIETY OF KANSAS:

601 North Water, Wichita. In the old Calvary Church, African artifacts and exhibits honor the black culture of our area and nation. Open Monday, Wednesday, and Friday 10 a.m. to 2 p.m. and Sunday 2 to 6 p.m. Donations appreciated. Phone 316/262-7651.

GREAT PLAINS TRANSPORTATION MUSEUM:

700 East Douglas, Wichita. Railroad buffs will appreciate the efforts to preserve the history of the railroad. Climb into the caboose and the huge steam locomotive. Open Saturday 9 a.m. to 4 p.m. and Sunday 1 to 3 p.m. April through October. Admission fee. Phone 316/263-0944.

MCCORMICK MUSEUM:

855 South Martinson, Wichita. Wichita's oldest school building is open for tours. Call for an appointment. Phone 316/833-3760.

WICHITA ART MUSEUM:

619 Stackman Drive, Wichita. Permanent exhibits of American masterpieces complement traveling exhibits and sculptures. Open Tuesday through Saturday 10 a.m. to 5 p.m., Sunday noon to 5 p.m. Restaurant open for lunch daily except Monday and Saturday. Free. Phone 316/268-4921.

MID-AMERICA ALL INDIAN CENTER MUSEUM:

650 West Seneca, Wichita. See paintings, photos and descriptions, clothing, baskets, arrowheads, and pottery exhibits with Indian music setting the mood. Indian tacos and honey fry bread available on Tuesdays. Museum open 10 a.m. to 5 p.m. Tuesday through Saturday, Sunday 1 to 5 p.m. $2 adult admission. Phone 316/262-5221.

PICCADILLY GRILL AND MARKET:

7728 East Central, Wichita. This modern market has an old-fashioned

good food, fun atms, nice wines

flair, and the adjoining restaurant provides a light and airy atmosphere for a great meal. The market deli provides excellent carry-out choices. Open for lunch and supper daily. Phone 316/681-1100.

SPICE MERCHANT: 1308 East Douglas, Wichita. It smells great to step inside this store that sells coffees, teas, spices, and gifts. A cafe in the back serves a soup or sandwich of the day. Lunch served 11:30 a.m. to 2 p.m. Phone 316/263-4121.

NU-WAY RESTAURANT: 1416 West Douglas, Wichita. The reputation of the Nu-Way burger with the crumbled beef, mustard, pickle, and onions dates back to 1930. There are several locations in Wichita, but this one, with its horseshoe shaped counter and stools, has the most nostalgia. Open daily 10:30 a.m. to 9 p.m., Sunday 11 a.m. to 9 p.m. Phone 316/267-1131.

HOLIDAY HOUSE RESIDENTIAL BED-AND-BREAKFAST: 8406 West Maple, Wichita. Fireplaces and porches, antiques, and a decor reflecting Diane and Carroll's love of the theater and holidays make this a fine getaway. Phone 316/721-1968.

THE INN AT WILLOWBEND: 3939 Comotara, Wichita. This is a resort-type setting that includes 22 rooms with private baths. Overlooking golf course. Phone 1-800/553-5775.

MAX PAUL... AN INN: 3910 East Kellogg, Wichita. Fourteen rooms and private baths. Some suites offer fireplaces and private balconies . Breakfast included. Phone 316/689-8101.

INN AT THE PARK: 3751 East Douglas, Wichita. This may be the ultimate urban bed-and-breakfast experience. This restored 1909 Cyrus Beachy home now provides a roman-

tic, elegant, and private setting. Phone 1-800/258-1951.

CLIFTON SQUARE: 3700 East Douglas, Wichita. Enjoy this collection of shops in 19th-century houses. Includes Best of Kansas, a great place to buy Kansas products and souvenirs. Shops open daily 10 a.m. to 6 p.m., Sunday 1 to 5 p.m. Phone 316/686-2177.

KANSAS SOUVENIRS AND PRODUCTS: Shop at The Hay Market, 5426 East Central, Wichita (316/685-0611) or The Sunflower Shoppe, 400 North Seneca, Wichita (316/265-0837).

LAWRENCE-DUMONT STADIUM: Maple and Sycamore, Wichita. This newly remodeled minor-league ballpark, home of the Double A Wichita Wranglers, also hosts the annual National Baseball Congress tournament. Phone 316/292-2900.

Nice Stadium [handwritten annotation]

JOYLAND AMUSEUMENT PARK: 2801 South Hillside, Wichita. This amusement park is open April through October daily 2 to 10 p.m., closed Monday and Tuesday. Fee per ride. Phone 316/684-0179 to confirm hours.

WICHITA GREYHOUND PARK: Exit 16 from Interstate 135. Watch the rituals that take place at a race track and enjoy the exciting races, or try your luck at pari-mutuel betting. Dining by windows if you prefer during the races. Open Wednesday, Friday, and weekends for races starting at 1:30 p.m.; evening races starting at 7:30 p.m. on Tuesday, Thursday, Friday, and Saturday. Phone 316/755-4000.

KANSAS COLISEUM: Exit 17 from I-135 north of Wichita. The coliseum is home of the Wichita Wings, a professional soccer team, and the Wichita

Thunder, a professional hockey team. Call for other entertainment. Phone 316/755-1243. Box office 316/755-1246. An RV park is available in front of the coliseum with full hookups and dump station.

JOHN MACK BRIDGE: Broadway and Pawnee, Wichita. This seven-arch cement bridge was designed by John Mack.

WATSON PARK: Just south of 31st and Broadway, Wichita. This huge park is a great place for groups or family fun, with paddle boats, pony rides, train rides, miniature golf, playground equipment, concessions, picnic areas, and fishing. A walk down the Yellow Brick Road takes you by wooden statues of Wizard of Oz characters. Fun place! Phone 316/522-3211.

HORSE POLO: South field: South Broadway and 95th, Haysville. Take Haysville-Derby turnpike exit, then go three miles south on Broadway. East field: Andover Road and Harry, Andover, behind the PKD Arena. Chuckers, divots, and mallets are polo terms not often associated with Kansas. There are six 7-1/2-minute chuckers, and the players change horses between each one. Spectators drive their vehicles right up to the sideline. Bring lawn-chairs and a cooler full of goodies. It often seems the action is at the far corner of the field,

but when the horses come near, the heavy breathing and sounding of hooves are exciting. At half-time spectators get out on the field and help put the divots back. Free. Matches usually take place on Sunday at 2:30 p.m. between May and October. Usually 20 tournaments a season. Call the Fairfield Polo hotline to find times and places, 1-800/280-5425.

CRAFT COUNTRY CO-OP: 6346 South Broadway, Haysville. Over 20 local craftspeople have their wares for sale behind this yellow western storefront. Open Tuesday through Saturday 10 a.m. to 5:30 p.m., Sunday 1 to 5 p.m. Phone 316/524-4265.

PRAIRIE PINES CHRISTMAS TREE FARM: Three miles west of Wichita on K-96 to Ridge Road exit, south to 37th, one mile west to Tyler, then 1/4 mile north to 4055 North Tyler. Buying a christmas tree here will certainly put you in the Christmas spirit! Catch the first hayrack out to the trees, pick your own, then enjoy hot chocolate back at this wonderful renovated old barn. Get your trees starting the day after Thanksgiving. A reception room upstairs and a garden, waterfall, lily pond, and three decks behind the barn are available for receptions and groups year-round. Phone 316/722-1145.

SOUTHEAST KANSAS

COFFEYVILLE SECTION: Caney, Chanute, Cherryvale, Coffeyville, Elk City, Fredonia, Independence, Neodesha, Thayer. *Page 119 to 123.*

EL DORADO SECTION: Andover, Augusta, Benton, Beaumont, Douglass, El Dorado, Eureka, Fall River, Hamilton, Towanda. *Page 123 to 127.*

EMPORIA SECTION: Burlington, Burns, Cassoday, Cedar Point, Cottonwood Falls, Emporia, Florence, Hartford, LeRoy, Madison, Matfield Green, New Strawn, Olpe, Strong City, Williamsburg. *Page 127 to 133.*

FORT SCOTT SECTION: Fort Scott, Garnett, Humboldt, Iola, Neosho Falls, Piqua, Pleasanton, Trading Post, Yates Center. *Page 133 to 139.*

PITTSBURG SECTION: Baxter Springs, Chetopa, Columbus, Frontenac, Galena, Girard, Hallowell, Oswego, Parsons, Pittsburg, Riverton, St. Paul, Scammon, West Mineral. *Page 139 to 143.*

WINFIELD SECTION: Arkansas City, Cambridge, Cedar Vale, Dexter, Elgin, Elk Falls, Geuda Springs, Grenola, Howard, Moline, Oak Valley, Sedan, Winfield. *Page 143 to 148.*

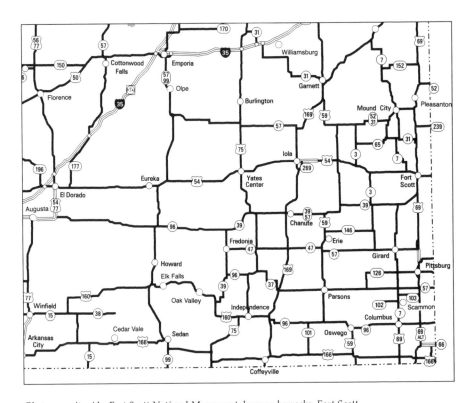

Photo opposite side: Fort Scott National Monument dragoon barracks, Fort Scott

The Little Ozarks, the Chautauqua Hills, the Mined Land areas, Osage cuestas, and the heart of the Flint Hills — all are words that, once experienced, call forth soul-stirring images — quiet woodland lanes, gold-finches streaking golden contrails, mellow afternoons spent fishing, woodpeckers drilling, and wildflowers dotting a carpet of green.

Not always has this idyllic corner of Kansas been a tranquil place. Nowhere else in Kansas is the upheaval caused by the "hand of man" more apparent than in the coal-, lead-, and zinc-mining areas of Cherokee and Crawford counties. As you travel, view this region from a layered-time perspective: Start with the present — cities and towns, agriculture, and many fishing lakes; then let the mining remnants take you back to the early days of white domination; let subtle relics recall for you the red people; and finally think about the ancient cataclysmic times when the coal beds and veins of zinc were formed.

The travail of Kansas's pre-Civil War era is still evidenced in many ways along the Missouri border — monuments in cemeteries, signs along the road, and artifacts in visitor centers and museums.

Southeast Kansas is unique, beautiful, and a pleasure to visit. The citizens remark, "We are the forgotten corner of Kansas, yet we have so much to offer." Go visit southeast Kansas and see what it is all about. You'll have a good time.

COFFEYVILLE

1990 population 12,917; 1970 15,116. The town is near the lowest point in Kansas, where the Verdigris River enters Oklahoma at 700 feet above sea level. For lodging and food information call the Convention and Visitors' Bureau, 1-800/626-3357 or 316/251-1194.

OLD CONDON BANK: 811 Walnut, Coffeyville. Beautifully restored, this is one of the banks robbed by the Dalton Gang that tragic October day in 1892. Other nearby buildings involved in the episode are the old First National Bank; Isham's Hardware store, where the defenders borrowed guns; Death Alley; and the jail where the bodies were laid out. Pass by any time, go inside weekdays during business hours.

Condon Bank, Coffeyville

DALTON DEFENDERS MUSEUM: 113 East Eighth Street, Coffeyville. This museum captures the drama of the Dalton story and duly honors the townsmen who died in the gunfight. The museum also includes mementoes of Coffeyville's baseball hero, Walter Johnson, and Coffeyville schoolteacher Wendell Willke. Admission fee. Open June, July, and August daily 9 a.m. to 5 p.m. Phone 316/251-5944.

BROWN MANSION: On U.S. 169 just south of Coffeyville. This mansion may be the ultimate expression of personal affluence and opulence found in Kansas. It is large, it is ornate, and it is worth seeing. The mansion is a Kansas Visitor Center from May 15 to September 15, open 9 a.m. to 5 p.m. Admission fee. Closed in January and February. The rest of the year it's open 1 to 5 p.m. Phone 316/251-0431.

COFFEYVILLE MURALS BY DON SPRAGUE: Various places in Coffeyville: Walter Johnson mural at 223 West Ninth, Dalton murals at 912 and 807 Walnut, an attractions map at 811 Union, and eight more around town.

PEPPERMILL GRILL: 104 West Eleventh (at the Fountain Plaza Inn), Coffeyville. Your taste buds will like this quiet restaurant because Monty Lynch and his wife, Lori, believe each delicious plate served should be as good as they can make it. Monty is the grandson of Dorothy Lynch of salad-dressing fame. Open Monday through Saturday for breakfast, lunch, and dinner. The Sunday buffet, 11 a.m. to 2 p.m., features Monty's specialty, strawberry crepes. Phone 316/251-7755.

MIDLAND THEATER: 208 West Eighth Street, Coffeyville. An attractive 1928 art-deco-style theater, still showing movies every night. Phone 316/251-0280.

KANSAS SUNSHINE SHOP: 132 West Ninth, Coffeyville. Full of Kansas-made gifts and souvenirs. Open Monday through Friday 9 a.m. to 5:30 p.m. and Saturday 9:30 a.m. to 4 p.m. Phone 316/251-6061.

COCA-COLA SIGN: 713 Union, Coffeyville. An authentic 70-year-old five-cent Coca-Cola sign restoration.

CANEY

1990 population 2,062; 1970 2,192.

SAFARI PARADISE EDUCATIONAL ZOO: From U.S. 75 and 166 intersection north of Caney head south on U.S. 75 until you reach a Phillips 66 station. Turn east for 1-1/2 miles. Look for the gate. For a group fee, one to 50 will enjoy a guided tour that encourages a close-up and personal experience with exotic animals like bobcats, bears, primates, rhesus monkeys, alligators, cougars, foxes, and a python, as well as animals native to Kansas. They let you feed certain animals, handle others, and play games with the primates! It's a visitor-friendly place. In the museum and trading post are stuffed animals and animal hides to look at and touch. A tour usually lasts up to two hours. This is a privately funded family enterprise. Must call 316/879-2885 for a reservation.

ELK CITY STATE LAKE: Southeast of Elk City on U.S. 160. Elk City 1990 population 334; 1970 432. Several hiking and nature trails are located here including the nationally recognized Elk River Hiking Trail, a rugged 15-mile one-way trail. Phone 316/331-6295 or 331-0315 for more information.

INDEPENDENCE

1990 population 9,942; 1970 10,347. For Independence area lodging and food information call the Convention and Visitors' Bureau, 316/331-1890.

LITTLE HOUSE ON THE PRAIRIE: Thirteen miles southwest of Independence near U.S. 75. Follow markers along county roads. A replica of the original "Little House" where Laura Ingalls Wilder lived as a child. Wayside Post Office and a schoolhouse are on the site too. Donations appreciated. Open May to September Monday through Saturday 10 a.m. to

5 p.m., Sunday 1 to 5 p.m. Phone 316/331-6247.

RIVERSIDE PARK AND RALPH MITCHELL ZOO: North on U.S. 75 to Oak Street, then east to the park, Independence. A beautiful park and zoo. Lots of animals and birds including pileated woodpeckers along the river drive. This park was one of the settings for the movie *Picnic*.

NEODESHA

1990 population 2,837; 1970 3,295.

NORMAN NUMBER ONE: First and Main, Neodesha. A replica wooden derrick with working mechanisms commemorates the first commercial oil well west of the Mississippi River. Oil was found here November 29, 1892, at a depth of 800 feet. The park and museum are open Monday through Saturday 9 a.m. to 5 p.m. Phone 316/325-5316.

WILDWOOD LIMITED GENERAL STORE AND BED-AND-BREAKFAST: 411 Main, Neodesha. This discriminating gift shop has been renovated with hardwood floors and wall display cases for a turn-of-the-century look. Merchandise includes antiques, Kansas products, books, and other gifts. The second floor, with beautifully painted pressed tin ceilings, wainscoting, and period wood carvings dating back to 1871 is available for lodging for one to six family members. Eclectic furnishings, plants, magazines, and a dining area make this an elegant home away from home. Continental breakfast included. The gift shop is open Tuesday through Saturday 9 a.m. to 6 p.m. and Sunday 1 to 5 p.m. Open daily in December 9 a.m. to 8 p.m. Phone 316/325-2448.

COBALT BOATS: Take Eighth Street in Neodesha north to the factory. An opportunity to see the boat-building process from start to finish. Please call a week in advance for a guided tour of the entire factory. Weekdays only. Call Jim Casper at 316/325-3019.

FREDONIA

1990 population 2,599; 1970 3,080. The Fredonia Chamber of Commerce is located in the 1884 Gold Dust Hotel at 402 North Seventh, Fredonia. Stop here for information or call 316/378-3221.

ROCKY RIDGE RESORT AND RESTAURANT: Four miles south of Fredonia on K-96, then one mile east. This is a wonderful getaway area in the Chautauqua Hills on the Fall River. The staff will organize float trips on the Fall River for your group starting at the Fredonia Mill Dam and ending at Rocky Ridge. Six comfortably furnished cabins, RV hookups, a swimming pool, a small petting zoo, horseshoes, and walks along the river make this a great place for families and groups! Dine inside or outside on the patio deck overlooking Rocky Ridge Bluff. Enjoy a menu of charbroiled steaks, seafood, Mexican food, and pasta. The salad bar is located in the belly of a 1923 Ford Model T! You don't have to be staying at Rocky Ridge to come and enjoy the restaurant. Open Tuesday through Saturday at 6 p.m. for supper. Phone 316/378-3303.

FREDONIA MILL DAM: Take K-96 south from Fredonia to the golf course, turn west, drive under a railroad trestle into the Fredonia Water Supply area, bear left as you go. A picturesque "down by the old mill stream" spot. Drive across the Fall River on the low-water bridge if the water isn't too high. See a mural of

the mill dam in Fredonia at Madison and Seventh.

FRIEND'S BIRD FARM AND ANTIQUES: One mile farther on K-96 than the Fredonia Mill Dam turnoff. What a combination: exotic birds and antiques! Stop at the house to let J.W. and Keri know you're on the yard or call 316/378-3946 first to make sure they'll be home.

THE MOUND: Go south on Seventh and follow winding road to the crest of the hill, Fredonia. Park your car and take the stairs to the top of this lookout. The view is excellent.

WILSON COUNTY MUSEUM: 420 North Seventh, Fredonia. Many county exhibits are displayed in the old ironclad cell block. Unlike earlier occupants, you can leave when you're ready. Open Monday through Friday 1 to 4:30 p.m. Free. Phone 316/378-3965 or 378-2632.

BAGGAGE CART ANTIQUES: K-39, Fredonia. This old depot has crafts, collectibles, and some antiques. Open daily 10 a.m. to 4 p.m. Closed Wednesday and Sunday. Phone 316/378-3052 or 378-3031.

KANSAS COUNTRY MEATS AND MERCHANDISE: 631 Monroe, Fredonia. Fresh-cut meat and Kansas food products can be found here. Phone 316/378-2672.

STONE HOUSE GALLERY: 320 North Seventh, Fredonia. Nationally known artists exhibits on display Monday through Friday 9 a.m. to 1 p.m. Free. Closed for art classes in summer. Phone 316/378-2052.

CHANUTE

1990 population 9,488; 1970 10,341. For accommodations and attractions informa-

tion call the Chamber of Commerce, 316/431-3350.

MARTIN AND OSA JOHNSON SAFARI MUSEUM: 111 North Lincoln, Chanute. This is an all-American adventure story. A 16-year-old Chanute girl marries Martin Johnson, a globe-trotting friend of Jack London. They go on to explore and record on film the lands untouched by civilization — Borneo, the South Seas, and East Africa. This museum tells the exciting story. Admission fee. Open Tuesday through Saturday 10 a.m. to 5 p.m., Sunday 1 to 5 p.m. Phone 316/431-2730.

SANTA FE DEPOT: 111 North Lincoln, Chanute. Circa 1903. The people of Chanute deserve a lot of credit for this beautiful restoration job. This building now houses the Martin and Osa Johnson Safari Museum and the Chanute City Library. The building itself is worth a stop; it reflects the spirit of the railroad passenger era.

CHANUTE ART GALLERY: 17 North Lincoln, Chanute. Located in four adjoining restored downtown buildings. Free. Open Tuesday through Saturday 10 a.m. to 4 p.m. Phone 316/431-7807.

HARMS'S BARN: U.S. 169, Thayer. 1990 population 435; 1970 430. You can get wrought iron, planters, pottery, paintings, onyx, and owner Ernie Harms's views on the farm situation and the economy. You just might learn something. Phone 316/839-5568.

BIG HILL LAKE: East of Cherryvale on a county road. This clear-water lake offers excellent camping and fishing. A well-developed equestrian trail is perfect for hiking.

of Coffeyville on U.S. 169. A town strug-
gling to survive. A beautiful red brick
depot, well-restored, stands in the middle of
town as a reminder of glory days gone by.

BENDER MURDER MYSTERY:
Cherryvale Museum, 215 East Fourth, Cherryvale. Why did pioneer travelers disappear near a lonely country inn? By appointment, meet the author of *Keepers of the Devil's Inn.* Hear the chilling story from Fern Morrow Wood at the Cherryvale Museum, and look at haunting artifacts. Phone 316/336-2090.

EL DORADO

1990 population 11,504; 1970 12,308.
For additional lodging, restaurants, or
area attractions information call the
Chamber of Commerce at 316/321-3150.

KANSAS OIL MUSEUM AND BUTLER COUNTY HISTORICAL MUSEUM:
383 East Central, two blocks east of downtown on U.S. 54, El Dorado. These county and oil industry exhibits are displayed in a very interesting manner. Take special note of the detailed 1/16-scale working rotary drilling rig and the oil-field lease house and central power unit. Men like Al Derby and W. G. Skelly are featured in the Kansas Oil Hall of Fame. Open daily 1 to 5 p.m. Closed on holidays. Phone 316/321-9333.

WALKING TOUR:
Pick up a brochure for this 2-1/2-mile loop of historical and architectural sites at the Butler County Historical Museum, 383 East Central, El Dorado. Phone 316/321-9333.

ELLET MEMORIAL MARKER:
383 East Central, El Dorado. This monument honors six members of the Ellet family who provided distinguished service during the Civil War.

STAPLETON #1 AND OIL HILL:
Northeast of El Dorado. You have to be observant to realize you're in Oil Hill, an oil-boom town that died in 1957. Twenty-five hundred people once lived here in "shotgun houses" like the one displayed at the Kansas Oil Museum. Stapleton #1, discovery well of the El Dorado oil fields in 1915, is located just beyond the ghost town. Visit the Kansas Oil Museum first and ask Bob or Kevin for directions.

GALLERY OF THE HILLS ATRIUM:
Enter south side of Walnut Valley Bank, 112 East Central, El Dorado. This is a tribute to the mystique of the Flint Hills. Rolla Clymer quotes accompany an art collection of the hills. "And so, may all those whose senses are stirred by the warmth of this magic prairie dominion lift their voices and cry, 'My heart is where the Hills fling up green garlands to the sky.'" Open during banking hours, usually Monday through Friday 9 a.m. to 3 p.m. Phone 316/321-1250.

WARREN HALL COUTTS III MEMORIAL MUSEUM OF ART:
110 North Main, El Dorado. This gallery is a rare Kansas find. You'll feel like you're in someone's elegant home viewing a Picasso lithograph, Prairie Print Makers, Joe Beeler western portraits, Frederic Remington's work, and the largest Makk collection in Kansas. Open Monday through Friday 1 to 5 p.m., Tuesday and Thursday 9 a.m. to noon. Free. Phone 316/321-1215.

BLUESTEM ART GALLERY:
111 South Main, El Dorado. Local artists staff this cooperative sales gallery. Featured exhibits change bimonthly. Open Tuesday through Saturday 11 a.m. to 4 p.m. Phone 316/321-4344.

Open Tuesday through Saturday 11 a.m. to 4 p.m. Phone 316/321-4344.

NORTH WARD JUNCTION ANTIQUES: 518 North Star, El Dorado. A red brick sidewalk takes you to this old white stucco and brick school building with dark green window trim. An open ceiling supported by bridge girders and timbers draws your attention to additional antiques in the loft. Great place to rummage around. Open Monday through Saturday 10 a.m. to 5:30 p.m. Phone 316/321-0145.

SUSI'S CHILI PARLOR: 117 West Second, El Dorado. This place only seats twelve at the counter so avoid high noon. The specialties are a Frisco Melt and homemade pie.

IRON HORSE FOLK HOUSE: Second and Main, El Dorado. Don and Marianne Koke are trying to keep folk music alive and offer everything from bluegrass to blues on Saturday nights during the school year in the repair shop of a 1918 John Deere garage. Some performances during the summer. Admission fee. Phone 316/321-6348.

EL DORADO RESERVOIR: Northeast of El Dorado. There are 98 miles of shoreline and 1,100 campsites ranging from full hookups to primitive. There are two swimming beaches and great fishing because of standing timber, submerged railroad beds, and old river channels. Phone 316/321-7180.

TETER NATURE TRAIL: From Twelfth and Main go east 2-1/2 miles. Take south fork at lake. Trail is 3/4 mile west of park office. The trail is 3/4 mile long, with sumac, honey locust, and wild plum bordered by prairie grasses. A sign reminds hikers that this is how the county looked before settlement. Obtain informative brochure at Butler County Historical Museum.

FLINT HILLS TOURS: Pick up a self-guided auto tour brochure at the Kansas Oil Museum/Butler County Historical Museum and select one of the tours through the prairie grasses to such places as Council Grove, the Beaumont Hotel, Marion and Chase counties, and ghost towns. Phone 316/321-3150.

BENTON

1990 population 669; 1970 517.

BENTON ANTIQUE MALL AND OL' GUYS CAFE: Benton corner and K-254. This is one huge antique mall. What sets it apart are the classic cars on display and the Ol' Guys Cafe. Sit at antique oak tables or at the antique bar and order anything from steak to salad. Open for lunch and supper. The mall is open Tuesday through Saturday 10 a.m. to 9 p.m., Sunday noon to 6 p.m. Phone 316/778-1700.

FLINT HILLS WINDMILL AND PUMP SERVICE: Downtown Benton. If Lucy, the red truck, is in front of the shop there's a good chance that Chuck will be inside. Go on in. It's not every day you get to see a unique shop like this full of windmill heads, tails, pumps, and all sorts of tools and supplies. Phone 316/778-1191.

TOWANDA ANTIQUES MALL AND BLUE MOON SALOON: Downtown Towanda. 1990 population 1,289; 1970 1,190. You'll find a classy red-and-black tiled soda fountain and a fun restaurant tucked inside this multi-room antique mall. Old-fashioned fans hang from the pressed tin ceilings. An upright grizzly bear greets you as you enter. The

Chuck Jones in front of Flint Hills Windmill and Pump Service, Benton

chicken, fish, and steak are excellent. A fun and unique dining experience is guaranteed here. The restaurant is open Thursday through Saturday 11 a.m. to 2 p.m. and 5:30 to 10 p.m., Sunday noon to 4 p.m. and 5 to 9 p.m. Antique mall open Thursday through Sunday. Call 316/536-2544 to make reservations.

ANDOVER

1990 population 4,047; 1970 1,880.

PKD ARENA: 16197 East Harry, Andover. This is the place to watch bull-riding indoors during the winter and rodeo during the summer. Admission fee. Phone 316/733-0385 for a schedule.

TERRADYNE RESORTS: 1400 Terradyne Drive, Andover. Whether you treat yourself to a meal or an overnight stay, this place is top of the line with marble floors and dark woodwork. The restaurant is open Tuesday through Saturday 6 to

10 p.m., Sunday 11 a.m. to 2 p.m. for brunch. Phone 316/733-2582.

AUGUSTA

1990 population 7,867; 1970 5,977.

AUGUSTA THEATRE: 525 State, Augusta. The art deco ceiling and wall murals with an Egyptian flavor are more than impressive. This theater, built in 1935, was the first in the world to be lit by neon. Movies are shown the first and third weekend of each month, but a day tour is the only way to really see this place. Kandi is usually in the building between 10 a.m. and 5 p.m. on weekdays, but call 316/775-3661 to be sure. Free tour.

CIRCA 1890 ANTIQUES: One mile west of Augusta on U.S. 54, then 1/4 mile south and 1/2 mile west on gravel driveway. (Keep your eye out for red fox or deer.) You'll like the atmosphere as you look at well-preserved furniture. Glass chandelier and other items hang from wooden beams, and a wood-burning stove keeps the place warm in the winter. Open Wednesday through Saturday 10:30 a.m. to 5 p.m. and Sunday by chance. Phone 316/775-3272.

AUGUSTA HISTORICAL MUSE-UM AND C.N. JAMES LOG CABIN: 303 State, Augusta. This log cabin was the first building in Augusta and is on the national register. The town was named after C.N. Jones's wife, Augusta. Open Tuesday through Saturday 11 a.m. to 3 p.m. Free. Phone 316/775-5655.

SHIRLEY'S DECORATIVE FUR-NITURE STRIPPING AND REFINISHING: 715 Ohio, Augusta. This place has character, with stripped chairs hanging from every-where and a wooden floor covered with paint, sawdust, and wood chips. Shirley or Calvin will be glad to show you their furniture stripping process. Open Monday through Friday 8 a.m. to 5 p.m. Phone 316/775-2279 or 775-6885.

DOUGLASS PIONEER MUSE-UM: 312 South Forest, Douglass. 1990 population 1,722; 1970 1,126. Area exhibits are housed in this old furniture store and city hall. Open Monday, Wednesday, and Friday 10:30 a.m. to 2:30 p.m. Phone 316/746-2122.

EUREKA

1990 population 2,974; 1970 3,576.

123 MULBERRY STREET BED-AND-BREAKFAST: 123 South Mulberry, Eureka. Jay Jordan spotted this house while on vacation and liked it so much that he and his fami-ly sold their California home and moved to Eureka! Jay and his wife, Linda, thought others would enjoy the home, too, so they converted three

upstairs bedrooms into pleasing guest rooms and added a deck and hot tub. The wide open kitchen, with yellow pine ceilings, is conducive to conver-sation and relaxation. A walk through the neighborhood is a good way to unwind. Phone 316/583-7515.

HAWTHORNE RANCH TRAIL RIDES: North of Eureka. Sally Hawthorne offers a two- to three-hour trail ride through the rolling hills and across a creek on her Arabian horses. She even provides boots if you don't have any! Begin-ners are welcome. The 1993 fee is $15. Phone Sally at 316/583-5887.

FALL RIVER CANOE TRIPS: 106 South Main, Eureka. The most popu-lar trip is an eight- to ten-mile stretch on the Fall River that takes about four hours. The 1993 prices are $20 to $22 per canoe. Phone 316/583-6481 or 583-6345 to make arrangements.

THE PADDOCK RESTAURANT AND SUPPER CLUB: 502 North Main, Eureka. Breakfast, lunch, and dinner are offered. If Joy is there, ask her any questions you might have about things to do in Greenwood County. Phone 316/583-7572.

EUREKA AREA CHAMBER OF COMMERCE: Eureka ranchers and the Chamber of Commerce invite the public to come learn about their part of the world. From early spring until fall, the rolling hills are filled with grazing cattle. In the spring, with wildflowers peeking from behind thick and lush grasses, the cattle become part of the picturesque Flint Hills scenery. If you'd like to watch cattle being gathered up in their pas-tures and loaded into trucks call Joy at 316/583-5452 or 583-7572 for dates. Ranch tours also available for groups. A plan for monthly cattle drives is being developed.

COUNTRY FLEA MARKET:
One mile north of Eureka on K-99
from U.S. 54. This old auditorium and
schoolrooms are filled with flea market clutter. Phone 316/583-5242.

**HOLMES DRUG STORE AND
SODA FOUNTAIN:** Downtown
Hamilton. 1990 population 301; 1970
349. The marble base and swivel
stools of this soda fountain have been
around for a long time and it seems
that no one is very interested in
changing one thing about this drug
store. Open every day early to late.
Phone 316/678-3341.

**BEAUMONT HOTEL RESTAU-
RANT:** Downtown Beaumont (unincorporated) off K-96. Drive or fly to
the restaurant in this deserted cowtown. Open Thursday, Friday, Saturday, and Monday 8 a.m. to 8 p.m.,
Sunday 8 a.m. to 6 p.m. Rooms available also. Phone 316/843-2422.

SCENIC DRIVE: Go west from the
Beaumont Hotel restaurant, then
immediately south on an unpaved
road. Travel a few miles until the first
road east. It will be about 17 miles
until you get to the first blacktop,
K-99. These rolling back roads will
take you through the heart of the Flint
Hills. Note the groves of trees along
the creeks. The unpaved road is lined
with a tremendous variety of wildflowers during their peak season.

FALL RIVER

1990 population 113; 1970 191.

**GRANNY'S COUNTRY CONVEN-
IENCE STORE:** North end of Fall
River. This is the place to get groceries, a fishing license, hamburgers,
or information. If you're interested in
rappelling, Helen can tell you about
some excellent nearby limestone

cliffs! Open daily 6 a.m. to 8 p.m.
Phone 316/658-4941.

DOWNTOWN FALL RIVER:
These sidewalks were raised because
of the mud during the horse-and-
buggy days.

**FALL RIVER RESERVOIR AND
STATE PARK:** Southeast Greenwood County. This reservoir offers
boating, camping, swimming, hiking,
and fishing. Canoe enthusiasts will
enjoy the route on Fall River or Otter
Creek. This is a good place for bird-
watching. A park naturalist does
interpretive programs in the summer.
Phone 316/658-4445.

EMPORIA

*1990 population 25,512; 1970 23,327.
Just east of the Flint Hills, adjoining two
rivers and at the junction of four major
highways, Emporia was the home of
Pulitzer prize-winner William Allen
White. As an educational center Emporia
has nine public schools, a school of nurs-
ing, a technical school, and a four-year
state university. For more information
visit or call the Emporia Visitors' Bureau,
427 Commercial, phone 316/342-1600.*

**NATIONAL TEACHERS' HALL
OF FAME:** 1320 C of E Drive,
Emporia. This beautiful center is dedicated to the classroom teachers of the
United States. Each year five new
members are inducted into the
Teachers' Hall of Fame, and their stories are told here. Open Monday
through Friday 9 a.m. to 4 p.m. Phone
316/341-5660.

**LYON COUNTY HISTORICAL
MUSEUM:** Market and Sixth,
Emporia. Housed in a 1904 Carnegie
library, this museum interprets the
history of Lyon County. Free. Open
Tuesday through Saturday 9:30 a.m.
to 5 p.m. Phone 316/342-0933.

Sixth Avenue, Emporia. A striking bronze sculpture by J. Seward Johnson, Jr., of a little boy and girl sharing an ice cream cone.

SODEN'S GROVE AND EMPORIA ZOO: South Commercial north of the Cottonwood River, Emporia. A nice park with picnic areas, comfort stations, and an interesting zoo. Zoo hours vary with season. Phone 316/342-7306.

FISHING BRIDGE: Soden's Grove just west of Commercial, Emporia. This beautiful Marsh design bridge over the Cottonwood River has been preserved for fishing enthusiasts.

THE EMPORIA GAZETTE AND WHITE MEMORIAL PARK: 517 Merchant, Emporia. This is the newspaper made famous by William Allen White, and it is still in operation today. The *Gazette* newspaper offices are open weekdays 8 a.m. to 5 p.m. The park is open year-round. Phone 316/342-4800.

ONE-ROOM SCHOOL: 18th and Merchant, Emporia. An authentic 1800s stone one-room school with period furnishings. Phone 316/341-5454.

LUJAN'S WATER WORKS: 402 Merchant, Emporia. Mesquite-grilled steaks and sandwiches, chicken, and everything else from Irish stew to the most delicious apple, cherry, or peach cobblers. The old wood and western decor vie with the food as the main attraction. Open Monday through Friday 11 a.m. to 2 p.m. and Monday through Saturday 5 to 10 p.m. Phone 316/343-9980.

PLUMB HOUSE BED-AND-BREAKFAST: 628 Exchange, Emporia. Enjoy this venerable Victorian home in air-conditioned comfort. Call Barbara Stoecklein for reservations, 316/342-6881.

WHITE ROSE INN: 901 Merchant, Emporia. Just three blocks from the university, you can enjoy the luxury of yesteryear in this Queen Anne Victorian home. Each suite has a private bath and several have kitchenettes. A large wrap-around porch is complete with porch swing. Phone 316/343-6336.

CHASE COUNTY

Located in the heart of the Kansas Flint Hills. The recent book PrairyErth *by William Least Heat-Moon has brought national attention to the culture of Chase County. The population of the county is only 3,021, but the story of this particular rectangle of land and its people from deep time to the present is astounding. Contact the Chase County Twin Cities Main Street Association for a county guide and map. Then, with a full tank of gas, good tires, and an open mind follow the highways and back roads of this timeless land. Write Box 362, 318 Broadway, Cottonwood Falls, Kansas 66845, or call 316/273-8469.*

The relatively few roads range from primitive to blacktop highways. The rewards of exploring the back roads are great: getting in touch with vanishing towns such as Wonsevu, Bazaar, Hymer, and Clements, listening to the sandpiper in spring, thrilling to the color of the prairie in bloom, and experiencing the solitude of the everlasting hills.

CLOVER CLIFF RANCH BED-AND-BREAKFAST: 3-1/2 miles west of Elmdale on U.S. 50. This imposing limestone home built in 1861 overlooks some of the finest rangeland in Kansas. Most of the house, including the woodwork, is restored or replicated to its original splendor. Bedrooms are furnished with fine antiques and the deep window sills are good places to sit and splendor. Bedrooms are furnished with fine antiques and the deep window sills are good places to sit and take in the view. You'll love the square grand piano in the music room. Meals are served by a fireplace or out on the big front porch. Phone 316/732-2665 or 273-6698.

COTTONWOOD FALLS

1990 population 889; 1970 987.

CHASE COUNTY COURTHOUSE: South end of Broadway, Cottonwood Falls. Built in 1873, this is the oldest operating courthouse west of the Mississippi River. Open weekdays 8 a.m. to 5 p.m., Saturday 10 a.m. to 5 p.m., Sunday 1 to 5 p.m. A guide will assist you on weekends. Call 316/273-6493 or 316/273-8288.

MUSEUMS: Cottonwood Falls. Two museums, the Roniger south of the courthouse and the Chase County Historical on Broadway, offer good information about the region. Open daily 1:30 to 4:30 p.m. Closed Mondays and Thursdays. Roniger, 316/273-6310, Chase County Historical, 316/273-8500.

FLINT HILLS ART GALLERY: 226 Broadway, Cottonwood Falls. This is the studio of Judith Mackey, Flint Hills artist. From her deep personal knowledge and love of the Flint Hills, Judith's paintings reflect the beauty and spirit of the land. Open daily 10 a.m. to 5 p.m. and Sunday 1 to 5 p.m. Phone 316/273-6454.

GRAND CENTRAL ICE CREAM AND CANDY COMPANY: Across from Flint Hills Art Gallery, Cottonwood Falls. Renovated to look like an old-fashioned ice cream and candy store, this is a great place to stop for ice cream treats or sandwiches. Phone

316/273-6454 or 273-4470. A bed-and-breakfast is being planned.

PRAIRIE ROSE: 200 Broadway, Cottonwood Falls. A lovely little gift shop that offers Flint Hills memories. Phone 316/273-8151.

STRONG CITY

1990 population 617; 1970 545.

CAROL'S BED-AND-BREAKFAST: Strong City. Rustic Flint Hills ambience. Phone 316/273-6683

WAGON WHEEL CAFE: Main Street, Strong City. This is where the local folks eat. Join them for good food.

SPRING HILL RANCH: Two miles north of Strong City on K-177. Also known as the Z-Bar Ranch. Circa 1884. The unusual feature here is that the three-story stone house with mansard roof is surrounded by original stone outbuildings. Spring Hill may be open to the public in the future. Stop for a few minutes on grass highway shoulder to view.

FOX CREEK SCHOOL: Three miles north of Strong City. Built in 1882. Outside viewing only, very photogenic.

FOX CREEK GALLERY: Four miles north of Strong City on K-177. Debbie offers her original oil paintings and notecards here. Usually open weekdays 1 to 5 p.m. Call 316/273-6310 to be sure.

COWBOY TRAIL: Flint Hills scenery from Cottonwood Falls to Elmdale via a scenic county road.

DENA'S HOME STUDIO: At K-177 and Bazaar turn west for four miles, Chase County. This gallery features Dena's original work plus that of Flint Hills artists. Get prints and postcards of historical Chase County spots. Open by chance or appointment. Call Dena at 316/273-6912 for an appointment or to find out about other home studios in the Flint Hills.

PRAIRIE WOMEN ADVENTURES AND RETREAT: Rural Matfield Green. This is an opportunity to spend time on a working ranch in the Flint Hills. You'll sleep in the bunkhouse and do things like mend fences; put out feed; and help with calving, weaning, branding, castrating, roundups, and a host of other ranch chores. This is a grand opportunity to learn new skills and enjoy rural life in the Flint Hills. Women only. Phone 316/753-3465 for information.

MATFIELD GREEN: 1990 population 33; 1970 77. The Land Institute is expanding its research to tiny Matfield Green. Interns are presently living here and are remodeling the school and other buildings.

C A S S O D A Y

1990 population 95; 1970 123.

CASSODAY CAFE: Downtown Cassoday. Whether you're interested in good food or want to rub elbows with modern-day cowboys, this is the place to start your day in the Flint Hills. The owner, Norma, can tell you when and where you can see cattle being loaded or unloaded. She can direct you to the ghost town of Teterville or tell you the best route to take for wildflower viewing. She also caters to groups in her cafe or out in the hills. Open Monday through Friday 6:30 a.m. to 3 p.m., Saturday 7:30 to 3 p.m., and the second Sunday of every month 11 a.m. to 2 p.m. Phone 316/735-4432.

CASSODAY ANTIQUES AND PRAIRIE CRAFTS: These two stores are located next to the Cassoday Cafe. Open by chance or appointment. Phone 316/735-4210.

CASSODAY MUSEUM: This old depot is filled with railroad memorabilia. One room is devoted to exhibits about old-time Flint Hills cowboys. Phone Chet Unruh for an appointment, 316/735-4286.

FLINT HILLS OVERLAND WAGON TRAIN TOURS: Become a pioneer for a day or two and take advantage of these grain-bed covered wagon tours through the Flint Hills. You'll camp in a grove of trees by a stream with a multitude of stars overhead. Enjoy storytelling, music, and meals by the campfire. In early June the wildflowers will pave the route. Tours begin in Cassoday June through September. Phone Ervin at 316/321-6300 for fee and reservation information.

CASSODAY COUNTRY INN AND RANCH: 1-1/2 miles west of Cassoday on First Street, north side of road. Guests can stay in the Grunder home or in cabins among a grove of trees. The best part, though, is the opportunity to get involved in the lifestyle of a Flint Hills cowboy. Bring in stray cattle or do other ranch work with Carl, or just enjoy horseback rides over the hills. You can watch some calf roping or go fishing or canoeing in the creek that runs through his ranch. Phone 316/735-4425.

THE SUNBARGER GUEST HOUSE: Near Cassoday Turnpike Entrance. For guests only, this turn-of-the-century farmhouse is surrounded by bluestem prairie. Four bedrooms. Catered meals or kitchen privileges available. You'll wake up in this peaceful setting ready for a day of Flint Hills exploration. Phone 316/735-4499.

WALNUT VALLEY DULCIMER COMPANY AND BRUNER GUITARS:
Northeast corner of Washington and Broadway, Burns. 1990 population 226; 1970 268. Visit this four-man craft shop where dulcimers and children's guitars are hanging everywhere in various stages of construction. Open Monday through Friday 7:30 a.m. to 4 p.m. Best to call first at 1-800/633-9477.

HARVEY HOUSE MUSEUM:
Third and Marion, Florence. 1990 population 636; 1970 777. The chug-chug, choo-choo, and clickety-clack of the trains are gone, but the sumptuous dining that Santa Fe rail travelers enjoyed a hundred years ago is still simmering and sizzling for you at the first Fred Harvey Hotel. Luncheons and dinners are served to groups of 12 to 32 by "Harvey Girls" dressed in period costume. Call Bessie Suffield for reservations at 316/878-4474. You might just want to peruse the museum collection of Harvey House-era exhibits. Open daily 2 to 5 p.m.

VAN'S TIME PAST:
413 Main, Florence. Buy antiques, collectibles, or an entire soda fountain! Open daily 9 a.m. to 5 p.m. Closed Sunday. Phone 316/878-4621.

CLEMENTS STONE ARCH BRIDGE:
One-half mile south of Clements (unincorporated). Since Clements is missing on new maps look for the one remaining building about 15 miles west of Strong City on U.S 50, south side. The venerable bridge (1886) is a massive work of art worth searching for.

OLD MILL:
Cedar Point, on the Cottonwood River. Better see this one soon, it's crumbling. Cedar Point 1990 population 39; 1970 73.

HARTFORD

1990 population 541; 1970 478.

BILL'S HARDWARE:
Main Street, west side, Hartford. If Bill and Theda can't find it here for you, you probably didn't need it anyway. Everything from bale hooks to fly swatters, fabric, noodle cutters, nostalgia signs, seeds, and underwear is here somewhere, and it's all new merchandise. Bill says others may sell washboards as antiques, he orders them new from the factory. These people don't advertise; big-city columnists do stories on them. Open Monday through Saturday 8 a.m. to 5:30 p.m. Phone 316/392-5573.

LOVE'S CAFE:
Downtown Hartford. Ritzy this is not, but what do you expect when you get breakfast and change for a five-dollar bill? Do expect to meet heartland country people as they really are: friendly, talking politics, busy, joking, dressed in work clothes, and proud of their home town. Antiques line the walls; John Deere aficionados will love the JD posters and the cast-iron model.

OLD COLLEGE BUILDING:
One block east of Bill's Hardware, Hartford. Built in 1862 by the Methodist Church out of stone freighted by wagon from Leavenworth. Students received their education here all the way from first grade through college. The building now serves as a senior center.

FLINT HILLS NATIONAL WILDLIFE REFUGE:
Hartford, 18,500 acres with headquarters three blocks west, one block north of Hartford High School. Activities here include wildlife observation, photography, hiking, boating, fishing, camping, picnicking, and hunting.

Special feature is eagles, as many as 50, in the winter. For information call 316/392-5553 or write Refuge Manager, Box 128, Hartford, Kansas 66854.

THE CHICKEN HOUSE: Eleven miles south of Emporia on K-99 in Olpe. 1990 population 431; 1970 453. For 35 years people who take fried chicken seriously have been coming to Olpe to partake with gusto. Leonard and Theresa Coble and staff dish out prodigious amounts of chicken, tasty breads, and all the usual goodies seven days a week. They also serve fine steaks and seafood. Open daily 11 a.m. to 10 p.m., Sunday till 3 p.m. Phone 316/475-3386.

LITTLE OLDE SHOPPE ANTIQUES: Downtown Madison. 1990 population 845; 1970 1,061. Unique shop with ever so many French display cases full of cut glass, art glass, glass of every color, and much more. Open six days a week 10 a.m. to 4 p.m. Closed Tuesday. Phone 316/437-2080.

LUTHER'S SMOKEHOUSE BAR-B-Q RESTAURANT: West Highway K-57, LeRoy. 1990 population 568; 1970 551. Along with the great Smokehouse cuisine and decor Luther offers free outrageous humor and loves to entertain tour groups. Open 8 a.m. to 8 p.m. except Saturday and Sunday 10 a.m. to 8 p.m. Buses and groups please call in advance. Phone 316/964-2500.

BURLINGTON

1990 population 2,735; 1970 2,099.

FLINT HILLS OPRY: 404 Neosho, Burlington. The Opry showcases Kansas talent as well as hosting Nashville entertainers. Every Saturday the 350 seats in the air-conditioned auditorium fill up at 8 p.m. for the two-hour show. Check for summertime Friday night shows. The building itself is a gem, a striking art deco movie theater remodeled for live stage shows. Call 316/364-5712 for reservations. Tour buses welcome.

BLUE MOON CAFE: 320 Neosho, Burlington. One-half block east of the opry house. A good place to enjoy dinner before the show. Dinner served Friday and Saturday 5 to 9 p.m. Check their deli at noon Monday through Friday. Call 316/364-5560 daytime, evenings 316/364-8830.

COUNTRY CRITTERS: 217 Neosho, Burlington. You have to see this to believe it — the largest puppet manufacturer in the world in Burlington, Kansas! They also make realistic Country Critter plush toys: papa bear, 52 inches tall; mother pig with six little hand-puppet piglets; ride-on elephants and buffalo; and the list goes on. Visit the showroom Monday through Friday 8 a.m. to 4:30 p.m. Call 316/364-8623 for tours.

COFFEY COUNTY HISTORICAL MUSEUM: 1101 Neosho, Burlington. Strike the word "stuffy" from your museum vocabulary here. This is one of the most enjoyable museums in Kansas. Annual summer quilt shows are featured. Open Tuesday through Saturday noon to 4 p.m. and Sunday 1 to 4:30 p.m. Phone 316/364-2653.

JOHNSON'S PHARMACY: 312 Neosho, Burlington. Pressed tin ceilings, wooden back bar with mirror and glass display cases, and neon lights make this soda fountain experience one to remember. Open daily 7:30 a.m. to 5:30 p.m., closed Sunday. Phone 316/364-2142.

VICTORIAN MEMORIES BED-AND-BREAKFAST: 314 North Fourth, Burlington. An elegant guest house, circa 1889, hosted by Clarence and Donna Knapp. Phone 316/364-5752.

OLD EXCELSIOR MILL: In Burlington follow Kennebec to its extreme east end. View the ruins from the street only.

WOLF CREEK NUCLEAR GENERATING STATION: One mile east of U.S. 75 on access road beginning six miles north of Burlington. Not every town can boast one of these. Free two hour tours are available for groups. Call 316/364-8831 in advance.

JOHN REDMOND RESERVOIR: Extends from north of Burlington, near Hartford, to Neosho Rapids. The main entrance is just south of New Strawn on U.S. 75. John Redmond offers all the usual reservoir recreational benefits. Unique features are pedestrian and equestrian trails going through hardwood, tall grass, and marshy areas plus 140 acres for off-road ATVs. Call 316/364-8614 or write Project Manager, John Redmond Project Office, Route 1, Box 91, Burlington, Kansas 66839 for information.

PEGGY SUE'S RESTAURANT: Take exit 155 from I-35, Beto Junction near Lebo. Beto Junction is not a town but a service spot where those coming from Burlington, Emporia, Topeka, and Ottawa often stop. Truckers like Vernon say that Peggy Sue's has put the junction on the map. Open 24 hours a day. Phone 316/256-6754.

GUY AND MAE'S TAVERN: Downtown Williamsburg. 1990 population 261; 1970 268. Year after year, still serving the famous barbecue with newspaper as the drip catcher. Prepare for a wait and a smoky environment. Open Tuesday through Saturday 11 a.m. to 10:30 p.m. Phone 913/746-8830.

SILKVILLE: Three miles southwest of Williamsburg on old U.S. 50. An old stone schoolhouse identifies the region. Little evidence remains of an 1860s French colony here that reportedly sought to introduce silk production to Kansas. Some mulberry trees, a house, and several stone buildings on private property south of the schoolhouse are remnants.

FORT SCOTT

1990 population 8,362; 1970 8,967. The military fort, now restored, sets the stage here. Its historical and architectural influence is readily apparent in the city of Fort Scott and surrounding communities. The city has done an excellent job of preserving turn-of-the-century houses and businesses. Between 1838 and 1845 a military road running from Fort Leavenworth through Fort Scott and on to Fort Gibson in Oklahoma was marked out. Modern U.S. 69, designated as a scenic byway, roughly parallels the old Military Road. The days when heavy wagons rolled on the Military Road, streetcars clattered on the city streets, and Indians began their reluctant trek from their homeland are easy to imagine in restored Fort Scott.

VISITOR INFORMATION CENTER: 231 East Wall, Fort Scott. Make your Fort Scott expedition easy and exciting. Pick up information here and ride "Dolly the Trolley" through the city. Fee. Trolley runs daily from 11 a.m. to 3 p.m. leaving on the hour. Call 1-800/245-FORT for details. For lodging and food information call 1-800/245-FORT or 316/223-3566.

FORT SCOTT NATIONAL HISTORIC SITE: Northeast section of Fort Scott city. A National Park Service project. This restored frontier fort was garrisoned from 1842 to 1853 to police what was projected to be the permanent Indian frontier. Eleven original and nine reconstructed buildings are open to the public. The dragoon barracks and stables are especially interesting. Admission fee. Open daily 8 a.m. to 5 p.m. Phone 316/223-0310.

HISTORIC FORT SCOTT CITY:
Old Fort Boulevard, Main Street, and various places in town. This city has done a great job of bringing out the original essence of frontier and turn-of-the-century business places. Some buildings house shops catering to the visitor trade, others are occupied by modern businesses. Enjoy browsing the streets and stores.

MEMORIAL GRAND THEATER:
Third and National, Fort Scott. Refurbished and proudly bringing its marquee display back to life, this grand old theater reopens in 1993. For theater information call 1-800/245-FORT.

MICROWAVE TOWER: West
Wall, Fort Scott. Built by Southwestern Bell in a Romanesque arch design to blend into the city's historical architecture. Drive by any time.

HUNTINGTON HOUSE BED-AND-BREAKFAST: 324 South
Main, Fort Scott. A lovely home away from home. More turn-of-the-century elegance found in this old mansion. A five-minute walk from Fort Scott attractions. Call Wendy McDonald for reservations. Phone 316/223-3644.

THE LYONS HOUSE: 742 South
National, Fort Scott. An outstanding 1876 vintage Victorian mansion. Sterling silver, fine china, and sparkling crystal are hallmarks of teas and dinners served here for groups by Pat Lyons. Pat is happy to coordinate meals, bed-and-breakfast lodging, sightseeing, and "Parlors on the Prairie" tours for groups. She also invites people to tour her house and then enjoy tea and crumpets every

Friday and Saturday at 3 p.m. for $5 April through December. Phone 316/223-0779.

THE CHENAULT MANSION BED-AND-BREAKFAST:
820 South National, Fort Scott. The curved glass; stained and leaded windows; ornate cherry, gum, ash, and oak woodwork; and crystal chandeliers are still as beautiful as they must have been in 1887. Call 316/223-6800 for reservations.

CEDAR CREST BED-AND-BREAKFAST: Four miles east of
U.S. 69 and Pleasanton on county road 552. This one is special. Mary Jo Leisure, an instructor in the art of decorative painting and author of art instruction books, invites you to enjoy her hospitality. The beautiful decor in Harold and Mary Jo's home reflects her artistic philosophy. Phone 913/352-6706.

TOMMASSI'S ITALIAN/AMERICAN RESTAURANT: 101 State in
the Fort Scott Inn, Fort Scott. Expect great food, good service, relaxed atmosphere. Open 24 hours.

MINE CREEK CIVIL WAR SITE:
One mile west of U.S. 69 and K-52 intersection, near Pleasanton. In the process of development. Phone 913/352-6174.

LINN COUNTY MUSEUM:
Dunlap Park, Pleasanton. 1990 population 1,231; 1970 1,216. Depicts county history — first Kansas lead mines, bullet-proof Blue Mound Bank tellers' cages, Civil War-era displays. Open Tuesday, Thursday, Saturday, and Sunday 1 to 5 p.m. Phone 913/352-8739.

TRADING POST: Six miles north of
Pleasanton on U.S. 69. Claims to be the oldest existing settlement in Kansas. Established 1825 by French

traders. A museum complex here has John Brown memorabilia and early Kansas items. Donations appreciated. Open Tuesday through Saturday 9 a.m. to 5 p.m., Sunday 1 to 5 p.m. Phone 913/352-6441.

MARAIS DES CYGNES MASSACRE PARK: From intersection of U.S. 69 and K-52 north of Trading Post go one mile north, then four miles east, follow markers. Site of the massacre of free-state men by pro-slavery ruffians in 1858. Small circa 1862 visitor center, excellent picnic and playground facilities. Brad Woellhof, curator, can tell you the story of turbulent "Bleeding Kansas." Open Tuesday through Saturday 10 a.m. to 5 p.m., Sunday 1 to 5 p.m. Phone 913/352-6174.

MARAIS DES CYGNES WILDLIFE AREA: North of Pleasanton on U.S. 69. Over 7,000 acres of water and woodlands for hunting, fishing, birding, and photographing. Call 913/352-8941 for information.

ALLEN COUNTY

In July of 1951 a flood devastated Allen County. For 10 days the Neosho River was out of its banks. It crested at 33 feet, four inches — 18-1/2 feet above flood stage — and flooded 165 county farms covering 21,646 acres of farmland. In Iola, 930 homes were affected.

IOLA

1990 population 6,351; 1970 6,493. For area accommodations or attractions information call Linda at 316/365-5252. The Greenery on U.S. 169 South and the China Palace at the junction of U.S. 169 and U.S. 54 are good places to eat. General Funston's boyhood home can be found several miles north of Iola on U.S. 169.

KING'S SANDWICH SHOP: 321 South State, Iola. Step up to the counter to order, then find a booth to sit in. You'll find Elvis or Marilyn Monroe staring at you from every corner of this 1950s hamburger joint. Squeaky clean. Picnic tables outside in the summer. Open Monday through Friday 10 a.m. to 8 p.m., Saturday 10 a.m. to 3 p.m. Phone 316/365-6271.

HAWK RURAL WESTERN WILDLIFE GALLERY: Inside Classy Attic, 20 West Jackson, Iola. Gary Hawk has received wide acclaim for his historical paintings of the Midwest. There's a story of rural culture in each painting. His prints are for sale, but you're welcome to just look. Open Monday through Saturday 9 a.m. to 5 p.m. Phone 316/365-5343.

ALLEN COUNTY MUSEUM AND OLD JAIL: 207 North Jefferson, Iola. County photographs and exhibits are on display here. The jail next to the museum was used for 90 years. Open May through October Tuesday through Sunday 1 to 4 p.m. Phone 316/365-3051.

IOLA COURTHOUSE SQUARE: Downtown Iola. Four square blocks make this the largest courthouse square in the U.S. Take a slow tour around the square and look at the original store fronts.

CLOCK AT COURTHOUSE SQUARE: South and Madison Avenue side of the square, Iola. Yes, this large clock keeps time! Look through a glass window and see the clockworks.

SHEPHERD-EVERETT PARK: Turn right just past Kentucky Fried Chicken on U.S. 169 North, Iola. Plenty of room to stretch your legs here amidst the trees and next to the

Neosho River. Lots of playground equipment and a 1937 WPA swimming pool.

RIVER VIEW: West side of Iola on U.S. 54. Turn off just west of this cement arch bridge for a riverside view. Imagine this river when it was eight feet out of it's banks in 1951.

HUMBOLDT

1990 population 2,178; 1970 2,249. Located about seven miles south of Iola on U.S. 169. The town was a favorite target of rebel raiders during the Civil War. Humboldt was also the boyhood home of Walter Johnson, Hall of Fame pitcher.

HUMBOLDT HISTORICAL MUSEUM: 416 North Second, Humboldt. Open Memorial Day to Labor Day weekends 2 to 5 p.m. Agricultural exhibits are featured at this local museum. Phone Harold at 316/431-7834.

STONE BRIDGE: A seven-arch stone bridge, built in the late 1800s, can be found five to six miles east of Humboldt on Tank Farm Road. Call Harold at 316/431-7834 for information.

PIQUA: Unincorporated. On U.S. 54 12 miles east of Yates Center. Buster Keaton, the king of silent films, was born in Piqua. A Buster Keaton museum is in the works. Saint Martin's Catholic Church was built in 1884. Phone Linda at 316/625-3235 for information.

NEOSHO FALLS: Located about six miles north of Piqua on a county road. 1990 population 157; 1970 184. Once the county seat, this town began its rapid decline in 1951 after the big flood of the Neosho River. Main Street is full of abandoned buildings, but people still live in Neosho Falls.

ROUND BARN: One-half mile north of Yates Center on U.S. 75.

KALIDA: One mile east and 1-1/4 miles south of Yates Center. Circa 1870 to 1875. Kalida vied with Yates Center to be the county seat in 1875, but when Yates Center won, the people of Kalida cut down trees from nearby creeks and moved their homes to Yates Center. Reminders are stone gates to the town, a structure paradoxically referred to by local folk as a castle or cave, shrubs, and flowers. Phone Linda at 316/625-3235 for information.

YATES CENTER

1990 population 1,815; 1970 1,967. For Woodson County area attractions information and accommodations call Linda at 316/625-3235.

FRANNIE'S: Main and Rutledge, Yates Center. Enter a side door on Rutledge. You'll have to go up a wide set of 31 steps and down the hall to get to Frannie's. The cafe has been nicely painted and wallpapered to complement the old wooden floors, high pressed tin ceilings, and antique oak tables. But the real stories are the food, the price, and Frannie's way of thinking. Frannie makes one special entree daily and it costs $1, no matter what it is. Her fabulous pies are another dollar and the drinks are free. When it's time to leave, you just deposit money in the cash register and get your own change if you need it. Some people don't think a dollar bill can buy much any more. Good thing Frannie doesn't think that way. Open Monday through Friday for lunch until around 5 p.m. Phone 316/625-2325.

STEINER'S SUNDRIES: 115 North State, Yates Center. This drug store and soda fountain date back to 1920. Just look for the green neon fountain light in the window and the red and white awning. The black marble counter cracked when an overweight traveling salesman rested both elbows on the counter! Ice cream sodas are made with real ice cream. Notice corner gargoyle on pressed tin ceiling. Phone 316/625-2704.

PIONEER HERITAGE MEMORIAL WALL AND GARDEN: North side of square, Yates Center. This is an attractive way to pay tribute to the heritage and people of the county. The tiles are made by Bill Linde. Anyone is welcome to buy a tile and have it engraved to add to the wall. Phone Bill at 316/625-2960.

COURTHOUSE SQUARE:
Downtown Yates Center. The entire courthouse square district was placed on the National Register of Historic Places in 1986. Most of the 41 buildings are brick Italianate or are made from sandstone. Go to the Chamber of Commerce, 108 South Main, for a brochure that will tell you the history of many buildings on the square.

WOODSON COUNTY COURTHOUSE: Downtown Yates Center. Completed in 1900, this Romanesque Revival building was designed by George Washburn. Inlaid into the red brick at the courthouse entrance is the biblical verse, "Do unto others as you would have them do unto you."

WOODSON COUNTY HISTORICAL MUSEUM: 208 West Mary (U.S. 54), Yates Center. Located in the first Yates Center church, this museum is full of interesting county exhibits including photos of all the one-room schoolhouses, farm implements, and rotating exhibits from the Kansas Museum of History. The Daniels walnut log cabin, built in 1855, is in the

museum complex. Open Memorial Day to Labor Day daily 10 a.m. to 4 p.m. Closed Thursday and Sunday. Phone Dorothy 316/625-2220 or Kenny 316/625-2929.

ANTIQUE AUTO MUSEUM:
Washington and State, Yates Center. A handful of cars have been superbly renovated. Phone Linda, 316/625-3235 or Bill, 316/625-2960 for an appointment.

HERITAGE PLACE ANTIQUES:
119 West Butler, Yates Center. Open Monday through Saturday 10 a.m. to 5 p.m. Phone 316/625-3212 or 625-3272.

COTTAGE CRAFTS COLLECTIBLES: 215 West Butler, Yates Center. Open Monday through Saturday 9 a.m. to 5 p.m. and Sunday 1 to 4 p.m. Phone 316/625-3649 or 625-2843.

AMERICAN ANTIQUES: Located in the pink Victorian house at U.S. 54 and State, Yates Center. Open daily 10 a.m. to 5 p.m. Closed Sunday. Tuesday by chance. Phone 316/625-2375.

GHOST FORTS: The ghost forts of Woodson County are dramatic reminders of the area's history. It's thought that Fort Belmont and Fort Row were established to protect settlers from rebel raiders during the "bleeding Kansas" days before the Civil War. Osage, Seminole, and Creek Indians went to the forts for provisions. A marker commemorating Fort Row can be found where the Verdigris River almost meets the county road just southeast of Coyville in Wilson County. For a personal tour of these fort sites and county ghost towns call Linda at 316/625-3235 or Bill at 316/625-2960.

THE OLD YATES CENTER LAKE:
One-quarter mile south of Yates

Center on U.S. 75, turn west at Twin Oaks, then go south at the next road. The original source of water for Yates Center was expanded as a WPA project in the 1930s. Gone dry recently, there are plans to refill it and develop a paddle boat area, fishing, and camping sites. Phone 316/625-3235 for information.

YATES CENTER RESERVOIR: Three miles west of Yates Center on U.S. 54, then two miles south. This lake supplies the city drinking water and is said to have the purest water in the nation. The fishing is also exceptionally good. Phone Linda at 316/625-3235.

WOODSON STATE FISHING LAKE: Also known as Feagan Lake. Seven miles west of Yates Center on U.S. 54, three miles south, then 1-1/2 miles east. Some of the best fishing anywhere can be had at this deep 179-acre lake.The drive around the lake will take you along the wooded Big Sandy River area. Hawks abound here. Legend has it that when Indian chiefs died they came back to the area as hawks. Phone Linda at 316/625-3235.

TORONTO RESERVOIR AND STATE PARK AND WILDLIFE AREA: Southwest corner of Woodson County. Located in the Verdigris River Valley, the reservoir and park are at the northernmost tip of the Chautauqua Hills geologic region. Camping, fishing, and swimming are available. This lake is especially good for sailing and windsurfing. To really appreciate the area, attend one of the daily park interpretive programs in the summer or call the park naturalist (316/637-2213) for wildflower tours. This area also has an unusually high number of rare birds. The Toronto Point Trail has a 1.5-mile hiking loop and a four-mile loop.

GARNETT

1990 population 3,210; 1970 3,169. For area accommodations and attractions information call the Chamber of Commerce, 913/448-6767.

THE WALKER ART COLLECTION: Garnett Public Library, 125 West Fourth, Garnett. A collection of 20th-century American paintings, sculpture, prints, and drawings including works by John Steuart Curry, Robert Henri, Arthur Davies, Walter Kuhn, and more. Call ahead for a guide to experience true art at an intimate level. Phone 913/448-3388.

GALEY'S DELI: Fourth and U.S. 59, Garnett. A most delightful deli serving lots of Land of Kansas Products. They are happy to furnish box lunches for tour groups. Have some Lost Trail Rootbeer and ask DeeDee Galey for travel information. Monday through Saturday 9:30 a.m. to 5 p.m. Phone 913/448-3804.

BURNS PHARMACY: 122 East Fifth, Garnett. It's another old-fashioned soda fountain! This one has a wooden back bar with mirrors. Open Monday through Saturday 8:30 a.m. to 5 p.m. Phone 913/448-6122.

KIRK HOUSE BED-AND-BREAKFAST: 145 West Fourth, Garnett. Kirk House, a Colonial-Revival style mansion built in 1913, will give you a taste of luxury: tiger-grain oak woodwork and 24-carat gold on the fireplace inside, elaborate gardens outside. Hosts Robert Cugno and Robert Logan revel in discussing art displayed in the house and in the Walker Gallery. Phone 913/448-5813.

HARRIS HOUSE: One block west of Kirk House. This fine example of Victorian architecture (1888) was the first house designed by famous courthouse architect George Washburn in Garnett, while the Kirk House was his last Garnett venture. Ask to see display in carriage house — buggy, sleigh, yeast machine, and more. Call Stanley More for tour at 913/448-6334.

ANDERSON COUNTY COURT-HOUSE: Town Square, Garnett. An example of Romanesque architecture by George Washburn. Circa 1902.

ANDERSON COUNTY HISTORI-CAL SOCIETY MUSEUM: Sixth and Maple, Garnett. Schoolrooms full of Anderson County exhibits. Unusual items are WPA craft projects — toy wagons, oil derrick, stagecoach, and more. Open Mother's Day to October, weekdays and Saturday 1 to 4 p.m. Call Dorothy at 913/867-2966 for information.

GOODIES: 121 East Fourth, Garnett. Antiques, antiques, antiques on three floors. If it's not here it probably never existed. For more stuff see the adjoining Frog Store. Open Monday through Saturday 10 a.m. to 5 p.m., Sunday 1 to 5 p.m. Call 913/448-6712 or 913/835-6572.

EMPORIUM ON THE SQUARE: 415 South Oak, Garnett. Antiques, art, collectibles — numerous artists and collectors represented. Open Monday through Saturday 10 a.m. to 5 p.m., Sunday 1 to 5 p.m. Phone 913/448-6459.

ANDERSON COUNTY SALE BARN: On U.S. 59, Garnett. Everything sells from cattle and sheep to shrubs, bulbs, pies, and breads — if it's produced in the county it's sold here on Tuesday. Phone 913/448-3811.

RV CAMP: Garnett. Electric and water hookups. Call the police department for location and permit. Phone 913/448-6823.

PITTSBURG

1990 population 17,775; 1970 20,171. Pittsburg, the home of Pittsburg State University, once had visions of becoming a great industrial center like its namesake, Pittsburgh, Pennsylvania. Call the Crawford County Convention and Visitors' Bureau for accommodations and attractions information, 316/231-1212.

CRAWFORD COUNTY HISTOR-ICAL MUSEUM: U.S. 69 bypass, enter frontage road at 20th Street, then north, Pittsburg. The perfect place to get a geographical and historical overview of this region. Donations appreciated. Open Wednesday through Sunday 1 to 5 p.m. Phone 316/231-1440.

HAROLD BELL WRIGHT HOME: 410 West Kansas, Pittsburg. Once the home of Harold Bell Wright, author of *Shepherd of the Hills* and a host of other best-selling early 20th-century novels. The home is in the process of restoration. Drive by viewing only.

MOSTLY BOOKS: 111 East Sixth, Pittsburg. A book lover's store where books are treasured for the spirit of the authors' words. Open Monday through Friday 10 a.m. to 6 p.m. Phone 316/231-0999.

MEMORIAL AUDITORIUM: Fifth and Pine, Pittsburg. Originally built as a shrine mosque in 1926. Today it is a state-of-the-art-convention center. The Memorial Art Gallery in the main lobby features major exhibits on a rotating basis as well as local art. Gallery is free. Open Monday through Friday 8 a.m. to 5 p.m. Phone 316/231-7827.

NONA'S RISTORANTE: 3105 North Broadway, Pittsburg. Fine Italian food. Open daily 11 a.m. to

8 p.m., closed Tuesday. Groups call for reservations at 316/235-1737.

JIM'S STEAK HOUSE: 1912 North Broadway, Pittsburg. Excellent steaks — and try the onion rings! Open daily 4:30 p.m. to 10 p.m., closed Sunday. Phone 316/231-5770.

OTTO'S CAFE: 711 North Broadway, Pittsburg. Start your day with breakfast at Otto's in the old Hotel Stilwell, where yesteryear the tycoons of industry met to plot. Open daily 6 a.m. to 8 p.m., Saturday 6 a.m. to 2 p.m. Closed Sunday. Phone 316/231-6110.

MINED LAND WILDLIFE AREAS

Crawford and Cherokee counties. More than 14,250 acres of land and water are scattered over 45 units. Obtain a map for reference at most information stops or write Mined Land Wildlife Area Office, Route 2, Box 929, Pittsburg, Kansas 66762, or call 316/231-3173.

Take the time to study the Mined Lands; the project is so large and complex it's hard to grasp at first. Included are over 200 lakes and thousands of acres of woodlands. Here is the story in a nutshell: Before being mined, the area was flat grassland. Huge mining shovels like Big Brutus dug down to the layers of coal, leaving deep pits with large piles of overburden on the sides. Today this land is overgrown with woody shrubs and oak-hickory forests. The fishing is excellent in the pits, and wildlife abounds in the woods. Access is free.

MINED LAND UNIT #6: West of Pittsburg. From the U.S 69 bypass go west on 20th street about two miles. Turn in to the south. The Mined Land Wildlife Area office is located here. Enjoy the winding roads and natural beauty.

MINED LAND UNIT #1: One mile north of Frontenac on U.S. 69. A good place to get the feel of the Mined Lands. Three miles of walking trail. In season watch for bluebirds, indigo buntings, warblers, and pileated woodpeckers. Mining was abandoned here in 1926.

FRONTENAC BAKERY: 211 North Crawford, Frontenac. 1990 population 2,588; 1970 2,223. Italian and French breads baked in large brick beehive ovens. Irene says the only thing changed here in 90 years is the price. Buy bread and, if you time it right, you might see the ovens. Open daily 8 a.m. to 4 p.m. Closed Tuesday and Saturday. Phone 316/231-7980.

BIG BRUTUS: Six miles west of K-7 and K-2 Junction, then 1/4 mile south, West Mineral. 1990 population 226; 1970 232. The stellar attraction of the region. This 11-million-pound, 160-foot-tall power coal shovel has been converted into a museum. It's almost impossible to exaggerate the size of this machine, which could lift 150 tons in one massive bite. Younger kids will enjoy exploring the "belly" of Big Brutus, and if you're older than 13 you can climb clear to the top! Admission fee. Open daily 9 a.m. to 5 p.m. Phone 316/827-6177.

JOSIE'S RISTORANTE: Main Street, Scammon (south of Pittsburg on K-7). The best in Italian food. Imagine how good the pasta must be to bring busloads of hearty eaters to this deserted Main Street. Open Wednesday through Saturday 5 to 9 p.m. Phone 316/479-8202. Scammon 1990 population 466; 1970 457.

COLUMBUS

1990 population 3,268; 1970 3,356. Pick up a driving tour brochure that shows historic homes and points of interest at the Chamber of Commerce office, 320 East Maple, and get to know Columbus. Phone 316/429-1492.

COUNTRY LOFT BED-AND-BREAKFAST: Two miles north of Columbus on K-7, then 2-1/4 miles east. This cozy restored barn provides one of the most delightful lodging experiences in Kansas. It's filled with antiques, quilts, and crafts, and the fireplace makes it great for wintertime getaways. Bedrooms are upstairs, bathroom downstairs. Call Mary or Marva at 316/674-3348.

COLUMBUS MUSEUM: Maple and Tennessee, Columbus. Advertised as a town within a museum. Open Tuesday through Friday 1 to 4 p.m., Saturday 10 a.m. to 4 p.m., and Sunday 2 to 4 p.m. Phone 316/429-2160.

MERIWETHER HOUSE BED-AND-BREAKFAST: 322 West Pine, Columbus. Enjoy a night in this lovingly restored cottage. Antiques, lace, and home decor items on display may be purchased. Phone 316/429-2812.

AGRICULTURE AND INDUSTRIAL TOURS: Columbus. Free one-hour tours to a turkey farm, a longhorn ranch, or a computer-forms manufacturer can be set up for groups of 15 or more. Call Columbus Chamber of Commerce for details, 316/429-1492.

CLAYTHORNE HUNTING LODGE: Nine miles west of Columbus on K-96 and two miles north. Fifty-bird sporting clay course, wobble trap, fishing, archery, lodging, food, and RV hookups. Open Wednesday, Saturday, and Sunday Phone 316/597-2568.

SPRING RIVER INN: K-66, Riverton (unincorporated). The atmosphere of an early-20th-century country club makes dining an elegant

pleasure. Features include a smorgasbord, cinnamon rolls, and squaw bread. Open daily 4:30 to 9 p.m., Sunday and holidays 11 a.m. to 8 p.m., closed Mondays. Phone 316/848-3645.

GALENA MUSEUM: On U.S. 66 two blocks west of the stop light, Galena. 1990 population 3,308; 1970 3,712. This restored depot is a treasure trove of railroad, mining, and labor history. Open Monday through Saturday 10 a.m. to noon, 2 to 4:30 p.m., Sunday 2:30 to 4:30 p.m. Phone 316/783-2192.

KANSAS OZARKS: South of Galena and east of Baxter Springs. Drive the highways and back roads here just to enjoy the scenic beauty of the Kansas Ozarks. Stop at Schermerhorn Park south of Galena to let the children play or to see Jesse James's cave hideout. West and north of Treece the landscape alternates among woodland splendor, oppressive poverty, and barren wastelands of mining vomit.

BAXTER SPRINGS

1990 population 4,351; 1970 4,489. For lodging and food information call the Chamber of Commerce, 316/856-3131.

BILKE'S WESTERN WEAR: 1041 Military Avenue, Baxter Springs. The smell of leather and the sight of saddles, boots, and cowboy hats makes this a fun store to stop at. Jim Bilke makes custom hats and does hat renovations, so bring in that old hat that needs fixed up! Make sure you ask Jim about his western museum upstairs. Open Monday through Saturday 9 a.m. to 6 p.m. Phone 316/856-5707.

BAXTER SPRINGS MUSEUM: Eighth and East Avenue, Baxter

Springs. Baxter Springs' rich and diverse history — Indian, bleeding Kansas, cow town, pioneer, and zinc mining — is skillfully displayed. Open 10:30 a.m. to 4:30 p.m. weekdays from May to mid-October. Sunday 1 to 4:30 p.m. Closed Mondays. Winter hours on Saturday and Sunday. Phone 316/856-2385 or 856-5708.

NATIONAL CEMETERY: West of Baxter Springs on U.S. 166. Federal troops massacred by the notorious Quantrill raiders are buried here.

CHETOPA

1990 population 1,357; 1970 1,596.

CARDEN PECAN COMPANY: Five miles east of Chetopa. What a nutty store! Driving along U.S. 166 you'll see groves of pecan trees. Observe harvesting and processing in November and December. This store sells all kinds of local products — nuts, sorghum syrup, honey, and gifts. Open weekdays 8 a.m. to 4:30 p.m., weekends 10 a.m. to 4:30 p.m. Phone 316/597-2661.

PADDLE FISH FISHING: Below the dam on the Neosho River, Chetopa. Paddle fish (or spoon-billed) fishing is a very rare sport. Snagging is permitted here from March 15 to May 15 for licensed fishers. Regulations require that you weigh your catch in at the nearby Johnson General Store located just west of the U.S. 166 Neosho River bridge. For information call Paula, 316/236-7430.

BUCKBOARD CAFE: Main Street, Chetopa. You can tell the food's going to be good at this full-menu restaurant when they serve real mashed potatoes. Open for breakfast, lunch, and dinner. Open daily. Closed Wednesday and Thursday. Phone 316/236-4295.

CONRAD'S TRADING POST: Junction of U.S. 166 and U.S. 59, Chetopa. Lots of antiques are well organized here. Four more antique stores on Chetopa's Main Street.

GOLDEN MILL SORGHUM: Two miles west of Bartlett on U.S. 166, then two miles south and 1/4 mile west. The Eck family produces and markets the golden syrup made from sorghum cane. October is when the cane is pressed and cooked. Call 316/226-3368 for a visit.

MOSLER RESORT: Hallowell (unincorporated). From Columbus go about eight miles west to Angelo's Grocery, then one mile north and 1/2 mile west. This is the place to stay while exploring Cherokee County, a place to get the feel of the land, woods, and lakes. Country cabins with air conditioning and RV hookups. Guided hunting. Call 316/597-2799 or write for brochure.

OSWEGO

1990 population 1,870; 1970 2,200.

OSWEGO RIVERSIDE PARK: Oswego. North on Oregon to the Neosho River. Scenic overlook is above the river where Osage Indians forded the Neosho. Fitness trail with exercise stations.

JOHN MATTHEWS SPRING WELL: Fourth and Union, Oswego. Matthews, a southern sympathizer, built the first settlement here in 1841. In 1861 Union Army Colonel James Blunt's troops killed Matthews and burned the settlement. Blunt's troops were later massacred by Quantrill's guerrilla forces near Baxter Springs.

PARSONS

1990 population 11,924; 1970 13,015. For lodging and food accommodations call the Chamber of Commerce, 316/421-6500.

PURPLE MARTIN CAPITAL:
Parsons. Parsons has gone all out in its war against insects. About 70 purple martin nests are located near Corning and 18th (near the museums), and 230 more nests are distributed across town. The martins usually arrive on March 17 and depart the first week in August. For information call Bill Brewer, 316/421-9011.

IRON HORSE MUSEUM:
Eighteenth and Corning, Parsons. A reproduction of a typical Katy (Missouri, Kansas and Texas Railway) railroad depot. The depot houses an extraordinary collection of Katy artifacts including silver, china, and oil paintings from the dining cars . The outdoor display features a 1946 yardage diesel, the first diesel purchased by the line. Donation optional. Open May through October Friday, Saturday, and Sunday afternoons. Call Maynard Harding for details, 316/421-1959.

PARSONS HISTORICAL SOCIETY MUSEUM: 401 South Eighteenth, Parsons. This museum displays furniture, clothing, tools, and pictures of early Parsonians. Donations appreciated. Open May through October Friday, Saturday, and Sunday afternoons. Phone 316/421-6500.

SAINT PAUL/OSAGE MISSION: East side of Saint Paul on K-57. The story of this Catholic community intertwines with the history of displaced Osage Indians. Local men quarried stone for nine years to build the present church, Saint Francis. Go in and pick up brochures that tell the story. Saint Paul 1990 population 687; 1970 804.

SAINT ALOYSIUS: Eight miles west of Girard at the former townsite of Greenbush. A bittersweet story awaits you here. A beautiful church, built in 1881 and refurbished a hundred years later, serves parishioners now; less than a hundred yards away lie the ruins of a once-magnificent edifice built in 1907.

GIRARD

The town bills itself as the printing capital of the world. In 1913 The Appeal To Reason, *a Socialist newspaper published in Girard, had the largest circulation in the world at 750,000. The paper advocated reforms such as the eight-hour day and child-labor laws. Call the Chamber for a drive-by tour guide of historic landmarks, 316/724-4715. Girard 1990 population 2,794; 1970 2,591.*

LARGEST FLAG IN KANSAS:
Just east of Girard on K-57. Flag is 30 by 60 feet and flies at 108 feet. Erected by American Legion Post #26.

CRAWFORD STATE PARK:
Girard, nine miles north on K-7, then one mile east. Truly one of the most beautiful of Kansas state parks, especially in spring when the many redbuds bloom. Swimming beach, lovely picnic areas, electrical hookups, dump station, limited boating. Good food at Geier's Marina. State permits required. Phone 316/362-3671.

WINFIELD

1990 population 11,931; 1970 11,405. For additional information about lodging, restaurants, or area attractions call Cathy Gage at the Winfield Convention and Visitors' Bureau, 316/221-5500. Winfield is home to the annual Walnut Valley Bluegrass Festival.

HIATT'S RESTAURANT: 508 West Ninth, Winfield. A fine restaurant that reflects the grand style of 19th-century cattle barons. Lunch and dinner Wednesday through Friday, Saturday dinner only, and Sunday lunch only. Call 316/221-7101 for reservations.

IRON GATE INN BED-AND-BREAKFAST: 1203 East Ninth, Winfield. An 1885 Victorian home that's preferred lodging for many traveling executives. A hand-carved walnut staircase, imported handmade parquet floors, and Italian tile fireplaces augment the feeling of luxury here. Call Donna or Larry for reservations. Phone 316/221-7202.

COWLEY COUNTY HISTORICAL MUSEUM: 1011 Mansfield, Winfield. Everything from a mint-condition V-12 American LaFrance fire truck and excellent agricultural tools to looms, a spinning wheel, dolls, and an early soda fountain complete with ornate back bar. Open Saturday and Sunday 2 to 5 p.m. For an appointment call Jeanette at 316/221-3864.

VIETNAM WAR MEMORIAL: East of the courthouse on Ninth, Winfield. A replica of the Washington, D.C., Vietnam Memorial. Engraved on the memorial are the names of 759 Kansans who were killed or missing in action in Vietnam.

JENNY'S TREASURES: 919 Manning, Winfield. Collectibles, antiques, and gifts. Open daily 11 a.m. to 5 p.m., closed Friday and Sunday. Phone 316/221-9199.

CRAYOLA PRODUCT TOURS: 2000 Liquitex Lane (20 blocks east of Main on Nineteenth), Winfield. An exciting tour of the Binney and Smith Crayola factory. Reservations must be made one year in advance. Call 316/221-4200 for tour regulations.

LITTLE HOOKER BAIT SHOP: Six miles east of Winfield on U.S. 160, five miles north on Cowley 1, then three miles east. You might call the style here modern rustic. Mouth-watering barbecue food, clean, casual atmosphere, and a drive through the Flint Hills make this a fun experience. Open Tuesday through Saturday 6 a.m. to 8 p.m., Sunday 6 a.m to 7 p.m. Phone 316/438-2806.

ARKANSAS CITY

1990 population 12,762; 1970 13,216. For additional information about accommodations in Arkansas City call 316/442-0230.

CHEROKEE STRIP MUSEUM: Near state line on U.S. 77. As you walk around the museum think about these wagons moving at breakneck speed vying for a choice land claim. Interesting exhibits and newspaper accounts. Open Tuesday through Saturday 10 a.m. to 4 p.m. and Sunday 1 to 4 p.m. Admission fee. Phone 316/442-6750 for information about historical dinner theater productions at the museum.

BRYANT HARDWARE AND COLLECTIBLES: 104 South Summit, Arkansas City. This red brick building with the old-fashioned street lamps out front is even more nostalgic inside.

OTIS SCOTT MUSEUM: South Summit, Arkansas City. This fascinating private collection of early Arkansas City is displayed in a unique setting. Tours by appointment. Phone 316/442-1076.

WINDOW MURAL PROJECTS: 316-324 South Summit, Arkansas

City. If you aren't alert you'll miss the second-story window panels painted with pre-1900 Arkansas City scenes. This is a joint project of the Chamber of Commerce and Cowley County Community College.

STAN HERD MURAL: 100 block of North Summit, Arkansas City. This 1984 mural depicts the Cherokee Strip Land Rush.

J.S. GALLERY: 3413 North Summit, Arkansas City. Local artists display their watercolor and oil paintings, woodcarving, pottery, and china. Available for sale or for viewing. Call next door to Jean at 316/442-5464 and she'll come open the gallery.

NATIONAL HISTORIC SITE: Second and Central, Arkansas City. Vermillion pigment was poured in the mortar of this 1890 high school to accentuate the beauty of the limestone, but the pigment wasn't weatherproof. Rains have given the stone a crimson tint.

GARDEN GATE WOOD-WORKS: 211 East Chestnut, Arkansas City. Watch furniture being built and an artist painting in the shop where Walter Beech got his start.

CONEY ISLAND: 200 South Summit, Arkansas City. Great place for short-order foods and a cold drink like a Blue Moon. Open daily 10:30 a.m. to 7 p.m., closed Sunday. Phone 316/442-2533.

GREEN DOOR LA FAMILIA: 714 West Madison, Arkansas City. Good Mexcian food. Open Tuesday through Saturday for lunch and supper. Phone 316/442-1685.

CHAPLIN NATURE CENTER: Three miles west of Arkansas City on U.S. 166. Kids will love touching nests, eggs, feathers, and animal skulls in the information center. Five miles of walking trails offer adventure through thick woodlands and over footbridges. Keep on the lookout for lizards, deer, wild turkeys, and a great variety of birds . Visitor Center open Tuesday through Saturday 9 a.m. to 5 p.m., Sunday 1 to 5 p.m. Trails open daily. Phone 316/442-4133 or 442-7227.

POST MUSICAL HOMESTEAD: On U.S. 166, southwest of Geuda Springs. 1990 population 219; 1970 223. Enjoy a musical tour of the 100-year-old Post homestead. Bill Post, an internationally known songwriter and composer of the Kansas state march, "Here's Kansas," takes you through the barn, granary, and house and sings his songs in front of murals and fiberglass animals that make his family's history come alive. Bill's wife, Orvaleen, leads the chapel tour and gives a short message of inspiration. Tours available in the spring and fall. Fee. Phone 316/442-4336 for reservations.

HENRY'S CANDIES: North of Dexter. 1990 population 320; 1970 286. They make candy here. Watch it being made or buy some! Open seven days a week. Phone 316/876-5423.

WEE KIRK OF THE VALLEY: From small sign just west of Cedar Vale on U.S. 166, three miles south, one mile west, three miles south, and 1/4 mile west. 1990 population 760; 1970 665. A stepladder helps you over the fence. Be careful of cow patties as you make your way through the pasture to this tiny chapel. This peaceful memorial seats 12 and is always open. Hymns play when you close the door.

SEDAN

At junction of U.S. 166 and K-99. This charming little town of 1,300 people (1970 population 1,555) has made a remarkable comeback in the last ten years. Twelve new businesses have opened, most of them catering to the tourist trade. One of the town's claims to fame is the Yellow Brick Road. You can buy a brick in this legendary sidewalk and have your name (or someone else's) engraved on it. Call Nita Jones at 316/725-5797 to become part of Sedan's Yellow Brick Road.

TORNADO ALLEY: Munchkin Mall on Main Street, Sedan. You might just run into the Tin Man, the Scarecrow, or the Cowardly Lion on your way to the Yellow Brick Road Castle. Open Monday through Saturday 10 a.m. to 4 p.m. Phone 1-800/892-1355.

EMMETT KELLY MUSEUM: Old Opera House, Main Street, Sedan. Remember Weary Willie, the clown? Well, he was born in Sedan in 1898 and his memory lives on here. Free. May through October daily 9 a.m. to noon and 1 to 5 p.m., Sunday 1 to 4 p.m. Phone 316/725-3470.

CHAUTAUQUA HILLS JELLY COMPANY: 125 East Main, Sedan. Watch jelly being made while you have a tornado malt at an authentic 100-year-old soda fountain. The delicious jams and jellies are for sale here. Open Monday through Saturday from 10 a.m. to 5 p.m. Phone 1-800/637-4101.

MRS. BURDEN'S CANDY COMPANY: 112 West Main, Sedan. Oh, that delicious candy. Watch it being made. Gift shop, too. Monday through Friday 9 a.m. to 4 p.m. Saturday gift shop only. Phone 316/725-3500.

OLD BATH ANTIQUES: 161 East Main, Sedan. Featuring an English Tea Room and a select assortment of antiques. Open Wednesday through Saturday 10 a.m. to 5 p.m. Phone 316/725-3130.

HARMON HOUSE RESTAURANT: 105 North Hooper, Sedan. Dine in a refurbished old house. Buses welcome. Open Tuesday through Saturday 11 a .m. to 8 p.m., Sunday 11 a.m. to 3 p.m. Phone 316/725-5355.

MARGARET'S CAFE: Downtown Elgin. 1990 population 118; 1970 115. The trek to this border town will take you on unpaved roads west from K-99. Unless there are pickups in front of Margaret's Cafe it may appear to be closed. Look closer and step inside for Margaret' s delicious food. She makes two entrees a day and serves until it's gone. She'll pack your plate with numerous items. Serving hours usually start at 11 a.m. Monday through Saturday. Phone 316/346-2213.

ELK FALLS

1990 population 122; 1970 124. This little town on U.S. 160 is proof of what can happen when a group of enthusiastic people combine their talents and energies. Elk Falls is fast gaining a reputation as one of the most unique towns to visit in the state. The last surviving frame building in Elk Falls is in progress of being turned into a visitor center.

SUNDAY-AT-THE-FALLS: Every Sunday afternoon from May through October Elk Falls puts out the welcome mat. Phone 316/329-4433.

THE SECRET GARDEN AND PATH OF WISDOM: Southwest corner of Elk Falls. A beautiful flower garden has softened charred ruins and represents the spirit of the people in this little town. Sayings from the Bible, Gilbert and Sullivan, and Shakespeare add to the spiritual feeling here. Continue beyond the flower garden to the Path of Wisdom. Look among the trees and vegetation to find verse and sayings scrawled on barn wood. At its best mid-May through October. Donations appreciated.

ELK FALLS POTTERY: East side of Elk Falls. This is a popular stop in Elk Falls for pottery enthusiasts and anyone who wants to take a souvenir home. Porcelain pins are made from traditional quilt patterns. Steve and Jane Fry use native Kansas clays to make their traditional and functional pottery. This is a good place to ask questions about Elk Falls attractions. Usually open daily all year. Closed Sundays and holidays. Phone 316/329-4425.

THE SAWMILL: Elk Falls. Follow the redwood chip trail (Ye Olde Cow Path) south of the 1880 Little White Church. Wayne loves to demonstrate the gang saw, lineshaft equipment, and planer. He lets you get so close you almost feel like you're doing it yourself. The smell of the wood chips, the seldom-seen sights around you, and, on Sunday, a nearby blacksmithy bring thoughts of a simpler life. Get refreshment at the rustic canteen and step inside the gift shop. Demonstrations on Sunday from 2 to 5 p.m. Memorial Day weekend until frost. Weekday hours are variable. Phone 316/329-4445.

VILLAGE VARIETY THEATRE: Downtown Elk Falls. The old-fashioned wooden chairs (complete with hat rack underneath the seats) and the homemade stage provide a great atmosphere in this narrow building. The vaudeville shows most often include music, magic, and a puppet show for all ages. The star of the show is Barry McGuire, a retired Hollywood actor. Fun! Every Sunday at 3 p.m. May through October. Special performances for tour groups. Admission fee. Phone 316/329-4433.

1893 IRON TRUSS BRIDGE AND FALLS: Northeast corner of Elk Falls. Only foot traffic allowed over this old bridge, so make your way out to the middle for a great view of the natural falls and the Elk River. Listed on National Register of Historic Places.

LITTLE WHITE CHURCH: Elk Falls. This church was built in 1880 and is presently being used by the United Methodists. It has been modernized somewhat, but it's always open, so feel free to go in and find some peace.

THE SHERMAN HOUSE RESTAURANT: Northwest side of Elk Falls. Imagine that you just stepped off the train in the 19th century and into this railway restaurant for a meal. Roy wasn't serving his famous barbecue back then, so you get a bonus for living in the 20th century. The building has been moved about a half-mile from its original site and restored in period style. Jane and Steve Fry's pottery throughout the building is a pleasing touch. Open Friday and Saturday from 5 to 8:30 p.m. Phone 316/329-4320.

CAPE COD BAKERY AND COFFEE SHOP: Downtown Elk Falls. Anyone who knows Rebeka knows she can cook and bake up a storm. Doughnuts and bakery items daily, family-style dinner on Sunday. Open Tuesday through Saturday 5 a.m. to noon, Sunday 5 a.m. to 3 p.m. Phone 316/329-4379.

SUNNY LANE CAFE: Elk Falls. This concession is open daily 11:30 a.m. to 8 p.m. for take-out sandwiches, barbecue, smoked turkey and ham, and Mexican food. Picnic table nearby.

TIFFANY'S GALLERY: One block east of Main, Elk Falls. Fine crafts, antiques, and collectibles. Open Friday through Monday 9 a.m. to 5 p.m.

PRUDENCE CRANDALL STATE HISTORICAL MARKER: West side of Elk Falls on U.S. 160. This new historical marker commemorates a courageous woman who established a boarding school for black girls in Connecticut in the 1830s. She lived in Elk Falls from 1874 till her death in 1890 and is buried in the local cemetery north of the highway.

OAK VALLEY PUMP: U.S. 160. Once you've found this pump, you've found the center of Oak Valley (unincorporated)!

H O W A R D

The county seat of Elk County, which has lost population in every census but one since 1890. The county's population in 1890 was 12,216, in 1990 it was 3,327. There's a poignant beauty on Howard's crumbling Main Street. Howard population 815; 1970 918.

BENSON MUSEUM: Downtown Howard. See county exhibits here and antique farm implements at the Gragg Museum May through October Wednesday and Friday 2 to 4 p.m. Phone 316/374-2142. Stop at Batson's Drug Store downtown for a soda fountain treat.

JERRY'S LITTLE OPRY: South Wabash, Howard. Folks from all over the county get together for this foot-stompin' music bash. Bring finger foods and your family, if you'd like. The fun starts at 7 p.m. every Thursday except holidays. It's not

over until everyone goes home! Free. Phone 316/374-2142 or 374-2012.

MOLINE SWINGING BRIDGE: One block west of Main Street on the river, Moline. 1990 population 473; 1970 555. A picturesque photo combo — a suspended footbridge and a little natural waterfall.

GRENOLA MUSEUM: Old elevator along the railroad tracks just east of Main Street, Grenola. 1990 population 256; 1970 290. An early grain elevator complete with lift and all other working mechanisms. The aroma of the grain and heavy timbers still lingers. Rural artifacts displayed. Open Saturday and Sunday 2 to 5 p.m. or by appointment. Call Shirley, 316/358-2570 or Dorothy, 316/358-3241.

GRENOLA SENIOR CENTER: Downtown Grenola. Retirees: Call a day in advance for a delightful lunch with the Grenola seniors. Call Wanda Lodgson, 316/358-3601.

STOCKMEN'S CAFE: U.S. 160, Cambridge. 1990 population 74; 1970 110. An original, as-it-was, Flint Hills cowboy cafe. Open Monday through Friday 6 a.m. to 8 p.m. On Saturday and Sunday they close at noon. Call for information about their twice-a-month mountain oyster party, 316/467-2481.

SOUTHWEST KANSAS

DODGE CITY SECTION: Ashland, Bucklin, Cimarron, Dodge City, Fort Dodge, Ingalls, Jetmore, Kingsdown, Offerle, Sitka, Windhorst. *Page 149 to 153.*

GARDEN CITY SECTION: Alexander, Coolidge, Dighton, Garden City, Kendall, Lakin, Leoti, Ness City, Scott City, Syracuse, Tribune. *Page 153 to 159.*

LIBERAL SECTION: Copeland, Elkhart, Hickock, Fowler, Hugoton, Johnson City, Liberal, Manter, Meade, Montezuma, Plains, Ryus, Satanta, Sublette, Tice, Ulysses. *Page 159 to 166.*

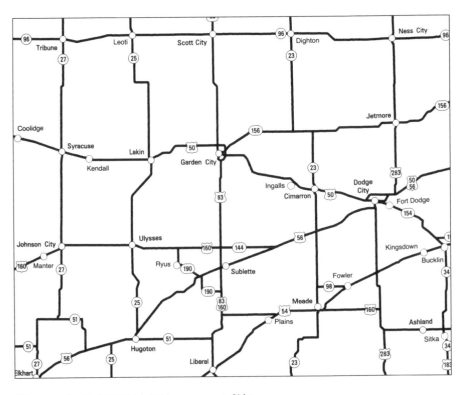

Photo opposite side: Old Weigh Station restaurant, Sitka

Southwest Kansas has changed dramatically in the last thirty years. Green fields of irrigated corn, feed lots, and packing plants on a scale that can be described only with superlatives have defeated the Great American Desert and the 1930s Dust Bowl. Clearly natural gas production, irrigation, and meat packing drive the economy here. One farmer has described the ideal farm as having an irrigation well in the middle of each quarter section and a gas well on each forty acres.

Few trees or farmsteads catch your eye as you travel here. Instead white grain elevators, marking small towns, appear along the line between land and sky. Only from an airplane can you see the geometric pattern of irrigation circles, generally one-half mile in diameter.

Nothing is merely large here. Things are huge, enormous, colossal. Mighty Samson, the railroad bridge over the Cimarron River, typifies the measure of things in southwest Kansas. The circle of the horizon about you is vast, the gas field is the worlds's largest, the feedlots and packing plant statistics are beyond comprehension, steaks are larger than platters, and ambitions reach into outer space.

The National Grasslands near Elkhart attest to the fact that sod breakers once were too ambitious with the plow, but the resulting Dust Bowl of the 1930s was bigger than big also, and the measures taken to overcome Dust Bowl conditions were even greater.

Leave your Hollywood image of the West and Dodge City behind as you travel here and discover that reality is truly grander than a video screen.

DODGE CITY

1990 population 21,129; 1970 14,127. For additional information on lodging, restaurants, and area attractions call 316/225-8186.

CARNEGIE CENTER FOR THE ARTS: 701 Second, Dodge City. This town has more to offer than Wild West history. The stained glass and roomy feel of the Carnegie library offer a wonderful background for changing exhibits, which include some traveling national exhibits. Open June, July, and August Tuesday through Friday 10 a.m. to 5 p.m., Saturday 10 a.m. to 3 p.m. Free. Phone 316/225-6388.

STAN HERD MURAL: Second and West Spruce, Dodge City, on the side of the First National Bank building. The stagecoach in this mural is flying furiously down a hill and was fashioned after Frederic Remington's painting *The Old Stagecoach of the Plains.* Another Stan Herd mural can be seen on the Hy-Plains Beef Packing Plant on East Trail.

EL CAPITAN: Wyatt Earp Boulevard and Second, Dodge City. This sculpture commemorates the cattle

El Capitan, Dodge City

drives of the 1870s that made Dodge City famous.

STATUES: Fourth and Spruce in front of the Chamber of Commerce office, Dodge City. It's worth a stop to read these poignant inscriptions for the cowboy and oxen sculptures.

WALKING/DRIVING TOUR BROCHURE: An area-wide historical brochure is available at the Dodge City Convention and Visitors' Bureau (Fourth and Spruce, Dodge City) and the Dodge City Visitors' Center. Buy or rent accompanying tape cassette for background on 1870s and 1880s area history. Phone Nancy Jo at 316/225-8186 for more information.

THE HOME OF STONE: 112 East Vine, Dodge City. This three-story limestone home was built in 1881. Guided tours are offered during the summer daily 9 a.m. to 6 p.m. and Sunday afternoon. Phone 316/227-6791.

WINTER LIVESTOCK SALE BARN: East Trail, Dodge City. This weekly livestock auction is one of the nation's largest. Every Wednesday starting at 8 a.m. Phone 316/225-4159.

KANSAS TEACHERS' HALL OF FAME: 603 Fifth, Dodge City. Yesterday's and today's teachers are recognized here. Nick Schmidt, inducted in 1988, was this author's seventh grade teacher. Free. Summer hours are daily 8 a.m. to 8 p.m., rest of the year 11 a.m. to 3 p.m., Sundays 1 to 5 p.m. Call to check hours. Phone 316/225-7311.

BOOT HILL MUSEUM: Front Street, Dodge City. During the summer season, tour reconstructed 1870s buildings at your own pace. See medicine shows and gunfights, take stagecoach rides, and enjoy a chuckwagon dinner. There's a Long Branch Variety

Show each evening at 7:30 p.m. A restaurant and ice cream parlor are on the grounds. Guided tours are available in the winter. Call for times at 316/227-8188. Admission fee. Open in the summer daily 8 a.m. to 8 p.m., winter 9 a.m. to 5 p.m. September through May Sunday 1 to 5 p.m.

DODGE CITY ZOO: From Wyatt Earp Boulevard turn south on Fourth until you reach Wright Park. This small zoo is a great place to stretch your legs and meander past the timber wolf, black bear, mountain lion, buffalo, longhorn steers, and more. Free. Miniature golf course located beside zoo. Open daily 8 a.m. to 5 p.m.

DCF&B RAILROAD: 818 South Second, Dodge City. Train rides. Admission fee. Phone 316/225-3232.

EL CHARRO: 1209 West Wyatt Earp, Dodge City. Excellent Mexican food. Open daily for lunch and supper. Closed Sunday. Phone 316/225-0371.

WATERSPORTS CAMPGROUND: East Cherry, Dodge City. This campground has a lake with paddleboards and water bykes. Showers, laundry. Phone 316/225-9325 or 225-9003.

SCENIC OVERLOOK: East of Dodge City on U.S. 50 an observation point overlooks one of the largest area feedyards. A historical marker tells about Dodge City the cowtown. Nearby Excel Corporation processes 5,500 head of cattle daily.

FORT DODGE

FORT DODGE LIBRARY-MUSEUM: Fort Dodge, K-154 east of Dodge City. From the grocery store on K-154, turn south. At the third corner turn west. Fort Dodge was established in 1865 to protect Santa Fe Trail travelers. Today it's a home for veterans. Open daily in the summertime 10 a.m. to 4 p.m. The rest of the year it's open daily 1 to 4 p.m. Free. Phone 316/227-2121.

FORT DODGE GROCERY: East side of town on K-154. This small store tells part of the story of Fort Dodge life and is on the site of the original fort supply store. Open Monday through Friday 8:30 a.m. to 4:30 p.m. and Saturday 8:30 to 11:30 a.m.

FORT DODGE CEMETERY: North of K-154 just east of Fort Dodge. Soldiers and their spouses from the Civil War to the Korean War are buried here. Phone 316/227-2121.

CORONADO'S CROSS: 1-1/2 miles east of Fort Dodge on K-154. This memorial is the site of the first Christian service held west of the Mississippi River. Franciscan friar Juan de Padilla, a member of Coronado's 1541 expedition, led the service.

BUCKLIN

1990 population 710; 1970 777.

BURTON FLORAL AND GIFTS AND JC'S DELI: 107 North Main, Bucklin. Order sandwiches, home-made cinnamon rolls, or frozen yogurt in this little deli among the plants and gift shop. Jean and Chuck are delightful to visit with. Open Monday through Friday 8 a.m. to 5 p.m. and Saturday 9 a.m. to 3 p.m. Phone 316/826-3661.

FERRIN HARDWARE: Main Street, Bucklin. It looks a bit modernized when you first step into this store, but observe carefully and you'll see original wall cabinets, old-fashioned turntables with drawers full of nuts and screws, and a ladder that moves across the store. Open Monday through Saturday 8:30 a.m. to 5 p.m., closed for the noon hour.

MURAL: Oak and Main, Bucklin. At the intersection behind the depot you can see a scene from the town's early days.

KINGSDOWN: On U.S. 54 seven miles west of Bucklin. This dying town is a relic of the early 1900s.

ASHLAND

1990 population 1,032; 1970 1,244. A soda fountain can be found at Milligan's Pharmacy, downtown Ashland.

PIONEER MUSEUM AND HAROLD KRIER FIELD AEROBATIC MUSEUM: On U.S. 160, Ashland. An outstanding museum judiciously displaying airplanes, chuck wagons, barbed wire, cast-iron seats, pioneer stores, and more. Open daily 1 to 5 p.m. Donations appreciated. For group tours and information call Floretta Rogers, 316/635-2227.

WALLINGFORD INN BED-AND-BREAKFAST: 519 Maple, Ashland. Experience the lavish surroundings of an early 1900s grain baron in this large Victorian home. Enjoy the historical furnishings, formal dining room, and lovely English garden. Call Susan and Aaron for reservations. Phone 316/635-2129.

THE SLATON HOUSE BED-AND-BREAKFAST: 319 West Seventh, Ashland. A nice contemporary home for a pleasant night in Ashland. Phone 316/635-2290.

HARDESTY HOUSE: 712 Main, Ashland. An old-fashioned hotel from the early 1900s. Some rooms are furnished in antiques from the headboard to the bathtub. Lunch served to the public in a spacious dining hall Tuesday through Friday 11 a.m. to 1 p.m., Sunday 11:30 a.m. to 1:30 p.m. Open as a dinner club Tuesday through Saturday evenings 5 to 9 p.m. Phone 316/635-4040.

BIG BASIN AND SAINT JACOB'S WELL: West of Ashland 12 miles on U.S. 160, then about three miles north on U.S. 283. Look for a historical marker and signs leading to Big Basin. Keep your eyes open for buffalo roaming freely in this vast land. Follow the signs to Saint Jacob's Well. After checking for the whereabouts of the buffalo, take the path down to the well. A bench is provided at the legendary water for relaxation.

CLARK COUNTY LAKE: South of Kingdown on K-94 or north of Ashland on unpaved road. The water of this picturesque lake looks especially blue against the white rocks and lush flora.

MOUNT JESUS: 1-1/4 miles east of Ashland on U.S. 160, then seven miles north on winding dirt road. Undulating blue-green hills provide spectacular vistas on the way. The destination is anticlimactic — a high promontory with a cross on it. Note working windmills in the pastures.

OLD WEIGH STATION: Sitka. Turn west on K-34 from U.S. 160 for one mile. Look for the lone building near the railroad tracks. The romantic Old West comes alive when you take a look across the flat prairie, then stomp across the wooden porch to enter a room with guns, cast-iron tractor seats, harnesses, and old tools hanging above the wainscoting. The aroma of hamburgers spreads across the room from the open grill. You'll find the menu written on the chalkboard and blue-checkered tablecloths softening this rustic cafe. Open daily 5 a.m. to 10 p.m., closed Sunday. Phone 316/635-2671.

CIMARRON

1990 population 1,626; 1970 1,373.

SANTA FE TRAIL MARKER AND TRACKS: Between Dodge City and Cimarron on U.S. 50, just one mile west of Howell or nine miles west of Dodge City. Go through the turnstile and up to the markers that show where the ruts are. Look out to the west and imagine yourself a pioneer viewing that hilly horizon, seeing tall prairie grasses, and wondering what lay ahead. This site is on the national register.

KANSAS WHEAT HOUSE: 102 South Main, Cimarron. This is the home of wheat nubs! They're seasoned for all tastes — cajun, honey roasted, ranch — or made into yogurt clusters. If your timing is right you may get to see the wheat kernels being cooked and deep-fried. Other Kansas products available here. Open Monday through Friday 9 a.m. to 5:30 p.m., Saturday 8 a.m. to noon. Phone 316/855-3489.

CLARK PHARMACY: 101 South Main, Cimarron. Stop here for a soda fountain treat. Lots of folks do. No back bar but they've got the marble counter, foot rail, swivel seats, and ceramic tile front. Open 8:30 a.m. to 6 p.m. Monday through Friday, Saturday 9 a.m. to 5 p.m. Phone 316/855-2242.

CIMARRON HOTEL BED-AND-BREAKFAST: 203 North Main, Cimarron. This three-story red brick building is on the national register. The wide hallway on the second floor takes you to your individually decorated room. Shared baths. Breakfast area is a cozy place with plants, dried flowers, bookshelves, and a cat. Great house for whodunit weekends. Roast beef and chicken are served to the public Sunday 11 a.m. to 2 p.m. Phone 316/855-2244.

CIMARRON CROSSING PARK: Head south out of Cimarron on K-23. The park is just before the Arkansas River bridge. This grassy area with lots of shade trees is a great place for a picnic. Playground equipment here, too, and a historical marker telling about the Cimarron route of the Santa Fe Trail.

SANTA FE TRAIL MUSEUM: Downtown Ingalls. 1990 population 301; 1970 235. D.A.R. markers outside the museum and in the park relate Santa Fe Trail information. Museum displays tell about Gray County history, including the construction of the Soule Canal. The old Montezuma and Ingalls depots are used as museum buildings. Open daily May through October 9 to 11 a.m. and 1 to 4 p.m. Free. Closed Sunday. Phone Jean at 316/335-5451.

JETMORE

1990 population 850; 1970 936.

HAUN MUSEUM: Downtown Jetmore. See these county exhibits housed in the first building in Jetmore. It adjoins the first public school building. Open Wednesday and Saturday 10 a.m. to 5 p.m., Sunday 1 to 5 p.m. Free. Phone 316/357-8344.

MURAL: Across from the museum, one side of the lumber company, Jetmore. A local Point of Rocks scene was painted by the 1982 Jetmore High School art class. Explore side roads around Jetmore that will take you into the rolling hills and limestone bluffs.

WINDHORST: On U.S. 50/56 between Bellefont and Offerle watch

for the Windhorst sign. Turn north there, go three miles, then follow paved road to spire. It's seven miles from U.S. 50/56. All that's left of Windhorst is the Immaculate Heart of Mary Church. You can see the spire from miles away.

MURAL: Offerle. Slow down and note the mural on the east side of the Offerle Cafe. 1990 population 228; 1970 212.

GEOLOGICAL REGION CHANGE: Going east from Offerle, you'll notice that the countryside changes from the cattle country of the High Plains region to the sand hills of the Arkansas River Lowland.

GARDEN CITY

1990 population 24,097; 1970 14,790; 1900 1,544. The city was named after the beautiful flower gardens of the wife of city founder W.D. Fulton. The cattle industry dominates in Garden City, where there are some of the largest feedyards and processing plants in the world. For more information about lodging, restaurants, or attractions in this culturally diverse city call the Finney County Convention and Visitors' Bureau, 316/276-3264. Ask for a Finney County driving and walking tour guide.

LEE RICHARDSON ZOO: South Fourth in Finnup Park, Garden City. Ranked as the sixth most visited Kansas attraction, this zoo is home to more than 300 mammals and birds from South America, Africa, Australia, and North America. A "Wild Asia" exhibit is being developed. Make sure you spend some time in the aviary and watch for elephant demonstrations at 11 a.m. and 2 p.m. in warm weather. Open 8 a.m. until 1/2 hour before sunset. December through February open 8 a.m.

to 4:30 p.m. Drive through for $1, pedestrians free. Phone 316/276-6243 for group educational programs.

FINNEY COUNTY MUSEUM: South Fourth in Finnup Park, Garden City. County history comes alive with these revolving exhibits. There's a permanent exhibit on the history of the cattle industry in the area. Open daily June through August 10 a.m. to 5 p.m., September through May 1 to 5 p.m. Free. Phone 316/272-3664.

FINNUP PARK: South Fourth, Garden City. This 110-acre park is home to the world's largest free swimming pool. Among the shade trees find picnic areas, horseshoe pits, and tennis courts.

FINNEY COUNTY COURT-HOUSE: 500 block North Eighth, Garden City. This classical-styled courthouse was completed in 1929. Note the art deco detailing on the exterior.

C.J. BUFFALO JONES STATUE: In front of courthouse, Garden City. Buffalo Jones was one of the town founders and is credited with helping preserve the American bison. He was the first game warden in Yellowstone.

WINDSOR HOTEL: Main and Pine, Garden City. As you drive by, take a good look at this four-story hotel built in 1887. It was sometimes referred to as the Waldorf of the Prairies. It's listed on the National Register of Historic Places.

HISTORICAL MARKER: Just east of Garden City on U.S. 50. Tells about how the extermination of the buffalo meant the end of the Indian lifestyle as well.

BROOKOVER FEEDYARDS: Three miles south of Garden City and three miles east on U.S. 83. The south yard of the Brookover Feedyards welcomes visitors and strives to educate the public about the industry. Families or groups should call Jerry or Tom (316/275-0125) for tours of one of the area's largest feedyards.

IOWA BEEF PROCESSORS: Just west of Holcomb on U.S. 50. One of the largest meat-processing plants in the world. Observe from road; do not drive into the parking lot.

REEVE CATTLE COMPANY AND AGRI CENTER: Located about nine miles south of Garden City on U.S. 83. The Reeves are committed to conservative resource management. Grain grown on the farm is used to make ethanol and create by products used to feed cattle. The process produces a large volume of clean water, which the Reeves use to breed Tilapia fish. Water circulated in the fish tanks is used for crop irrigation, and the manure from the feeding lots goes for crop fertilization. The public is welcome to tour the fish barn and cattle pens, but call first (316/275-0234). Groups can make appointments for guided tours.

SIEGEE'S: 121 Grant Avenue, Garden City. Rest your feet on the brass foot rail as you sit on the swivel stools and sip on a strawberry malt or eat homemade pie or a sandwich. Open daily 9 a.m. to 5:30 p.m. Closed Sunday. Phone 316/275-1998.

THE GRAIN BIN SUPPER CLUB: 1301 East Fulton, Garden City. The dimly lit booths are a cozy place to enjoy hamburgers, fish, beef, chicken, and more. A dance floor in the center of the room brightens things up. A lively but tasteful place. Open Monday through Saturday 6 to 10:30 p.m. Phone 316/275-5954.

IGNAZZIO'S ITALIAN RESTAURANT: 222 West Main, Garden City. The exposed pipes of this old water works building, the dim lights, and the dark green and white cement block walls will put you in the mood to try something new. The diverse menu includes chicken, veal, beef, and pasta. Open weekdays 11 a.m. to 2 p.m. and Monday through Saturday 5 to 9 p.m. Phone 316/275-7556.

PHO HOA RESTAURANT:
107 Jenny Barker Road, Garden City. The locals highly recommend this Vietnamese food. Open daily for lunch and Wednesday through Sunday for supper. Phone 316/276-3393.

GOLF COURSES: Garden City has three golf courses. Buffalo Dunes, an 18-hole course, and Golden Locket Club are public courses. Southwind is an 18-hole private course. Phone 316/276-3264 for more information.

LAKIN

1990 population 2,060; 1970 1,570.

KEARNY COUNTY MUSEUM:
Six blocks south of U.S. 50 on Buffalo, Lakin. Exhibits depict rich Santa Fe Trail and county history. One display tells about Fred Harvey's Kearny County XY Ranch that produced beef for all his restaurants. Open Tuesday through Friday and Sunday 1 to 4 p.m. Phone 316/355-7448 or 355-7598.

COUNTRY PLEASURES BED-AND-BREAKFAST: 1107 South Bridge, Lakin. Near junction of U.S. 50 and K-25. Don and Mickie Thomas welcome you to their farmhouse. Phone 316/355-6982.

BEYMER PARK: Four miles south of Lakin. Sand pit fishing ponds, picnic area, and playground.

BOOTS ON FENCE POSTS:
Three miles west of Lakin on U.S. 50 then 1-1/2 miles north. People around

here don't throw their boots away, they just put them on fence posts.

HARTLAND TOWN SITE:
Six miles west of Lakin. Only a school foundation shows evidence of this town's existence. It was once the county seat with a population of 2,000.

HAMILTON COUNTY

For additional lodging, restaurants, and attractions information call Sandy at 316/384-5459. You'll see few trees on U.S. 50 in Hamilton County except along the river where cottonwood, locust, and tamarack grow. Sage and yucca abound in this rangeland. You'll notice the rise in elevation as you head towards Syracuse. Elevation at Syracuse is 3,230 feet; on the eastern Kansas border it is 800 feet.

KENDALL: The change to Mountain Time comes just west of Kendall. In the late 1800s, Kendall fought with Syracuse to be the county seat. Find a Santa Fe Trail marker at the telephone office intersection.

SYRACUSE

1990 population 1,606; 1970 1,720.

NORTHRUP THEATRE: A pastel marquee and mosaic tiles on the building front welcome you. The daughter of the original owner painted the art deco walls and ceiling in 1949. Multicolor fluorescent wall lights, original seats, and a naugahide wall add authenticity. Movies are shown, but you'll get to see the 1932 carbon arc movie projectors and a better view of the art if you call for a tour. Phone Sandy at 316/384-5459.

MURALS: A local father-and-son team, Mike and Jim Fallier, painted the four murals. Find three within a half-block of U.S. 50 and Main Street and one at U.S. 50 and Barber.

BARBER HOUSE: North of U.S. 50 and Barber intersection. Mr. Barber was one of the first settlers to come to what was then called Hollidaysburg from Syracuse, N.Y., in 1873. This white clapboard house was the first built in the newly named town of Syracuse and often served as a fort for townspeople.

HAMILTON COUNTY MUSE-UM: U.S. 50 and Gates, Syracuse. The museum is housed in an old hardware store. Syracuse newspapers dating back to 1938, old vehicles, tools, guns, and other early Hamilton County artifacts abound. Open Monday through Friday 1 to 5 p.m. in the summer; Monday through Wednesday 10 a.m. to 4 p.m. in the winter. Phone 316/384-7496.

CYNTHIA'S PIZZERIA: 202 North Main, Syracuse. Cynthia has developed a deep-pan bread dough recipe that brings people from miles around. Open Monday through Thursday 11 a.m. to 1:30 p.m. and 4 to 8:30 p.m., Friday and Saturday 11 a.m. to 1:30 p.m. and 4 to 10:30 p.m. Phone 316/384-5928.

UPTOWN CAFE: 207 East U.S. 50, Syracuse. Great food here. Open for lunch and dinner. Phone 316/384-7874.

BRADDOCK-AMES BED-AND-BREAKFAST: 201 North Main, Syracuse. This two-story brick hotel has been serving guests since 1930. The lobby is now packed full of interesting antique items, the specialties being neckties and pins! You'll enjoy the old-time experience here. Private bath and TV in each room. Phone 316/384-5218 for reservations.

PETTERSON'S ART GALLERY: On east end of bed-and-breakfast. A retired Syracuse doctor displays his descriptive watercolors here. Paintings available for sale. Open during the week 9:30 a.m. to noon. Phone 316/384-7554.

LIVESTOCK BARN: South Main, Syracuse. Every Friday at 10 a.m. the cattle auction begins. Hogs are auctioned off Saturday morning. For many people, the most fun occurs the first Sunday of every month. At 1 p.m. flea market items and small animals are auctioned off in the parking lot, followed by a horse auction in the barn. Cow Patty's Restaurant is open on sale day in the livestock barn. No admission fee. Phone Sandy at 316/384-5459.

SYRACUSE RIVER RUN: If there's enough water in the river, Syracuse enjoys a River Run stock tank parade down the Arkansas River in the early summer. Decorated tanks swirl down the river until they get to the bridge just south of town on K-27, where a picnic is held after the tanks come home. Phone 316/384-5459 to check date and river conditions.

CANOE TRAIL: Start your canoe trip down the Arkansas River near Syracuse. The Kansas Department of Wildlife and Parks is planning a canoe trail and camping sites for canoers. Call Sandy at 316/384-5459 for canoe trail information.

HAMILTON STATE FISHING LAKE: West of Syracuse 6-1/2 miles on U.S. 50 and then 2-1/5 miles north. This is the story of a state lake gone dry. It was fed by a natural spring, but terraces and dams north of the lake and irrigation have contributed to its present condition.

GRAVE: From U.S. 50, 5-5/8 miles north on K-27. An iron fence surrounds this solitary 1888 grave of the first white woman to die in Hamilton County.

COOLIDGE

1990 population 90; 1970 102. In the late 1880s, Coolidge had a population of 800 to a thousand people. The Santa Fe Railroad used Coolidge as a base of operations for its huge cattle trade. A marvelous opera house was built during this time but burned to the ground after one performance. The town's roads are unpaved, but there are some interesting limestone buildings, including the city hall that dates back to 1886. Find picnic tables, slipper slide, teeter totter, and swings near city hall.

WATER TOWER: Coolidge. Go north past the old Conard's Store, the city building, and the old school. This is private property, so please be respectful. This brick and limestone water tower is over a hundred years old. Walls are 3 to 4 feet thick as you can see at the arch entrance.

TRAIL CITY ART GALLERY: U.S. 50 on east edge of Coolidge. Ten regional artists display their work here and hope passersby will stop to browse and buy. Open Tuesdays year-round and on weekends in the summer. Larue Lennon (316/372-8671) will open the shop any time.

AMERICAN DISCOVERY TRAIL: From the Coolidge red round top, go south over the Arkansas River bridge and take River Road, the first turn east. This is sandy country here, and you'll note that most of the trees are found along the river bed. The large nests made of sticks belong to magpies, which are plentiful. Much of this area is cattle rangeland. If you start this journey early in the morn-

ing you're likely to see wild turkeys. The road is good for biking since traffic is very light. The trail continues through Hamilton County for 32 miles. Phone Sandy at 316/384-5459 for information.

GREELEY COUNTY

When most Kansas counties were booming in 1885, only ten people were reported on the Greeley County census and those people were believed to be herding livestock. The 1888 county census recorded 2,638 inhabitants, but by 1913 the population had decreased by more than 30 percent because of drought. Tribune, the county seat, and Horace are today the only incorporated towns in Greeley County. 1990 county population is 1,774. For additional accommodations and attractions call Wanda at 316/376-2548.

TRIBUNE

1990 population 918; 1970 1,013. Watch for jackrabbits! These long-eared animals seem to be more plentiful on the High Plains.

HORACE GREELEY MUSEUM: Next to the new courthouse on East Harper, Tribune. This old courthouse, built in 1890, is listed on the national register and houses the county museum. Step inside the old courtroom to admire the woodwork and take time to view the photos that line the hallways. The grand old limestone building is full of fine exhibits, but the marble collection, with all its color and design, especially captivates people. Open May through October 10 a.m. to 4 p.m., some Sundays 2 to 5 p.m. Donations appreciated. Phone Evelyn at 316/376-4569, Nadine at 316/376-4308, or Wanda at 316/376-2548.

DIXON DRUG: Downtown Tribune. This modern drug store carries a varied inventory, but one of the best reasons to step inside is for lunch. Order at the counter and then find your way to a booth or table. Open Monday through Saturday.

HIGH SCHOOL: 400 West Lawrence in the northwest part of Tribune. This high school, built in 1931, has an intriguing exterior.

L E O T I

1990 population 1,738; 1970 1,916.

MUSEUM OF THE GREAT PLAINS: North end of Main, Leoti. Come in and learn about the county of Wichita. Donations appreciated. Open Tuesday through Sunday 2 to 5 p.m. Phone 316/375-2316.

JUNIOR HIGH: West edge of Leoti. This old brick building with spreading shade trees and well-kept lawn looks like a great place to go to school.

S C O T T   C I T Y

1990 population 3,785; 1970 4,001. Scott County feedlots annually produce 350,000 to 400,000 finished beef cattle with a value of over $300 million. More than 40 truckloads of finished cattle are taken each day from county feedlots to packing plants. Seventy-six million bushels of grain per year feed the cattle at a cost of nearly a quarter-million dollars per day. For additional lodging, restaurant, or attractions information call 316/872-3525.

BJ'S ANTIQUES: West of Scott City 3-1/2 miles on U.S. 96. Dolls, reference books, old toys, and depression glass are among the antiques and collectibles sold here. Open Monday

through Saturday 10 a.m. to 6 p.m. Phone 316/872-5278.

SCOTT COUNTY COURTHOUSE: One block northwest of Scott City business district. The courtroom in this 1924 structure is virtually unaltered.

SCOTT COUNTY EL QUARTELE-JO MUSEUM: West Fifth, Scott City. With a completion date of 1994, this southwestern-style museum will emphasize the history and archaeology of the El Cuartelejo pueblo ruins. It also will feature a time line of Scott County history beginning in the fossil era and continuing through the prehistoric Indians, the El Cuartelejo Indians, the pioneers, early farming and ranching, irrigation, and present-day feedlots. Phone Marilyn at 913/872-5341 or 872-5718 for information.

SCOTT STATE PARK AND LAKE: Located about 12 miles north of Scott City on U.S. 83, then take K-95 to the park. Ladder Creek runs through the park made picturesque with rugged sandstone bluffs and canyons. Camping (hookups), fishing, swimming, nature and equestrian trails, and canoe and paddle boat rentals are available to visitors. Park entrance fees. Phone 316/872-2061.

BIG SPRINGS NATURE TRAIL: Southwest side of the Scott State Park, Scott County. Girl Scouts marked this trail. The dam and bridge were built in 1933 by the Civilian Conservation Corps.

EL CUARTELEJO INDIAN PUEBLO RUINS: West side of Scott State Park, Scott County. Pueblos in this area were built in the late 1600s by Pueblo Indian refugees who fled from Spanish occupation of the New Mexico area and joined Plains Apaches. The area was excavated in 1897 when the remains of a seven-room pueblo-like structure were uncovered. The stone ruins have deteriorated in the nearly 100 years since that first dig, but two sections of the outer walls remain.

STEELE HOMESTEAD MUSEUM AND MONUMENT: West side of Scott State Park, Scott County. Herb and Liza quarried the native sandstone and built their home on the side of a hill. They hosted many a fishing and hunting outing, and it was their wish that their paradise become a public park. Take a sip from the spring that still runs near the house. A granite monument on a ridge across the road overlooks the Steele home.

KEYSTONE GALLERY AND CHALK PYRAMIDS: See the Northwest Kansas section for information about these attractions found just north of Scott State Park on U.S. 83.

K-96: From Tribune on the western Kansas border to Great Bend, note that a county seat is located almost every 30 miles. One theory is that the spacing corresponds with the distance wagons could travel in a day.

DIGHTON

1990 population 1,361; 1970 1,540.

OLD BANK GALLERY: Long and Lane, Dighton. Patrycia Herndon has her studio in this old First National Bank Building, which she's restoring. Patrycia's pencil drawings, watercolors, and pastels are here to view or buy. Open Monday through Friday 10 a.m. to 5 p.m. Phone 316/397-2273.

LANE COUNTY HISTORICAL MUSEUM: 333 North Main, Dighton. See interesting old photos, Indian artifacts, a country store exhibit, a sod house, and more. Open Tuesday through Saturday 1 to 5 p.m. and May through September Sunday 2 to 5 p.m. Free. Phone 316/397-5652.

FRIGID CREME: U.S. 96, Dighton. In the 1950s there was a small chain of Frigid Cremes, most of them in Oklahoma. Ice cream and extended menu. The Coney Island on the round bun is the specialty. Open daily 10 a.m. to 10 p.m. but closes earlier or later depending on the season.

HISTORICAL MARKER: Just west of Beeler on U.S. 96. A brief history of the life and work of George Washington Carver, who homesteaded near Beeler, is told here.

NESS CITY

1990 population 1,724; 1970 1,756. Ness City is approximately 100 miles south of Nebraska, 100 miles east of Colorado, and 100 miles north of Oklahoma. For lodging and restaurant information call Evelyn in the mornings at 913/798-2413.

NESS COUNTY HISTORIC BANK BUILDING: 102 West Main, Ness City. The limestone walls and two heavy glass doors give you an idea of early Ness City elegance awaiting you inside. No exhibits here, just a chance to see the building interior. Open weekdays 9 a.m. to noon. Phone 913/798-2413.

FRIGID CREME: U.S. 96, Ness City. Another Frigid Creme! Grilled food and ice cream. Open daily 11 a.m. to 10 p.m. Phone 913/798-2424.

HISTORICAL MARKER: Just west of Alexander on U.S. 96. The marker tells about the Fort Hays to Fort Dodge Trail. Alexander 1990 population 85; 1970 129.

LIBERAL

Before the town was founded, one particular homesteader would give travelers water from his hand-dug well. Because of his generosity with the water, they'd say,

"That's mighty liberal of you." And that's how the town got its name. 1990 population 16,573; 1970 13,862. For lodging, restaurant, and additional area attraction information call Denise at 316/626-0170.

LIBERAL AIR MUSEUM: 2000 West Second, Liberal. The power and mystique of planes from early aviation days to modern times and the pride of the men and women who flew them in war and exploration make this a fascinating and powerful tour. Fifth largest air museum in the nation. Open Monday through Friday 8 a.m. to 5 p.m., Saturday 10 a.m. to 4 p.m., and Sunday 1 to 4 p.m. Admission fee. Phone 316/624-5263.

BAKER ARTS CENTER: 624 North Pershing, Liberal. The former Baker residence has been renovated in a way that inspires appreciation of visual and performing arts. It should not be missed! Diverse forms of artistic expression are represented in new exhibits each month. Open Tuesday through Friday 1 to 5 p.m., Saturday 1 to 3 p.m., Sunday 2 to 4 p.m., and Tuesday evening 6:30 to 8:30 p.m. Free. Phone 316/624-2810 for information about special events.

MURAL: Fourth and Kansas on First National Bank Building, Liberal. See an artist's portrayal of various Liberal scenes.

LIBERAL MEMORIAL LIBRARY: 519 North Kansas, Liberal. How clever! The doors on the library look like an open book. Take a look for yourself. Phone 316/626-0180.

CORONADO AND SEWARD COUNTY MUSEUM: Intersection of Yellow Brick Road and east U.S. 54, Liberal. Highlights are F.M. Steele's black-and-white photographs that capture the evolution of the West.

Plains Indian exhibit, too. Open Tuesday through Saturday 9 a.m. to 5 p.m. and Sunday 1 to 5 p.m. Free. Phone 316/624-7624.

CORONADO STATUE: Next to the museum, Liberal. A historical marker next to this bronze statue tells about Coronado's explorations in Kansas.

DOROTHY'S HOUSE: Located near museum, Liberal. This white clapboard house is a replica of the house used in the 1939 movie *The Wizard of Oz.* See the ruby slippers and Toto's bed, and take a walk on the Yellow Brick Road. You'll probably bump into the Tin Man, Scarecrow, and Lion! Admission fee for house.

RANDY'S ANTIQUES: Second and Kansas, Liberal. Rooms and rooms and rooms of antiques. Open Monday through Saturday 10 a.m. to 5 p.m. Phone 316/624-0641 or 624-2431.

BOB'S DINER: 1032 North Kansas, Liberal. If you're looking for a place with 1950s atmosphere to get breakfast or a hamburger, fries, and a shake, look no further. Read the menu on the outside walls of this tiny red and white building and then hope for room at the counter. Enjoy! Open Monday through Friday 8 a.m. to 8 p.m. and Saturday 8 a.m. to 6 p.m. Phone 316/624-6466.

LIBERAL BEEJAYS BASEBALL: Entrance off Western Avenue at the Seward County Fairgrounds, Liberal. This is the home of the semi-pro Liberal BeeJays. Call 316/626-0170 for a schedule.

HUGOTON

1990 population 3,179; 1970 2,739.

SANTA FE STEAK HOUSE: East U.S. 51, Hugoton. Start your day with

Santa Fe Scramble or end it with Steak Santa Fe in the old Ulysses and Elkhart depots. Owners Tom and Judy Pepper invite you to explore the buildings. Look for the railroad passenger lockers. Tom is a butcher, so meat is cut fresh on the premises. Open Tuesday through Saturday 6 a.m. to 2 p.m. and 5 to 9 p.m., Sunday 6 a.m. to 2 p.m. Phone 316/544-8543.

STEVENS COUNTY GAS AND HISTORICAL MUSEUM:

905 South Adams, Hugoton. The museum was established in 1961 to commemorate the Hugoton Gas Field. Plan on spending some time here to study exhibits like a miniature rotary drilling rig that can be turned on. You can even watch the slush come out! Fossils, a cable tool drilling rig, a 1929 Roosevelt with Teddy's picture on the grille, farming tools, WPA figurines, and a printing shop are just a few of the exhibits. Do ask Gladys to play the Sears and Roebuck pump organ! Museum outbuildings include a schoolhouse, an 1886 home, a jail, a grocery store, and a church. Open daily 1 to 5 p.m., weekends 2 to 4 p.m. Free. Phone 316/544-8751.

CITY PARK: Fourth and Main, Hugoton. Get some ice cream from the nearby Jet Drive-In and eat it in the cool of the big shade trees.

DUCKWALL'S: Eighth and Main, Hugoton. The old-fashioned red Duckwall's sign on the blond brick building and the recessed doors will beckon you to enter. Open 9 a.m. to 5:30 p.m. Monday through Saturday.

ELKHART

1990 population 2,318; 1970 2,089. For additional lodging, restaurant, and attractions information call the Chamber of Commerce at 316/697-4600.

CIMARRON NATIONAL GRASSLAND:

Grassland acreage begins just a few miles north of Elkhart on K-27. Established after the Dust Bowl days to prevent erosion, this national grassland includes 108,176 acres. Wildflower, bird, history, hiking, and camping buffs will love this area of sagebrush, yucca, and mixed prairie grasses. Late May and June are best months for wildflowers. There are over 389 species of birds to be found here. Camping is available at the Cimarron Recreation Area, located four miles east of K-27 on a gravel road. Hikers can access the nine-mile Turkey Trail from here and follow the dry Cimarron River corridor. Post rock fenceposts mark 23 miles of the Santa Fe Trail. A companion walking trail (18 miles long) parallels the Santa Fe Trail. A 50-mile self-guided auto tour is also available and takes about three hours. Phone 316/697-4621 for information or to obtain auto tour brochure, or pick one up at the grasslands office or at the museum on U.S. 56 just northeast of Elkhart.

MIDDLE SPRINGS: In the Cimarron National Grassland west of K-27. Middle Springs was a welcome oasis for settlers needing water on their long Santa Fe Trail route. Take footbridges over the springs and enjoy a nature trail. Picnic area, bathrooms, and information provided here.

POINT OF ROCKS: A location in the Cimarron National Grassland beyond Middle Springs. Use auto tour guide to locate. Indians used this place as a lookout for buffalo. Traders and settlers later found that the location offered a stunning view of what lay ahead.

EIGHT MILE CORNER: From U.S. 56, turn north on K-27, cross railroad tracks, and then take first road west for eight miles until you see a 1903 windmill with a weather vane that lets you know you're at the corner where Kansas, Colorado, and Oklahoma meet. Find the corner monument for each state. See the national grassland in Kansas, irrigated wheat fields in Colorado, and sage and cropland in Oklahoma. Phone 316/697-4600 for more information.

MORTON COUNTY HISTORI-CAL SOCIETY MUSEUM: East U.S. 56, Elkhart. See local art work, exhibits on Elkhart natives Glenn Cunningham and Thane Baker, a pioneer women's project, an authentic teepee, a dugout, a blacksmith shop, a steam engine, antique tractors, and much more. Open May through September daily 10 a.m. to 5 p.m., weekends 2 to 4 p.m. October through April daily 1 to 5 p.m. Donations appreciated. Phone 316/697-2833.

BEA RILEY'S PLANTATION: West of the Cimarron National Grasslands. Ask at the museum about Bea's unique and intriguing farmstead.

HISTORICAL MARKER: Southwest of Elkhart on U.S. 56. This marker tells about the Point of Rocks and La Jornada.

TROLLEY CAR: 420 Morton, Elkhart. Fun place to get sandwiches or fountain treats. Open Monday through Saturday 10 a.m. to 8 p.m., Sunday 1 to 8 p.m. Phone 316/697-4755.

THE CIMARRON BED-AND-BREAKFAST: Rural Elkhart. See the grasslands, take in a Dusters baseball game, and spend the night in Kyle and Linda Martin's roomy country home. Pool table and guest rooms downstairs. Phone 405/696-4672.

ELKHART DUSTERS: Ball park at K-27 and Southwest Street, Elkhart. Watch this semi-pro summer baseball

team! Phone 316/697-4600 for a schedule.

MANTER CAFE: Main Street, Manter. 1990 population 186; 1970 219. There's no sign to welcome you to the white stucco Manter Cafe in this tiny town, but two big shade trees mark the entrance. Usually just open weekdays for lunch. The aroma of Lois Von Hemel's cooking fills this little cafe. Call 316/493-3456 to make sure of the hours.

JOHNSON CITY

1990 population 1,348; 1970 1,038.

PARMAN BROTHERS LTD.: Main Street, Johnson City. Haven't you always wanted to step inside a kaleidoscope factory? Here's your chance. Steve and David Parman make the scopes out of black walnut, oak, beech, and Imbuia, and use everything from polished stones to dried flowers to create that whirling design of color. Ask to see the floral scope! They also make walnut and oak trunks. Open Monday through Friday (when not at a show) 8 a.m. to 5 p.m but closed during lunch hour. Phone 316/492-6882.

STANTON COUNTY MUSEUM: 104 East Highland, Johnson City. This new museum is located in a sandstone building constructed as a WPA project in 1936. Besides county exhibits inside, a depot, jail, store, and iron-clad grain elevator will be located on the museum complex. Plans are for the elevator to be a working model. Open Monday through Friday 9 a.m. to 5 p.m. Donations appreciated. Phone 316/492-1526.

NORTH NIPP STREET: Johnson City. The American and Chinese elms on this street form a wonderful tree tunnel spring through fall.

U L Y S S E S

1990 population 5,474; 1970 3,779. For additional lodging, restaurant, and attractions information call 316/356-4700.

FORT'S CEDAR VIEW BED-AND-BREAKFAST: 1675 West

Patterson, Ulysses. Earnest tourists will find this an ideal place to stay between adventures. Owner Lynda Fort can supply a wealth of inside information about places to see and things to do in the area as well as provide a country setting, an indoor pool, and comfortable accommodations. Phone 316/356-2570 for reservations.

GRANT COUNTY MUSEUM:

300 East U.S. 160, Ulysses. Museum housed in white adobe built by WPA funds in the 1930s. Listed on state historic register. Ulysses sits atop the largest natural gas reserve in the world, and displays tell that story. An adobe room, Indian artifacts, and a Grant County model railroad highlight the many exhibits. A mural of 1911 depicts the beginning of New Ulysses. Part of Hotel Edwards, the last building moved from the old townsite, is available to tour. Tapestry from the only American Needlepoint Guild chapter in Kansas is displayed there. Open Tuesday through Friday 10 a.m. to 5 p.m., Saturday and Sunday 1 to 5 p.m. Phone 316/356-3009.

ULYSSES OLD TOWNSITE: From

museum, two miles east on U.S. 160, just west of cemetery. In 1888, 1,500 people lived in Ulysses. Improvement bonds were issued, and by 1908 when they came due, drought and crop failures had reduced the population to 40. The citizens gave the town to the bond owners and moved three miles west to the present site. The museum offers more information.

SANDWICH PLUS: 117 South

Main, Ulysses. This little sandwich shop is among the dried, silk, and fresh flowers of The Arrangement and the custom matting and framing shop Artworks. Create your own sandwich and enjoy the homemade desserts. Open Monday through Friday 10 a.m. to 3 p.m. Phone 316/353-1452.

FRAZIER PARK: Go east on U.S.

160 to the edge of Ulysses and then 7/10 mile south on Stubbs Road. The dam of the dry lake bed is a good place to hang out in the evening and wait for wild turkeys and deer to come into view. Playground equipment, RV park, camping stations, public golf course, and driving range. Call Chamber of Commerce at 316/356-4700.

RUSTY WINDMILL: West U.S. 160

by Kenney's Auto Clinic, Ulysses. This antique store is packed from ceiling to floor with anything you might find inside or outside an old farmhouse. If they're closed, ask for help at the auto clinic. Open 10 a.m. to noon and 1:30 to 5:30 p.m. Monday through Friday. Phone 316/356-3632.

GRANT COUNTY FEEDERS:

Rural Ulysses. This is one of the largest feedlots in Kansas. There are more than 15 miles of feed bunks for the 280,000 cattle that go through the feedyard each year. About 1,500 tons of feed and 1.7 million gallons of water are consumed daily.

WAGON BED SPRINGS: Eight

miles south of Ulysses on K-25 at county line, 3-1/2 miles west on Wagon Bed Springs Road, then cross the cattle guard and follow signs into pasture. During the Santa Fe Trail days this was called Lower Cimarron Springs and was the first water available on a 60-mile stretch. The spring is dry now but an old wagon bed marks the area. It feels kind of funny to walk through a turnstile in the middle of a cow pasture, but take some time to read the sign and imagine this National Historic Landmark as a welcome sight for thirsty pioneers.

GHOST GAS CAMPS: A half-dozen abandoned gas plants and villages can be found around Ulysses. The KP&L site was located eight miles south on K-27 and included 16 houses. After the houses were moved, the location was converted into a habitat for birds and small animals. The Grant County museum can supply information on the other sites.

GAS CAMP HOUSES: These prefabricated homes once served as residences for the gas plant workers and were among dozens of similiar houses near the gas plant. When the plants closed down many of the houses were moved to Ulysses.

BASEMENT HOUSES: Many are found in Ulysses and Satanta. Most homes of this kind were built during the Depression. Ask for more information and locations at the Grant County Museum.

RYUS: Between Satanta and Ulysses on K-190. The Ryus plant was the largest carbon plant in the world and once included more than 100 houses for employees and families. Now there is a cow pasture and a field of dead trees where the village once stood. The abandoned plant gives an eerie feeling.

ULYSSES WATCH AND CLOCK SHOP: Eight miles east of Ulysses on U.S. 160 or one mile east of Hickock. Bring along an antique clock that needs repair or your everyday watch that no one can fix. Leonard can fix it. Open Monday through Friday 8 a.m.

to 5:30 p.m. Phone 316/356-4913 or 356-4919.

IRIS'S COUNTRY KITCHEN: Adjoining Watch and Clock Shop, one mile east of Hickock. Buy loaves of bread for a picnic or enjoy a sit-down lunch. The aroma will entice you to purchase any of a number of delicious baked goods. Great place for cinnamon rolls! Open Monday through Friday, bakery open 8 a.m. to 5 p.m. Phone 316/353-2020.

HASKELL COUNTY HISTORICAL MUSEUM: Just south of U.S. 56 on Watkins Avenue at the fairgrounds, Sublette. 1990 population 1,378; 1970 1,208. County exhibits are housed in a depot and metal building. Open Wednesday through Sunday 1 to 5 p.m. Donations appreciated. Phone Irene at 316/649-2981.

GRAIN ELEVATOR ROW: In Haskell and Gray counties from Satanta to Montezuma, including the towns of Sublette, Tice, and

Grain elevator, Sublette

Copeland, grain elevators dominate the landscape and make it easy to locate each town. Haskell County is ranked first in the state in corn production with 90,000 irrigated acres. Gray County ranks third in corn production; and 23 percent of the county cropland is planted to corn.

ARKALON PARK: Just west of Mighty Samson of the Cimarron or 10 miles northeast of Liberal on U.S. 54. The town of Arkalon was founded in 1888 at the junction of the Cimarron River and the railroad line. The town never fully blossomed because the deep sandy soil made movement of horse-drawn freight so difficult. A nature trail and a quiet camping area are here now; electricity is available. Open April through October 1 from 8 a.m. to 10 p.m. daily. Phone 316/626-0101 for more information.

MIGHTY SAMSON OF THE CIMARRON: About four miles southwest of Kismet on U.S. 54. This railroad bridge, built in 1939, is 1,269 feet long and was considered an engineering marvel in its day. Rest area.

WIDEST MAIN STREET: Downtown Plains. Population 957. This main street is more than 155 feet wide, with room for parking in the center.

STAN HERD MURAL: Downtown Plains. Take the bank drive-through to study this 1980 mural of a Meade County farming scene.

MEADE

1990 population 1,526; 1970 1,899. Vegetation found west of Meade is unlike that in any other part of the state. Yucca and sage replace pastureland and trees.

DALTON GANG HIDEOUT: 502 South Pearlette, Meade. When the city purchased the house in 1940, the tunnel was a dirt-walled crawl space with beam supports. The WPA boys came in, enlarged the 95-foot tunnel, and lined it with stone. No doubt Bob,

Countryside around Meade

Grant, and Emmet Dalton would have preferred this roomier passage from their sister's house to the horse barn. A new barn holds guns, saddles, arrowheads, and photos of western heroes. The barn entrance door is from the county's first jail. Adult admission $1.50. Open Monday through Saturday 9 a.m. to 5 p.m., Sunday 1 to 5 p.m. Phone 316/873-2731.

SEYBERT FOOD PROCESSING: 112 East Carthage, Meade. This is where Aunt Vi's Sand Hill Plum Jelly is made. Using locally gathered sand hill plums, Vi is still using her grandmother's recipes to make jelly, jam, topping, fruit spread, pancake syrup, and wild game meat sauce. Apple and orange pumpkin butter are other specialties. Open weekdays 9 a.m. to noon and 1 to 5 p.m., Saturday 9 a.m. to noon. Phone 1-800/441-1781.

MEADE COUNTY HISTORICAL MUSEUM: U.S. 54, downtown Meade. Displays show what pioneer homes and shops looked like. Photos of dust storms and jackrabbit drives are fascinating. Ask Ora about the touching story of the World War I veteran's uniform and his grandson's Desert Storm uniform. Open May 1 through October 1 daily (except Monday) 10 a.m. to noon and 2 to 5 p.m. During the winter open weekends 2 to 5 p.m. $1 donation appreciated. Phone 316/873-2359 or 316/873-2242 for appointment.

MUSEUM OUTSIDE DISPLAY: One block east and 1/2 block south of museum. Examine antique farm implements, peer into furnished one-room schoolhouse, and watch progress of sod house reconstruction. Open May through September daily, closed Monday. Free. Phone 316/873-2359.

CITY PARK: East end of U.S. 54, Meade. The stone fence around the park was a WPA project. Playground equipment here.

GRACELAND CEMETERY: Intersection of U.S. 54 and U.S. 160, Meade. This area was the farmstead of Hoodoo Brown on the Jones-Plummer Trail. After his daughter Grace, his son, and his aunt died, Hoodoo sold land to a cemetery association, which named the cemetery Graceland after his daughter. A reddish marble memorial with bronze plaques stands out in the southeast corner of the cemetery.

JO MAMA'S DRIVE-IN: West U.S. 54, Meade. Drive under the roof into a parking slot, call in your order for a chili cheese coney and limeade, and wait for delivery. Open daily 10 a.m. to 9 p.m. Phone 316/873-2153.

MEADE STATE LAKE AND PARK: South on K-23 14 miles. The terrain changes from farmland to prairie to the Red Hills. Camping with electrical hookups and dump station, swimming, and nature trail. Fish for channel cat, black bass, and bluegill with permit. Check out the wildlife area with the artesian well and more secluded picnic area. If you head west to Liberal from here you'll see Red Hills and High Plains scenery.

7L GENERAL STORE: South Main, Fowler. 1990 population 571; 1970 588. Fun store with bulk spices, Kansas products, crafts, green plants, antiques, much more — and a soda fountain! Open daily 1 to 5:30 p.m. Closed Sunday. Phone 316/646-5475.

CREEKSIDE BED-AND-BREAKFAST: Rural Fowler. Enjoy a night in this country farmhouse located on the banks of Crooked Creek. Phone 316/646-5586.

This abbreviated index lists bed-and-breakfasts; galleries and studios; historic sites; lakes, natural landmarks, and nature areas; museums; and group tour suggestions. These categories are followed by an index of towns and cities listed in this guidebook.

An excellent supplemental book about Kansas annual events is *Kansas Event Guide* by Mil Penner and Marci Penner. Write to Sounds of Kansas, RR 1, Box 176, Inman, Kansas 67546, or call 316/585-2374.

INDEX

INDEX OF TOWNS AND CITIES

ABOUT THE AUTHORS

Milferd Penner and his wife, V. Lee, live on the farmstead near Inman where Mil was born and raised. For much of his life he worked closely with the land as a farmer, as a soil conservation contractor, and in irrigation sales. In 1983, Mil started a career in writing and photography. He produced *Kansas Journeys* and *Prairie: The Land and Its People* with Carol Schmidt. Prior to this book, Mil and daughter Marci published the first *Kansas Weekend Guide* and *Kansas Event Guide*.

Marci Penner played intercollegiate sports at the University of Kansas where she obtained her undergraduate degree in radio, TV,and film. She received her master's degree in counseling and guidance at the University of Wisconsin and spent five years in the Philadelphia area as an elementary guidance counselor. She currently conducts seminars for the Kansas Sampler Foundation.

Liz Penner King, another daughter, designs all the Penner books. Her business, Origins Design, is based in Boulder, Colorado, where she lives with her husband, Tom King, and daughter, Sofia.